D1614920

THE

HAPPY
TRAITOR

THE

HAPPY TRAITOR

SPIES, LIES AND EXILE IN RUSSIA:
THE EXTRAORDINARY STORY OF
GEORGE BLAKE

SIMON KUPER

P

PROFILE BOOKS

First published in Great Britain in 2021 by
PROFILE BOOKS LTD
29 Cloth Fair
London ECIA 7JQ

www.profilebooks.com

3 5 7 9 10 8 6 4 2

Typeset in Sabon by MacGuru Ltd
Printed and bound in Great Britain by Clays Ltd, Elcograf S.p.A.

A CIP catalogue record for this book is
available from the British Library.

ISBN 978 1 78125 937 5
eISBN 978 1 78283 398 7

For Pamela, Leila, Leo and Joey

Contents

1

Finding Blake

George Blake had spent the last forty minutes hiding in a passageway just inside the wall of Wormwood Scrubs Prison, waiting to escape. Sean Bourke, his accomplice on the outside, was supposed to throw a rope-ladder over the wall. But Bourke had gone quiet. Blake, soaked by the torrential rain, was getting desperate.

As the clock ticked to 6.50 p.m. on 22 October 1966, Blake began to suspect he wouldn't hear from the Irishman again. He grew so despondent that he almost switched off his walkie-talkie. He heard the bell calling the prisoners back to their cells. When they were counted at 7 p.m., his absence would be discovered. Police around the country would be alerted. In 1961 the Briton of Dutch origin had been unmasked as a KGB spy and had become the first officer in the UK's Secret Intelligence Service (SIS, known today as MI6) ever to be convicted as a traitor.[1] His forty-two-year jail sentence was the longest in British history. If he were caught trying to escape from the Scrubs, he could expect to be moved to a maximum-security jail, far from his wife and sons, and one day, decades later, to die there.

At about five minutes to seven Blake made his last bid for freedom. Using the agreed code names, he called Bourke on the walkie-talkie: 'Fox Michael! You MUST throw the ladder now, you simply must. There is no more time! Throw it now, Fox Michael! Are you still there? Come in, please.' Bourke on the outside wasn't sure the coast was clear, but chucked the ladder over the wall regardless.[2] Blake saw 'this thin nylon curling down like a snake'. Here was his moment of truth. He ran to the ladder and climbed up it. 'It seemed amazingly easy', he would recall many years later. Bourke, seeing his face appear at the top of the wall, shouted, 'Jump, jump, for Christ's sake, jump!'[3] Blake jumped, and, evading Bourke's clumsy effort to catch him, fell hard on the road, breaking his wrist and cutting his forehead. For a moment he lay still. Then Bourke bundled him into his old Humber car and whisked him away to a rented bedsit just a few hundred yards from the Scrubs. The streets of west London were almost empty. The rain had made it a perfect night for an escape.[4]

Within about forty-five minutes prison officers had found the rope-ladder and, lying against the prison's outside wall, like a clue out of Agatha Christie, a pot of pink chrysanthemums.

When Blake's fellow prisoners heard of his escape, they celebrated.[5] Zeno, a war hero who was in the Scrubs for murdering his ex-girlfriend's lover, wrote:

There must have been nearer a hundred than fifty escapes in the years I have spent here, but I have never known a reaction like this. By concentrating, I can distinguish words and snatches of conversation.

... 'He's fucked 'em ...' And then, far away and faintly from the south end of the prison, singing, 'For he's a jolly good fellow'... I have always known of his popularity, but until now had never appreciated the extent of it.[6]

'Blake the Spy Escapes from Scrubs Cell: Iron Bars Sawn Away', screamed the *Observer*'s front-page headline the next morning.[7] The newspaper reminded readers that at his trial in 1961 Blake had 'admitted that every single official document of any importance to which he had access as an intelligence officer was passed to his Russian contact'.

Some quotes from a safe-robber recently released from the Scrubs added personal detail on the double agent: 'He was very pro-British. He was a Communist, but an ideological one … He was very popular with the other prisoners … I have known men who went to him for Arabic, French and German lessons.'

Police were watching airports, south coast ports and Communist embassies in London. But a spokesman at the Soviet embassy told the *Observer*: 'We have nothing to say. Why should you think he has come here?'

* * *

I first became curious about Blake in 1999, when I came across an interview that he had given to a Dutch magazine from his exile in Moscow. I was immediately, selfishly, struck by how similar our backgrounds were. We were both mixes of British, Jewish and cosmopolitan, raised in the Netherlands.

His life story was remarkable, yet I had barely heard of him before. He had been front-page world news when he was jailed in 1961, and again when he escaped. But soon after his disappearance from the Scrubs he was practically forgotten, the sort of figure from a bygone age who is assumed to have died decades ago. I began to read about his life, and discovered a delicious cast of supporting characters that ran from Alfred Hitchcock to Vladimir Putin.

Then, in 2005, I met Derk Sauer, a Dutchman who had moved to Russia in 1989 and become a Moscow media mogul. (As well as founding the *Moscow Times* newspaper, he had the brilliant idea of starting Russian editions of *Cosmopolitan* and *Playboy*.) Sauer, a Maoist himself in his youth, had become friendly with his fellow Dutch Muscovite. Some years their families got together to celebrate *Sinterklaas*, the Dutch St Nicholas's Day. Before I flew to Moscow in May 2012, to speak at a conference, I asked Sauer if Blake might be willing to give me an interview.

This wasn't the sort of thing Blake did much. Being a spy, he was by nature secretive.[8] Except briefly around 1990, when he was plugging his autobiography, he very seldom spoke to English-language journalists (and always informed the KGB about his interviews, 'out of courtesy').[9]

By the time I was trying to find him, Blake had acquired a new reason for avoiding journalists: he didn't want to be asked about Putin. Though Blake retained some of his old Communist dreams, he had become a peace-loving democrat at heart, and he disliked his fellow KGB alumnus. However, Putin had the power to deprive Blake and his wife of their dacha and pensions, so Blake didn't want to offend him.

Before Blake agreed to let me interview him, he insisted on interviewing me. I rang him at the agreed time, from a friend's Russian mobile phone. I was standing in Moscow's Novodevichy cemetery, where I had been looking for the graves of Chekhov and Nikita Khrushchev. On the phone Blake and I spoke Dutch. His accent was pre-war chic, mixed with the hard tones of his native Rotterdam. He was chatty and quick to laugh. He skirted around the topic of Putin, so in the end I raised it: I promised not to ask him about contemporary Russian politics.

The other obstacle to an interview, he told me apologetically, was his family. He said his three British sons (establishment types) didn't like it when newspapers ran articles about their dad the Soviet spy. (In fact, I later learned that it was probably their mother, Gillian, Blake's ex-wife, who preferred to keep the whole story quiet.[10])

I agreed to publish the interview only in Dutch. That was good enough for Blake, and he invited me to his house. I think he did it because he trusted Sauer, because he welcomed having someone to speak Dutch with and because he liked the idea of being able to reach readers in his home country after seventy years of separation.

I later negotiated with Sauer that I would also be allowed to publish in English after Blake died, when his family was going to have to live with a rush of publicity whether I wrote anything or not. I have wrestled with my decision to publish in English at all. In part the decision is obviously selfish: I wanted to write this book. But I also felt that Blake owed the British an explanation.

The day after the phone call in the cemetery, Sauer's Russian chauffeur collected me at the Stalinist-Gothic Hotel Ukraina on the Moskva river, and drove me out of town to Blake's dacha – his former weekend house where by 2012 he was living full-time. Even on a Saturday morning there were traffic jams, but we got to Blake's neighbourhood early, so I went to sit in the sun in a local park. It could have been a middle-class suburb of London or Paris. Pleasant white apartment blocks fringed a children's playground. People in western clothes passed – a girl jogging, a man pushing a pram, a boy in a baseball cap riding a bike with training wheels. There were still some recognisably Soviet figures: a babushka with a cane and rotting teeth sitting on a bench chatting to a park keeper;

1. Blake and his dog, Lyusha, in the garden of his house, which was a gift from the KGB in recognition of his services.

a man carrying a plastic bag and his morning beer. But with hindsight, that spring morning in 2012 – when the oil price was over $100 a barrel, and before Putin invaded Ukraine – was about as good as Russian life has ever got.

Then I walked to Blake's house. In a quiet wooded lane a little old man with a cane in the shape of a dog's head stood waiting for me. George Blake had a straggly beard, false teeth, big ears, slippers and liver spots. His famous dapperness had gone, but he retained his deceiver's charm. He led the way through a door into his vast garden. Clothes hung on the washing-line, a grandchild's football lay in the sun, and there was a plague of mosquitoes.

The wooden exterior of the dacha was painted light green. 'This house, you would not believe it, was built before the Revolution', he marvelled.[11] It was here that the Blakes entertained Kim Philby on 1970s weekends, until the two defectors fell out.

Blake's Russian wife, Ida, and a noisy little terrier came out of the house to say hello. Blake took me into the conservatory. Many of the books on the shelves were from the library that he had inherited from Donald Maclean, his dear friend and fellow Soviet double agent. There were old jacketless hardbacks of Max Beerbohm's *Zuleika Dobson*, Faulkner, H. G. Wells, a biography of Dickens and the *Life and Teachings of Karl Marx* by somebody called Lewis, alongside histories of the Dutch resistance. In a windowsill stood a red-jacketed British Beefeater doll – perhaps a reminder of Blake's imprisonment as a traitor in London, or perhaps just a souvenir.

Ida brought us tea and salami sandwiches ('*buterbrod*', she announced in Russian). The dog, who was settling down to sleep at our feet, got his own portion. Blake and I sat side by side on a sofa, close together, so that he could at least hear me. His blue eyes were bloodshot. 'I cannot see you,' he explained. 'I see that somebody is sitting there, but who that is and what he looks like, I can't see.'[12]

That morning in 2012, Blake was eighty-nine-years-old, the last survivor of the British spies who had defected to Moscow. When he arrived there in 1967, after his jailbreak, Guy Burgess was already dead. Maclean and Philby died in Moscow in the 1980s.

I asked Blake whether he wanted to speak Dutch or English. He replied, in Dutch, 'When I get the chance – which happens very seldom – I find it very pleasant to talk in Dutch. Possibly that is how I feel most at home.' He added that he spoke Russian with 'a Dutch accent. I speak it very, errrr' – and here he shifted momentarily from Dutch to English – *'fluent, fluently*. With my wife, and the children, my grandson, my daughter-in-law.'[13]

I spent about three hours with Blake, trying to get him to reflect on his story: from the Dutch resistance in the Second World War to British spy to KGB colonel. Sauer later told me that it would be Blake's last interview. I had grown up in Leiden, twenty miles from Blake's childhood home in Rotterdam. During our time together, I felt that our shared language and origins created a certain intimacy. A Dutch-speaker who lives in a place where hardly anybody else speaks Dutch – as Blake and I had almost all our adult lives – can feel that he has a secret language, a distant perch from which to regard others. When you meet a fellow Dutch-speaker, that distance shrinks. This intimacy was exciting but also worrying: I didn't want to be seduced by Blake.

* * *

Blake's story is now known only to a few people, and then only insofar as anything can be known for certain in the world of deceit that is spying. There are still many mysteries about him. MI6 has never made its files on him public. Perhaps it never will, because his case was so embarrassing to the service.

In addition, Blake was a hard man to get to know. He had been something of a loner since childhood, and during his decade as a Soviet mole he appeared friendly but distant even to his wife. Many traitors present in this way. Donald Maclean's wife, Melinda, told her mother, 'Maybe you can be married to a man for a long time and really never know him at all.'[14] Philby's third wife, Eleanor, wrote apropos of him that 'no one can ever truly know another human being'.[15] (On the other hand, Guy Burgess, when drunk, had a habit of boasting that he was a Russian spy.[16])

Blake, during his years as a double agent, was living under two layers of subterfuge. On the surface he was pretending to be a British diplomat rather than a British spy; and beneath the surface he was pretending to be a British spy rather than a Soviet one. He must have been always on his guard. Then, in jail, he was always secretly plotting his escape. Certainly until he broke out of the Scrubs, aged forty-three, only his mother, Catharine, seems to have known him well. No wonder that descriptions of him by people in his orbit ranged from 'pleasant' to 'charming' to 'boring'.

The only way to understand a supremely international man is to use international sources. Because Blake emerged from anonymity in 1961 to disrupt the British national narrative, it has been mostly British writers, using British sources, who have tried to explain him. That approach doesn't work for Blake. He was fond of Britain (or 'England', as he always called it), but not obsessed by it. The longest spell he ever spent there were his five years in Wormwood Scrubs.

In this book I have supplemented earlier accounts of Blake's life, and my interview with him, with Dutch, German, French and Russian sources. Blake seems to have felt freer giving interviews in languages other than English, because he didn't have to worry about the publicity bothering his family in Britain.

I also drew heavily on the Berlin archive of the Stasi, the East German secret police. Archivists sent me thousands of pages of material on Blake (including, oddly, many West German articles that East German spies must have clipped from the imperialist press). Between 1976 and 1981 Blake made at least four celebrity-spy trips to East Germany to meet and greet Stasi chiefs, and give lectures about his life to their staff.

In the Stasi's internal report on his visit to Frankfurt an der Oder in 1976, 'Comrade Blake' was praised for his heroism and his sense of humour.[17] However, a Stasi officer who accompanied him on the visit noted that

> externally he had nothing heroic to offer ... Small, very slim, almost frail ... slowly thinning black wavy hair, bearded ... A man who – as he assessed himself – feels mentally and physically young, who swears by yoga, yet who also appears old enough to his own eyes to have grown a beard, though as he told us, only after passing the age of fifty.[18]

Blake's 1980 and 1981 lectures in East Germany were filmed. They make for wonderful period pieces. At the 1980 event a retired senior Stasi officer introduces Blake to the audience as an agent who came to work for Communism 'without our intervention – one of those who, as we say, the dear Lord sometimes sends'. The audience duly guffaws. Then Blake steps onto the podium. His beard and pointy chin give him a touch of the devil, but he is typically well dressed in a dark suit with a waistcoat – possibly the remnants of his pre-1961 British wardrobe that his mother had brought to him in Moscow. Standing before a large East German flag, he tells the story of his life in fluent if Dutch-accented German. The senior East Germans, all men in ties, sit in a long row, looking solemn and bored; there is occasional whispering and nose-picking. Bottles of beer sit tempting but unopened on the table beside them.[19]

What Blake said behind closed doors to fellow Communist spies adds new detail to his story. However, nothing in his Stasi lectures contradicts what he wrote in his 1990 autobiography (published at the peak of Soviet *glasnost*), or what he told me in 2012, or what his lawyer said at his trial in 1961. All his life the story Blake told about himself remained fairly consistent. He was a traitor, but I don't think he was a liar.

In this book I want to try to make sense of Blake's life. I also want to understand how, in old age, he looked back on it all. The little man I met in his dacha was a leftover from the Cold War. But he was also a harbinger of a twenty-first-century phenomenon, the 'foreign fighter': the westerner who sacrifices everything in a deadly struggle against the West. And his story prefigures Russia's hacking of the West during the Trump years. Blake betrayed western secrets and several hundred British agents to the Soviet Union. Dozens of those agents are presumed to have been executed. This intelligent, amiable, apparently well-meaning man then had to live with himself for decades afterwards. Who was George Blake? What impact did he have on history? And did he have any regrets?

An Ordinary Dutch Boy

Settling beside Blake on the sofa in the conservatory, I asked him what he missed when he thought back to his Rotterdam childhood. 'Well, of course I miss my parents,' he said, 'in the first place my mother, to whom I was very attached and who also loved me a lot and whose character I inherited.'[1]

He was born in the Dutch port city on 11 November 1922 – Armistice Day. His father, Albert Behar, a Jew from a wealthy family in Constantinople, had served in the French Foreign Legion and the British army in the First World War. A driver and motorcycle despatch rider on the Western Front,[2] Albert had been left with deep scars on each cheek from flying shrapnel, and bad lungs from a gas attack.[3] A month after the Armistice, the army posted him to Rotterdam to help repatriate British prisoners-of-war. There he met Blake's mother.[4] Blake would reflect in adulthood: 'If the Archduke Ferdinand had not been shot, I would not have been born.'[5]

At some point Albert Behar acquired a British passport, and so his son was born a British citizen.[6] On the way to the registry office Albert experienced a burst of British patriotism and decided to name the boy not Jacob, as he and his wife had agreed, but George – a name that Blake would always dislike and eventually ditch.

Albert doesn't seem to have transmitted any sense of either Britishness or Jewishness to his son and two daughters. During Albert's lifetime George never made the short journey across the sea to Britain. Albert himself would barely have known Britain. Nor was he at home in the Netherlands: he spoke hardly any Dutch, whereas his children, certainly when they were small, had little English. Blake's struggles to understand Albert's requests to him from his deathbed would stay with him forever. They may have inspired his later frenzied learning of languages.

George Behar never became a Dutch citizen but was raised 'as an ordinary Dutch boy',[7] under the aegis of his upper-middle-class Dutch Protestant mother, Catharine Beijderwellen. The family lived in a little street in Rotterdam's old city centre. He was known at home not as George but by his Dutch family nickname, 'Poek'.[8] As late as 1967, writing a letter to tell his mother that he had escaped from his British jail, he signed it 'Poek'.[9]

After Blake was unmasked as a traitor, journalists went in search of people who had known him in childhood. A picture emerged of a serious, polite, bright, conscientious, honest and rather solitary boy. Dina Regoort, who had worked as a maid in his mother's house, recalled young George, wearing a black dress and a black hat belonging to his mother, banging the table with a toy hammer as he pretended to be a judge doling out long prison sentences to Dina or his two little sisters, Adele and Elizabeth.[10] Dina's sister Johanna, who took over the maid's job in 1938, remembered Blake as a talkative teen-ager: 'He loved imitating. He'd imitate Hitler and lawyers. He wanted to be a lawyer himself, he said, or a pastor.'[11] Sometimes he would stand in front of a big mirror at home giving sermons to an imaginary congregation.[12]

As Blake later described it, he grew up in 'bourgeois circles',[13] 'conservative and, one could say, religious'.[14] His first book was an illustrated children's Bible,[15] and he grew up obsessed with Bible stories. His career plan was to become a *dominee*, or Dutch Reform pastor.

'You have strayed far from that path,' I remarked.

'I wouldn't use the word "strayed",' Blake replied. 'Let's say I was sent from that path.'

'Sent by what?' I asked.

'Sent by the circumstances.'[16]

Blake's mother's family were Remonstrants, a very liberal and generally posh variety of Protestants, who believed that not everything that happened was predestined by God. For Remonstrants the individual had room to exercise free will. But Blake as a boy embraced a sternly deterministic branch of Calvinism – one that, like his accent, has now almost died out in the modern Netherlands. He simply could not see how a human being could have free will. After all, God orders everything.[17] Blake seems to have stumbled on this extreme form of predestination largely because, like many Dutch people of his generation, he grew up idolising the country's royal family, the House of Orange. As this pious boy saw it, the royals followed a stern brand of Calvinism that left little space for free will.

In fact, his take on Orangeist religion was of dubious accuracy. He had probably absorbed it from Calvinist-nationalist children's books. Regardless, in his childhood Blake developed religious opinions that 'put me firmly in what is called today the fundamentalist camp', he wrote in his autobiography in 1990. 'My initial sympathies led to a genuine belief in predestination ... and later in determinism.'[18]

His royalism would endure to the end. When I asked him at the dacha to name his historical heroes, I expected him to come up with some pure-at-heart Communist believers like Rosa Luxemburg, but instead he said: 'William the Silent, Queen Wilhemina, Catherine the Great here.'[19] William the Silent led the sixteenth-century Dutch revolt against the Spaniards. Wilhelmina was the queen of Blake's childhood, who during the Second World War broadcast to the occupied nation over Radio Orange from London. And on Blake's kitchen table on the day we met lay a book (a present from Sauer) celebrating the then Queen Beatrix's seventieth birthday.

Somewhere along the way Blake stopped believing that Jesus was the son of God. However, all his life he continued to believe in some kind of predestination. He said that the one prayer he for ever considered valid was 'Thy will be done, on earth as it is in heaven'.[20] His autobiography has the deterministic title *No Other Choice* and mixes spy yarns with dense Calvinist theological passages. In it he writes: 'I believe it is justified for someone to say, "You cannot punish me for my sins because my sins were put inside me and are not my fault."'[21]

But Blake didn't believe that people should simply sit back and wait for God to reveal their destiny. On the contrary, they had to move fate along by taking action themselves.[22] His deterministic worldview – the only one that would last his whole life – was to prove momentous when he came into contact with Communism.

Blake told me his memories of his father:

He had a little factory – gloves for the ship-workers of Rotterdam – and he left early in the morning, and only came home at about eight in the evening. Then he'd come to our bedroom and tuck us in and give us a goodnight kiss, and that was really all we saw of him. And he wasn't healthy, because he had been wounded in the war – gas poisoning. So he never played as big a role in our lives as my mother.[23]

In 1929 Albert Behar's business was shaken by the Wall Street Crash. In 1936, when George was thirteen, Albert finally succumbed to his chronic illnesses.[24] At this point the boy had never met his father's relatives. They had cut off contact with Albert after he married a gentile. However, it seems that Albert had told his wife that after his death she should ask his sister Zephira in Cairo for help. Catharine Behar did so. Zephira, who was married to a wealthy banker named Daniel Curiel, wrote back. Her letter included a piece of information that bewildered George: Albert had been Jewish.

This news shook George's self-image. Albert had long concealed his Jewishness. He had told the British army that he was Catholic, the Rotterdam authorities that he was Lutheran,[25] and presented himself in society as an Englishman, not a Jew.[26]

There was a second surprise in Zephira's letter: she invited George to come and live with her family in Cairo for a few years.[27] Catharine, impoverished by her husband's death, accepted the offer. George himself was eager for an adventure.

3

A Jewish Mansion in an Arab City

Zephira Curiel may have hoped that her nephew would help fill the void left in her home by the death of her daughter at the age of four.[1] The Curiels already had a habit of picking up waifs and strays: some years before the invitation to George, Daniel had chosen a boy in a Cairo Jewish orphanage as a ward, and made his sons Raoul and Henri give him ten per cent of their pocket money. Once a week the orphan would visit the Curiel mansion for an awkward play date.[2]

In September 1936, five months after his father's death, George took the boat to Egypt.[3] Suddenly, the Dutch thirteen-year-old found himself living in an ochre-and-green Jewish mansion amid a park of palm trees in Zamalek, the most opulent neighbourhood in Cairo.[4]

Raoul Curiel would recall that, by the standards of their class, his family was relatively puritan: 'We had about ten servants, which wasn't enormous.'[5] The Curiels were Franco-phones, who revered French literature, summered in France and lived at a remove from their native Egypt.[6] In the phrase of Gilles Perrault, biographer of George's cousin Henri

Curiel, they 'had their stomachs in Cairo and their hearts in Paris'.[7]

Although their ancestors had arrived in Egypt over a century earlier, the Curiels had Italian passports. (The city of Livorno, whose municipal archives had burned down at some point, was particularly free in handing out Italian birth certificates on request. Many Egyptian Jews took advantage.[8])

The Curiels sent George successively to English and French schools, and he rapidly became fluent in both languages. By the spring of 1937, just months after his arrival in Egypt, he ranked fourth in a class of thirty-four at the English School in Cairo. The headmaster wrote in his school report: 'His work has given satisfaction in all subjects, and promises well for the future.'[9]

But the shift from Rotterdam to Cairo was emotionally wrenching. Blake later wrote: 'I am sure that I lived through an identity crisis in those years. Where did I belong? A Jewish cosmopolitan home, an English school, which reflected the glory of British imperial power of which I also felt a part, and in my heart, all the time, a longing for Holland and all things Dutch.'[10]

The Villa Curiel (as it was known[11]) contained thousands of books, and buzzed with political debate.[12] The Curiels kept an open table, and their mostly Jewish friends were always dropping by to eat and talk.[13] At the heart of the buzz was George's cousin Henri, eight years George's senior, a tall, spare figure known for his trademark shorts and sandals – an eccentric look in 1930s Cairo.[14] 'Immense charm and a dazzling smile made him very attractive, not only to women,' Blake would recall. 'He was, in a certain way, a hero for me.'[15] Henri was a charismatic extrovert of a kind that the strait-laced Calvinist schoolboy would scarcely have encountered before. The older cousin was to emerge as a central (though much misunderstood) character in Blake's life.

Like Blake, Henri had been given a partly Christian upbringing, attending a Jesuit *lycée*.[16] His father had then chosen him to take over the banking business, and Henri reluctantly obeyed. However, he was an intellectual – in French rather than Arabic, which at this stage he still barely spoke. In 1937 and 1938, during Blake's time in Cairo, Henri was reading Communist texts and becoming a Marxist.[17]

An energetic womaniser and brothel-goer,[18] Henri got to know his future wife, Rosette Aladjem, a nurse, while she was giving him daily injections against his pleurisy. She persuaded him to come with her to take care of the Egyptian peasants who farmed the vast Curiel estate on the Nile delta. Sometimes Blake accompanied the young couple.[19] Henri was shocked by what he saw on his own father's land, writes Gilles Perrault:

> A donkey was more expensive to rent than a man. In the cotton factories owned by their families, the workers were children aged seven to thirteen labouring under the whips of their European overseers ... Malaria killed whole villages.[20]

The main diseases that Rosette was trying to treat were trachoma and bilharzia.[21] At the time, average Egyptian life expectancy was between thirty and thirty-three years.[22]

It was exactly the sort of setting – unimaginable privilege alongside unimaginable suffering – that was bound to create radicals among both the richest and the poorest. Much later, Rosette would remark, 'I can say [Henri] never recovered from his shock at discovering the Egyptian misery.'[23] More directly than most wealthy Europeans of the time, Curiel and Blake witnessed deadly poverty at a formative age. Here was the exploitation that Marx talked about made flesh – and the exploiters were George and Henri's own family. It would have been natural for the cousins to feel that they owed penance.[24] Blake might have been thinking of his own cousin's radical circle when he said of the 'Cambridge Five' of Soviet double agents: 'Donald [Maclean] and his colleagues came from well-off, even rich families, so they felt guilty, even responsible for the poverty of the majority of people.'[25]

The late 1930s was the peak of the Communist craze among bright young people around the world. Many of Henri's bourgeois peers in Cairo converted too, although they were chiefly motivated by anti-fascism rather than by encounters with poverty.[26]

Henri handed out eye lotion and medicine to the Egyptian peasants, against the wishes of his father, who was a fervent anti-Bolshevik. However, the young man soon decided that charity wasn't enough; revolutionary change was required. Blake writes of his cousin: 'Later he became a co-founder of the Egyptian Communist Party.'[27]

The statement is repeated in even the best-informed English-language writings on Blake.[28] But, as Perrault shows, it isn't true – although Henri probably was indirectly the father of the Communist Party in neighbouring Sudan. A previous generation had set up a short-lived Egyptian Communist Party in the early 1920s.[29] In 1943 Henri founded the anti-colonial HAMETU movement,[30] which was not quite a Communist party. He had decided that Egypt's first priority – the will of the people, in his view – was national liberation from *de facto* British rule.[31] Communism could come later. And so Henri became an Egyptian citizen (the first in his family),[32] and gradually learned decent if strangely accented Arabic.[33] In 1947 HAMETU merged with the rival group Iskra (led by another Cairene Jew, Hillel Schwartz) to become the Democratic

Movement for National Liberation. Curiel briefly dominated the new movement, until Arab rivals rebelled against this 'leadership of foreigners'.[34]

Still, Curiel was probably the first Communist Blake ever met, and a famously persuasive one. The best recruiters to a radical cause are often close friends or relatives. Among recent European jihadis 'we have a lot of pairs of brothers: Kouachi, Abdeslam', notes the French scholar of Islam Olivier Roy.[35]

Henri explained his new creed to his bright young cousin.[36] Blake later wrote: 'His example and the discussions I had with him had little or no influence on me.'[37] It was certainly true that Curiel didn't convert him: the adolescent Blake continued to regard Communism as the enemy of God.[38] However, Blake's broad experience in Cairo, probably more than Curiel's influence in particular, does seem to have started a slow burn that erupted in flames years later.

In Cairo itself Blake underwent a different transformation: he morphed into a cosmopolitan like his father. The Egyptian years taught him that with his positive attitude and gift for languages he could cope anywhere in the world.

4

Deception Becomes Daily Habit

In September 1939 Blake was in Rotterdam on a summer visit from Egypt when the Second World War broke out. It was decided that he should remain in the Netherlands with his family. Back in Cairo, writes Perrault (presumably channelling Raoul Curiel's recollections), 'this studious, prim, boring little cousin was quickly forgotten'.[1] (The description probably says as much about the glamorous, high-living Curiels as it does about the Dutch Calvinist adolescent.)

George Behar endured the Luftwaffe's bombing of Rotterdam in May 1940 crouched under the dining table in his grandmother's house, holding a kitchen pan over his head. The old city centre in which he had grown up was devastated in a day. The Netherlands immediately surrendered to Germany.

During the bombardment Blake's mother and teenage sisters were living in The Hague. A few days later he cycled over to check on them, and found 'dirty teacups' on the table but the family gone.[2] A neighbour told the astonished boy that they had taken the boat to England. The Germans were already in control of the Netherlands by then, and it was too

2. Aged seventeen in 1940, Blake witnessed the Luftwaffe's
destruction of his hometown, Rotterdam. The experience
would shape his understanding of the American bombing of
Korea a decade later. It also meant that in 2017 he could easily
imagine nuclear war between the US and North Korea.

late for George to cross the North Sea. In any case, he didn't
want to leave his nation: 'In my eyes that would have meant
abandoning the sinking ship.' He and his grandmother went
to live with an uncle in the rural eastern Netherlands, near the
town of Zutphen.

The Germans briefly interned him with other British and
French citizens living in the Netherlands but released him
after less than a month: he was only seventeen, and they were
confident they would soon win the war. But on his eighteenth
birthday, in November 1940, he became an enemy alien of military age. 'I couldn't lead a normal life,' he told the Stasi agents
forty years later. 'From then on I lived on an illegal footing.'[3]
(His Jewishness would have complicated things further, but
that is something he never mentioned in his talks to the Stasi.)

In these early stages of the war the Dutch resistance was forming. A teenage Dutch patriot, part Jewish and 'passionately pro-British',[4] George Behar was a natural to join it. He fell under the spell of a pastor in Zutphen who was known to have resistance contacts.

Lost in thought on the sofa in Moscow, Blake anguished: 'What was he called? You see, I know that man so well, and now I don't know what his name was.'

All this was seventy years ago, I consoled him. (In his autobiography Blake names the pastor as Nicolaas Padt.)

Blake continued:

He taught us catechism, and this was a man who was anti-German, and who gave wonderful sermons in the church in Zutphen. I didn't have to work and I was already living on an illegal basis, and so I said I could do good work for the resistance. Because first of all I looked young for my age, I was an awkward schoolboy, and I could travel freely through the country and spread information and pamphlets. He helped me do that.[5]

The way Blake tells the story, he sounds like Tintin: a boy in plus-fours sitting on a train with a briefcase, carrying secret papers in the battle against evil.[6] Deception became a daily habit.[7] Few secret agents have started their careers so early. What would seem a strange profession to most people must have soon appeared quite normal to the young George Behar. He got used to risking his life in an ideological conflict.

His resistance work took a peculiarly Dutch form. The Netherlands, he recalled later, 'is utterly unsuited to partisan warfare', as it has no mountains or large woods where fighters can hide. The task of the country's wartime resistance was therefore to mobilise the population to the Allied cause, and above all to keep up hope that Hitler would eventually be beaten.[8] The teenaged George worked as a courier for the resistance group Vrij Nederland ('Free Netherlands'), distributing an underground newspaper of the same name.[9] (*Vrij Nederland* survives today, just about, as a struggling little leftist monthly opinion magazine.) Once, at a tram stop in the northern town of Assen, everything almost unravelled when a few illegal newspapers fell out from under his pullover. But an elderly German officer, who was waiting for the tram, kindly helped him pick them up.[10] Besides his illegal work, Behar/Blake helped out on the farm where he was staying in the village of Hummelo in the eastern Achterhoek (or 'Back Corner') region. His uncle paid for his lodging.

For decades, we knew almost nothing about Blake's resistance career except what he chose to tell us. However, in 2015 the wartime diary of Natalie Westerbeek van Eerten-Faure was published in the Netherlands. Faure, the wife of a country doctor, had lived in Hummelo. In May 1942 she wrote a letter to her son Bobbie in South Africa. Towards the end, she added an afterthought:

Rereading this long letter, I see that I have completely skipped Lous [her daughter, then aged eighteen] and so I shall tell you some things about her.

Lous has a boyfriend, a boy whom she has got to know here in Hummelo. He is staying with Weenink van de Koestert and (...) for the moment has to hide. He calls himself Gé Behar but his name is George Behar and he is an ... Englishman, and a forgotten Englishman. All the English have been interned, and thanks to all kinds of chance he has got out of it. (It is all too long to tell you how.) But now he is fairly safe in the Achterhoek. Luckily he speaks perfect Dutch, so that people don't notice what he is. You do always hear a more or less English accent, but if you have no suspicion, that could also be something personal. Apart from the Goedharts and us, nobody knows about his origins, and of course those have to be kept strictly secret until after the war. Gé, as we call him, is nineteen years old and the strange thing is that he looks a lot like you. Lous and he are serious, but of course there is no question of an engagement. He can come to our house, but they 'aren't at petting yet', as Lous says. He wants to become a preacher in England, but nobody knows when that will be. His family, mothers and sisters, live in England. His father, who was a consul, has died. Could you imagine that Lous might marry an English preacher? Time will tell. We find him a nice pleasant boy, who does look a lot older than nineteen, because he has travelled a lot and experienced a lot.[11]

That same day, Faure notes in her diary that every Jewish person now has to wear a small 'orange' star. She says that the Dutch treat the Jews 'with great respect (...) Many gentlemen greet ladies with the orange star'. Behar/Blake would also have noticed the fate of the Jews, though probably with less blitheness than Faure. But her letter mostly backs up his subsequent account of his resistance period. (Perhaps he had made up the story of his father being a consul, or Faure imagined it, just as she must have imagined his 'English' accent.)

In Moscow seventy years later, I asked Blake if he had taken any pleasure in his resistance work.

'Yes, yes, there was of course a strong desire for adventure in my character, undoubtedly.'

He elaborated on this point in his interview with the Dutch radio journalist Hans Olink in Moscow in 1999, saying of the resistance: 'The adventurousness, that appealed to me a lot. And really [*bursting out laughing*] it has appealed to me all my life. Otherwise I wouldn't have been sitting here. I must say that honestly too.'[12]

But Blake the determinist believes that his path chose him, rather than the other way round. He explained: 'You start something, and then it continues by itself, as it were. I began with my flight.'[13] In 1942 he set off on a daring underground journey through Belgium, France and Spain to Britain.

He told me:

I could have stayed in the Netherlands, but I wanted to be an agent for the English and Dutch service, and so I wanted to go to England and get sent back to the Netherlands. I thought – and it was true – that once I had got to England and had training there, then I could do much more than what I was doing in the Netherlands. I very much wanted to be a real agent.[14]

Leaving aside the wartime circumstances, there was something very Dutch about this quest to pursue his vocation in the wider world. Ambitious Dutch people often come to regard their own country as a marginal place. But, as Blake admitted to the Soviet newspaper *Izvestia* in 1970, he also had a pressing personal motive for fleeing: he missed his mother in Britain.[15]

He told his boss in the resistance, whom he knew only as 'Max', about his desire to leave. Soon afterwards Max placed him in the home of a family in the southern village of Zundert. After three weeks there, two daughters of the house offered to smuggle him across the border into Belgium. The

3. The identity card of twenty-three-year-old Greetje de Bie,
the resistance worker who, one summer's morning in 1942,
escorted George Behar across the Dutch border into Belgium.

three young people set off one beautiful Sunday morning in
the summer of 1942, but about 100 yards from the border, a
German soldier with a gun emerged from behind a haystack.
Luckily, he recognised the girls with delight. Blake writes in
his autobiography:

'What on earth are you doing here?' he said, half in Dutch,
half in German. 'This is a forbidden zone!' The eldest girl
hastily explained that we were cousins and wanted to visit
an aunt who was in a nunnery just across the frontier in
Belgium. The soldier smiled and nodded. 'All right, I'll let

you through and pretend I have not seen you. If you return this way this evening between nine and twelve, I shall be on duty again and let you back in. Good luck.' He gave us a friendly wave as we walked on.

Only later did George understand what had happened: the girls and the soldier (a homesick Austrian) were all pious Catholics. They had got to know each other through the local church and the Catholic youth organisation.[16] Otherwise their encounter might have ended differently: by one account, George had hidden his papers in his shoe, and could have been shot on the spot if discovered.[17] The girls brought him to their aunt in Antwerp, and from there he continued on to France.

On 23 July 1942 Faure in Hummelo wrote in her diary:

Lous' boyfriend, George Behar, has been gone for some weeks. Very probably he went to England. How and where, we have no idea.

He did tell Lous that he would try to go to England, and if she noticed that he was suddenly gone, she should just think that he had succeeded. Yesterday, all of a sudden, she got the dearest, most loving letter from him. It was a couple of weeks old, and for the sake of caution had only just been sent by some friend or another. The letter was sent from Holland. He says goodbye to her and writes at once that Lous should not feel bound, because the entire future is now completely uncertain. He doesn't want to stand in her way with a promise of fidelity, if she should happen to meet someone else.

Of course he doesn't know when he will next be able to give a sign of life. He writes so touchingly and so bravely, and for Lous it is even more of a bond than a real promise of fidelity. You feel that it is a big victory over himself for him to be able to write like this, and between the lines you can clearly read – keep loving me, I will keep loving you through it all (...) we like this young man a lot.

Very nice that from England he will write all sorts of things about us to Bobbie [in South Africa].[18]

On 15 November 1942 Faure notes:

Lous is very happy. A Red Cross letter has arrived from France from her boyfriend George Behar. Until then (the date was 12 September) the flight had succeeded, probably on foot from monastery to monastery dressed in a monk's habit. He has now reached Lyon, from where he sent this letter to his uncle. Now the journey to England! But again we have every hope that all this will work.[19]

Faure seems to have forgotten the young man after that: he does not appear again in her diary or letters.

Around the time of that last diary entry, he illegally crossed the Franco-Spanish border. The Spaniards interned him. However, by early 1943 the Spanish dictator Franco had understood that the Germans were going to lose the war, and he intended to stay on good terms with the Allies. After a couple of months, the Spaniards let Blake/Behar travel on to Gibraltar. There he boarded the RMS *Empress of Australia*, which managed to steer clear of German U-boats and make it to Britain.[20]

The whole journey was early training in coping with fear. 'You get used to being scared,' Blake said. 'So that is then a part of your life, you don't think about it any more. In any case, whether you are scared or not scared, it doesn't change the situation.'[21]

In 1943 he finally arrived in the country he barely knew. In wartime London he was reunited with Catharine and his sisters. Soon afterwards they changed the family name from Behar to the quintessentially English Blake. George was sloughing off his Dutch identity.

His passage to cosmopolitanism intriguingly resembles that of another Dutch international double agent – if indeed she was a double agent. Mata Hari grew up as Margaretha Geertruida Zelle in the provincial Dutch town of Leeuwarden. Her father too was a struggling local merchant: he had a shop selling hats and caps. Albert Behar died when Blake was thirteen; Zelle's father went bust and abandoned the family when Zelle was twelve or thirteen. Blake left the Netherlands for London at the age of nineteen; Zelle left the Netherlands for the Dutch East Indies aged twenty. Later she migrated between European cities as a dancer (and possibly a spy).[22] Blake's Egyptian uncle Max, a famous playboy, was said to have been one of her lovers in this period.[23] In 1917 Mata Hari was executed in Paris as a German spy.

A Legendary Centre of Hidden Power

In Britain, Blake volunteered for the Navy. He was just finishing his training in Hove when a visiting lecturer from the Admiralty changed his life. The man had been telling the trainees about the different branches of naval service they could enter – submarines, minesweepers and so on – and then added, 'There is one other branch, which I should mention. It is called "Special Service" and I cannot tell you very much about it because it is secret and, as far as we are concerned, the people who join it vanish.'

Blake writes in his autobiography:

> I at once pricked up my ears. This sounded exactly what I wanted. Special Service, secret, people not heard of again. It must be intelligence work, the landing of agents on the enemy coast.

He put his name down for the service that day.[1] But he was in for a disappointment: 'Special Service' turned out not to mean spying. Rather, Blake was to be trained as a diver for

4. Blake as a naval recruit (*c.* 1943) and Royal Naval Volunteer Reserve officer (*c.* 1945). Seen from the outside, his transition to a new name and a British identity appeared seamless.

'midget submarines' – one- or two-man vessels known as 'Sunday Hunters', he told the Stasi later. 'We were taught how to penetrate into enemy harbours to put a bomb under an enemy ship. And then try to get out again.'[2] It sounds like a kamikaze mission. Luckily for him, though, it was discovered during training that he passed out when deep underwater. This made him unarguably unsuited to the job.

A few weeks later he was summoned to an interview in London. He thought he was being considered for another position in the Admiralty; in fact, he had been headhunted by Britain's Secret Intelligence Service, SIS. A major who spoke fluent Dutch with a strong English accent interviewed him about his life and particularly about his time in the resistance.[3]

Blake's resistance work – the crucial and almost the only item on the young man's CV – seemed to establish his bona fides, not only then but all through his time in SIS. The service trusted him because he had had 'a good war'; importantly, so had his father, as a wounded British soldier in 1914–18. This seemed to confirm the family's patriotism. But, as Blake remarked much later: 'They didn't realise that, throughout the war, my loyalty was to the anti-Nazi cause, not to Britain.'[4]

After several interviews, to his great excitement, he joined 'the British Secret Service, this legendary centre of hidden power, commonly believed to have a decisive influence on the great events in the world'.[5] More precisely, he joined P8, SIS's Dutch section. One of his tasks was to escort members of the Dutch resistance who were to be parachuted into the occupied Netherlands. Before they were allowed to board their planes,[6] Blake would check their pockets to make sure they weren't carrying compromising items such as London cinema tickets (as had once happened[7]). He reflected: 'Many died, whom I knew personally and whom I took to the airfield myself.'[8] That tempered his envy of them.[9]

He also had to try to make sense of often garbled messages transmitted by agents in the Netherlands. The message might be, for instance, that the Germans were using a certain Dutch castle or country house as a headquarters. Blake would phone in the information to the Air Ministry.[10] 'The next morning, you might hear on the BBC that the castle had been bombed, and then you felt you were really participating in the war.'[11]

Blake found SIS 'so terribly English, part of the class system'. Nonetheless, he felt accepted into the British war effort, albeit as an outsider.[12] 'As a fairly conservative young man,' he recalled for the Stasi officers, he was proud to be serving in SIS – 'just as you would be proud to be chosen to serve the Staatssicherheitsdienst [Stasi].'[13]

And yet, he added, there was an important difference. Whereas Stasi officers received lots of training, 'I'm from the old days, when one could learn the trade, so to say, only in practice.'[14] SIS during the war was growing so fast there was scarcely any time either to vet or to train recruits. He gave the Stasi men his take on the service's history:

Before the war it was really an organisation of amateurs. They had no regular salary, no pension. They were mostly young people from good circles, who had money of their own, and only did it out of patriotism and a desire for adventure. It was a fairly small service then, but quite suited to the circumstances of the [pre-war] time. In many countries, the nobility dominated. The nobility to this day, in many western countries, has an important place in the foreign ministry and the army. And those young people, who came from these circles themselves, had natural connections to the European ruling circles. They had been selected because they were somewhat cosmopolitan, and that gave them the possibility to get information for the English secret services.

Of course, all that changed in the war. The service became very big – or quite big by English standards. I think at the time there were maybe 1,000 people, most of them officers.[15]

When the war ended, Blake again considered becoming a pastor, but SIS sent him to the Netherlands to wrap up its Dutch operations.[16] He found a half-starved country where some people were living off tulip bulbs. However, for young foreign military officers the months after Liberation were a time of abandon.[17] Blake writes:

Requisitioned cars, luxurious villas, stocks of champagne and brandy (hoarded by the defeated Wehrmacht), clubs located in the most expensive restaurants or the most picturesquely situated country houses, luxury hotels in famous spas and holiday resorts, attractive girls avid for a good time after the gloom of the occupation years, all these privileges normally enjoyed only by the very rich were now available to every officer.[18]

In the Netherlands, Blake combined hard work with hard partying. He had some sort of relationship with Iris Peake, a posh, young British secretary in SIS. Later, after his betrayal was revealed, this came to be regarded as significant.

He already spoke German well, and in April 1946 he moved on to Hamburg. One young colleague there, Charles Wheeler, later the BBC's longest-serving foreign correspondent and Boris Johnson's father-in-law, would remember that Blake 'smiled rather too much. Smiled at breakfast.'[19]

Blake's main task in Hamburg was to investigate whether German former U-boat officers – the wartime nemeses of British shipping – were founding an underground Nazi resistance movement. Many of the occupying forces in Germany were itching to go home now that the war was won, but Blake took his work very seriously. His first biographer, E. H. Cookridge, who as a British secret agent during and after the war briefly worked with Blake, describes him spending 'all his spare time studying marine technology and naval tactics with the result that, before long, he could talk with a fair degree of authority with Royal Naval officers and engineers who had spent a lifetime at sea'.[20]

'Making friends' with the former U-boat officers was simple, Blake reminisced to the Stasi:

We of the occupying forces had everything – cigarettes, schnapps, cars, ID cards – and the German population then had almost nothing. So I met many of them. And I could ascertain after some time that there was no question of an underground movement.

The officers had realised that resistance was pointless, and in any case they found daily life enough of a struggle in the bombed-out moon landscape of West Germany's 'zero hour'. In later years, Blake told the Stasi darkly, such former Nazis would follow other paths to power in the post-war Federal Republic.[21]

In Hamburg he lived through the start of the Cold War. SIS was shifting its attention from Germany to the Soviet Union. Blake said, 'They [SIS] had to fight an enemy that had a very big secret service, that was professionally trained, so to say, and it was necessary to build the service anew.'[22]

By 1947 Blake himself had switched to fighting Communism, as one of the very first Cold Warriors. He started learning the new language of espionage, Russian.[23] He recruited German 'former naval and Wehrmacht officers' and sent them as agents into Germany's Soviet zone.[24] He told the Stasi, possibly with some adjustment for tact and hindsight:

I succeeded in creating some groups here in the territory of the GDR [German Democratic Republic]. But I must say this task did not please me much personally – the fact that we were using our formerly hated enemies to fight against our former allies, to whom we owed a great deal. I tell you this only because this was the first breach in my ideological outlook.[25]

The Dutch-accented young SIS officer was a zealous worker, somewhat arrogant, uninterested in making an extra quid by selling drink or cigarettes from British army supplies on the black market. Naturally, he got up the noses of some of SIS's British dilettantes.[26] 'He was rude, fussy, vain and voluble, and he often struck his colleagues as a little mad', recounted the writer Rebecca West in the 1960s.[27]

But in his leisure hours he partook of post-Liberation party life, albeit more discreetly than many others in the occupying forces. In his autobiography he quotes from a Christian hymn: 'The world, the flesh and Satan dwelt around the path I trod.' His faith, he admits, had not been strong enough to protect him from 'temptations'.[28] He returned from Germany to Britain in 1947 feeling he was no longer worthy of a career in the church.

Luckily, the snobbish SIS had taken a liking to this foreign half-Jew. Blake had an impeccably British name, was an excellent operative, a resistance hero, anti-Communist, multilingual in a way that few Britons were,[29] apparently at home everywhere, and, importantly, he looked the part. Nicholas Elliott, a senior MI6 officer, thought Blake 'a good-looking fellow, tall and with excellent manners and universally popular'.[30] (Guided by the public school ethos of '*mens sana in corpore sano*', the British upper classes of the day often treated appearance as a guide to character. But either Elliott wasn't a very observant spy, or Blake shrank a fair bit in old age.) Blake also had no obvious weaknesses: he wasn't a blabbermouth, layabout, fantasist, gambler, alcoholic, uncontrolled womaniser or a homosexual vulnerable to blackmail. A listener rather than a talker, a self-contained man with no close friends, a mummy's boy rather than a barfly, he had the ideal temperament for a spy.

SIS decided to overlook his failure to meet two basic

requirements of entry: he didn't have a university degree, and neither he nor his parents had been born in Britain or its dominions.[31] The service offered him a job on the permanent staff – in effect, an upgrade 'from outsider to one of us'.[32] He accepted at once, ditching for ever the idea of becoming a pastor:[33] 'The work was very interesting, I had a good circle of friends', and 'I had no other prospects of interesting work.'[34] Spying gave him a new vocation in a booming post-war industry.

The novelist John le Carré has sketched the psychological profile of recruits to secret services:

> I understood the nature of the people who were drawn into that world. I knew what it was like to be unanchored, and drawn to a strong institution that took care of your moral judgements and ... your life. I knew the weaknesses that draw us into an institutional embrace which absolves us from personal decision ... I was a very mixed-up fellow. I became involved with that world when I was really very young, and it was everything for me. It seemed to be mother, father, priest and it gave me life's purpose.[35]

Blake, too, after the war was a 'very mixed-up fellow'. He had left behind both his motherland and his planned religious career, but he retained his moral impulse. He later noted that many members of SIS were pious Anglicans, while a lot of CIA officers were Quakers. The two most consequential Cambridge spies working for the KGB, John Cairncross and Donald Maclean, had Presbyterian backgrounds not so different from Blake's Calvinism. Presumably they, like him, had chosen to entrust their moral judgements to a 'strong institution'.[36]

In October 1947 SIS sent him on a 'sandwich course' at Cambridge University for a few months to learn Russian.

Though nobody then knew it, Cambridge was the place 'where all the top British traitors have been educated' (to quote from *Cell Mates*, Simon Gray's 1995 play about the Blake/Bourke relationship).[37]

Blake already admired the USSR for its role in winning the Second World War.[38] However, he would recall arriving at university as 'someone who maybe didn't yet have that much respect for Russians'.[39] That would change at Cambridge, thanks to his encounter with Elizabeth Hill, a staunch anti-Communist who became his first great unintentional mentor on the path to Communism. He gave me a version of the encomium that he always delivered to her:

> My attitude to the Russians was very much changed by the fact that I studied at Cambridge with Professor Hill. She was a very clever woman, of English descent, but before the Revolution there was a large English colony of businesspeople living here in St Petersburg. They lived here from generation to generation, and had many Russian contacts, and often married Russian women. Her mother was a Russian and she was the daughter of one of those rich businessmen.
>
> Of course, after the Revolution they went back to England, and she became a doctor in Slavic languages. She was a very well-known professor at the Slavonic faculty in Cambridge. And she was half-Russian, and she belonged to the Orthodox Church, and there were a couple of students she liked, among them me, and sometimes she'd take us to London on Sundays to the service at the Orthodox church. I thought that was beautiful. I still do.[40]

Hill was a rare female presence in the Cambridge of the time. She became the university's first ever professor in any branch of Slavonic studies in the same year, 1948, that Cambridge first awarded degrees to women. The blue-eyed, black-suited 'Liza' was 'known for her bamboozling Russian charm', which earned her the unheard-of privilege of parking her little Fiat car ('The Flea') in front of the British Museum. She was also so bilingual that she habitually mixed Russian and English in the same sentence.[41] '*Rabotat, rabotat, rabotat*' ('work, work, work'), she would urge her students. Blake claims that within a couple of months of starting her course, he read *Anna Karenina* in Russian.[42] He also imbibed Hill's 'romanticised image of the Mother Russia she had fled', writes the scholar of international relations Jonathan Haslam.[43] This emotional conversion, as Blake later noted, 'was probably not the intention of the English secret service'.[44] He was starting to discover a new motherland: not so much the Soviet Union, but Russia.

6

The Prisoner Converts

When Blake reported to the SIS head office in London in 1948 after leaving Cambridge, he hoped he would be posted to Afghanistan. Instead he was told he would be going to Urumchi, in western China, near the Soviet border. 'A few weeks later, without being given any reasons', he says in his autobiography, he was abruptly assigned to the South Korean capital, Seoul. He was disappointed: 'I had never felt much interest in Far Eastern culture ... and was much more attracted to the world of Islam.'

He did a lot of reading to prepare for his new posting, but one text in particular impressed him: 'a small handbook on Marxism', written by the SIS theoretician Carew Hunt. Blake writes:

> Entitled the 'Theory and Practice of Communism', its purpose was to acquaint SIS officers with the main tenets of Marxism on the sound principle 'Know your enemy' ... The booklet turned out to be an eye-opener to me ... I was left with the feeling that the theory of Communism

sounded convincing, that its explanation of history made sense and that its objectives seemed wholly desirable and did not differ all that much from Christian ideals even though the methods to attain them did.[1]

Armed with this new knowledge, Blake set off for Seoul as SIS's first ever head of station there.[2] 'It was just a very little residency', he modestly told the Stasi, using the Eastern-bloc term for a spy station.[3] His cover job was as a British diplomat.

Korea had been divided since 1945, when the Japanese occupiers had been driven out by American troops in the south and by Soviet troops in the north. Three years later, war between North and South Korea was expected. Blake was told that, if war came, Britain would probably stay neutral. That would allow him to remain at his post and observe events.[4] Some British consulates were at that moment doing exactly that in China, as the Chinese Communist Party took over the country in a civil war.[5]

Just before Blake left Europe, he had his last encounter with his cousin Raoul Curiel, in Paris. Raoul, by this time an archaeologist working in Afghanistan, would recall: 'He was a boring guy. He had the cult of the British empire and wanted to be more English than the English. A total Protestant … It seems that, at fourteen, he had already been like that.'[6]

Then Blake took a seaplane to South Korea. On a stopover in Cairo he visited Raoul's parents, Daniel and Zephira, and another aunt. Their lives had just been turned upside down. The creation of the state of Israel and the Arab-Israeli war of 1948 had made Egyptian Jews pariahs in their own country. Even the couple's phone had been cut off.[7] They told Blake that the Egyptian government had jailed his cousin Henri as a Communist. It was the last time Blake saw his uncle and aunts:

'With a heavy heart I said goodbye to these three lonely and aged people who had done so much for me.'[8]

Blake's boss in Seoul was the British consul-general, Captain Vyvyan Holt, 'a bachelor and truly eccentric Englishman'.[9] Bald, rake-thin and ascetic, Holt bore a curious resemblance to Mahatma Gandhi.[10] He soon became something of a hero to Blake. For the most part, though, Blake found Seoul frustrating. His main mission, while he waited for the war, was to recruit spies (especially among sailors) in Vladivostok, on the Soviet east coast. The city was only 450 miles north-east of Seoul. The problem was that both the North Korean and Soviet borders were in the way. 'That was a fairly naive idea [of SIS]', Blake complained later. 'They simply had looked at the map and thought, "What's the closest place to Vladivostok where we can open an intelligence section?" I had no success in building any agent network in Vladivostok, or even in North Korea.'[11]

Everything else went wrong too. Blake grew to despise Britain's corrupt and borderline fascist ally South Korea. He would for ever recall that the Oxford-educated minister of education had 'a big photograph of Hitler in his room'.[12] Blake began to equate the regime's opponents – whom the regime indiscriminately labelled 'Communists' – with the Dutch resistance. And he was appalled by the spectacle of Britain's American allies living the high life while homeless South Koreans lay freezing on the streets.[13]

In June 1950 the North Koreans invaded Seoul. Blake later recalled: 'It would have been easy to flee. We [in the British Legation] had four or five days' time. All the Americans fled, and offered to take us with them. But because we had orders to stay, we stayed.'[14]

Then, however, came a shocking BBC broadcast: Britain

would not stand aside after all, but was entering the war on South Korea's side. Blake told the Stasi in 1980:

> So we were not neutrals, as we had thought. We found ourselves enemies in the enemy camp. That was of course a very unpleasant situation ... Today no Englishman thinks of his country as a great empire ... but we then still thought we were an independent great power, and the evidence that England no longer acted in its own interests – because England didn't have any interests in Korea whatsoever – but only acted to please the Americans, that was a big shock for me. And another step in my future development [towards Communism].[15]

He was an ambitious man who had discovered he was serving a second-rate power. This second-rate power then landed him in horrible captivity. One Sunday, just after the North Koreans had invaded Seoul, three jeeps full of soldiers drove up to the British Legation and took Holt, Blake and his assistant Norman Owen for questioning at police headquarters.[16] The trio then became the first Foreign Office employees ever to be imprisoned by Communists.[17] The North Koreans added them to a group of about seventy civilian detainees, and marched them off north together with about 750 American prisoners of war. Around half of all the prisoners died that winter, mostly of starvation, illness, winter cold or at the hands of brutal Communist guards on a 'death march'.[18] Those who could no longer walk were doomed. Philip Deane, an *Observer* journalist who was in Blake's group, recalled: 'A young redheaded [American] kid who could still walk was trying, weeping, to carry his dying pal. A guard kicked him on. He stumbled off, sobbing ... We heard many shots ... the dying were pushed into the ditch.'[19]

Holt said afterwards: 'If it were not for George Blake and Philip Deane I would not have survived even the last lap of the death march. At Hadjang they nursed me and Consul Owen, and they gave us their rations, although they were themselves sick and hungry.'[20]

Blake spent nights sitting by the side of the desperately ill Holt and Owen. He persuaded the brutal camp commander, known as 'The Tiger', that there would be hell to pay if two British diplomats died on his watch. The North Koreans duly found both men penicillin. Still, Holt and Owen were permanently weakened, and would die within a few years of returning to Britain.[21]

Blake noticed that the mostly older European civilian internees – many of them quite elderly bishops and nuns – died at much lower rates than the captured American soldiers. He attributed the differences to the softness of American life.[22] When Americans were suddenly plunged into awful circumstances, he told the Stasi, they 'simply did not want to live any more. And perhaps one must conclude that it's not good to live too well.' (At this point there were sniggers from the Stasi audience, and Blake smiled.[23])

His account reflects a Calvinist suspicion of material excess, but it is unfair on the Americans. He didn't mention that some of them had previously been starved and tortured by the North Koreans, and that on the march they were often treated even worse than the civilians.[24] 'The soldiers died of pneumonia, they died of dysentery, they died of cold, they died of malnutrition, they died of thirst, and they died of exhaustion,' writes Steve Vogel in *Betrayal in Berlin*.[25] 'Some died because other soldiers stole their food.' None of this swayed Blake. Many educated Europeans at the time were turning against a supposedly materialist and imperialist US. Blake seems to have made that turn in Korea.

The horrors he witnessed there stayed with him for ever:

'Ten thousand were dying on my right and ten thousand were dying on my left. It was a period of violent conflict and I was in the middle of it. I saw the Korean war with my own eyes; young American PoWs dying and enormous American Flying Fortresses bombing small defenceless villages.'[26]

He told the Stasi officers that all of them knew, or had heard from their parents, about the wartime bombing of German cities. Indeed, Blake himself had witnessed the effects in post-war Hamburg and Berlin. However, he continued, the Americans had done much worse in Korea. They had flattened wooden farmhouses, poor villages and towns. 'Literally not one stone stayed on another.' He wasn't exaggerating. The US general Curtis LeMay, head of the Strategic Air Command during the Korean war, reflected in 1984, 'Over a period of three years or so, we killed off – what? – twenty per cent of the population.'[27] The bombing had inevitably reminded Blake of the Luftwaffe's destruction of his home town, Rotterdam, a decade earlier. He recalled: 'We, as representatives of the West, felt guilty and asked ourselves, "What are we doing here, what right do we have to come here and destroy everything?" These people, who live so far from us, should decide for themselves how to organise their lives.'[28] This was another step in his ideological journey, he later said.[29]

Finally, in February 1951 the horrors began to subside. Blake was one of a group of ten French and British prisoners, most of them diplomats and journalists, who were taken to a quiet farmhouse near Manpo, in the north. 'Our existence in that small wattle hut', he writes, 'was not unlike that of ten people who have to spend two years in a railway carriage, put on a siding and forgotten.' The eight men in the group slept on the floor in two rooms (while the women slept elsewhere), but at least they had food, shelter and some degree of security.[30]

Their suffering from then on was mostly psychological: 'First, because we never knew how long this would last, secondly, because we had absolutely nothing to do.'[31] These were intelligent people, hungry and bored out of their minds. Blake learned from this time that even a person with the richest set of experiences could tell his entire life story within three or four months, and would then have to start from the beginning again. There wasn't much to do except play fantasy games. Blake, recalled Deane later, 'loved to imagine himself … a great officer of the crown ennobled for gallant and devoted service. Lightly we would tap him on the shoulder and say solemnly: "Arise, Sir George." We promoted him to baron, earl, marquess. He never quite made duke; captivity ended too soon.'[32]

The rather half-witted North Korean propaganda lessons aimed at converting them to Communism – 'brainwashing', in the jargon of the day – succeeded mostly in irritating this group of intellectuals. Deane said later, 'We often had to help them with their quotations from Karl Marx.'[33]

To convert Blake would take something rather more thoughtful. It duly arrived. He told the Stasi, 'Luckily – or not so luckily for all of us – the Soviet embassy in Pyongyang felt sorry for us and sent us some books.'[34] The package, which arrived in the spring of 1951, contained only one book in English: Robert Louis Stevenson's *Treasure Island*. The prisoners drew lots for the privilege of reading it first, and then quickly read it to pieces. But there were also three books in Russian: Lenin's *The State and the Revolution*, and two volumes of Marx's *Capital*.

The only Russian-speakers in the group were Blake and Holt. The consul had lost his glasses earlier in the war while scrambling to hide from machine-gun fire from American planes.[35] 'Then he couldn't read any more himself,' said Blake, who by the time I met him was in exactly the same situation,

> and I read to him. We sat on a burial mound, and we read and discussed the books. I think he'd been political commissioner in Iraq for the English Foreign Office. He had been a civil servant of the English Indian government, and he was completely a servant of the English colonial system. But he was a very sensible man and he saw that it couldn't go on, and that something would replace it, and he thought that thing would be Communism. He wouldn't want to live in a Communist country, but that was his prediction. And since he was someone for whom I had a lot of respect – he was my boss, shall I say, and we had very good friendly relations – what he thought had a lot of authority for me.[36]

'So I have read *Capital*, two volumes, twice', he marvelled to the Stasi (prompting a few cautious chuckles).[37] 'For months, we spent hours every day reading … *Capital* and some works by Lenin.'[38] He and Holt would read a section of the text and then discuss it, 'problem by problem'.[39]

The readings with his boss must have made a deep impression on a bright young man whose education had been interrupted by war, and who suddenly had two years with little to do but think. He and Holt also studied the Koran together, in Arabic,[40] and discussed Marx and Lenin with their fellow prisoners.[41] (When Holt was interviewed by Blake's future biographer E. H. Cookridge soon after returning from Korea, he seems to have omitted to mention his Communist studies.[42])

Blake reflected later: 'I thought I was fighting on the wrong side … The main aim, if not the only aim, of the English secret service was to destroy Communism ... I came to the conclusion that if I had to die – and the possibility of dying in Korea was large – I wanted to die for a cause I could believe in.'[43]

I suggested to Blake that the Korean farmhouse had been his second university. He replied, 'Yes, yes. That is true, that is true. You can say that, up to a point. Yes.'[44] And so the old imperialist Holt unintentionally nudged him into Communism.

When people convert to an extreme creed, they usually do so in company. Indeed, company is part of the point. For most of the last century, if you joined the Communist Party, you were joining a club with outposts all over the world. In any country you went to, you would find soulmates and helpmeets (until something went wrong and the Party decided to purge you). The Cambridge spies of the 1930s, and most twenty-first-century European jihadis, were radicalised as part of a peer group. Many were recruited by close friends, lovers or siblings. Blake in Korea, however, was a solitary Communist without a 'cell'.

By this time, 1951, Communism was less fashionable than it had been in the 1930s. On the other hand, it was on a winning run: Communist regimes had recently taken over China and Eastern Europe.

Having become a Communist, Blake decided he would have three choices if he were ever freed from captivity and made it back to Britain: 1) leave SIS and find a different job; 2) join the Communist Party, and sell the party newspaper, the *Morning Star*, on the streets on Saturdays; or 3) become a Soviet double agent. Option 3, he decided, was the best way to serve his cause.[45]

One autumn evening in 1951 he secretly handed the North Korean camp commander 'Fatso' a note in Russian, addressed to the Soviet embassy. He had gone over to the other side. 'I must honestly tell you', he admitted to the Stasi, 'that it was a very difficult decision. But I felt I had to do it.'[46]

Blake, understandably, never revealed much about the inner workings of the KGB. Even when addressing Stasi agents behind closed doors, he said of his recruitment: 'It would take too long to tell you how we did that.'[47] However, his joining the KGB may have been more of a two-way process than he ever admitted, or even realised. The Soviets in 1951 were on the look-out for agents in the West, after many of the previous generation had been purged by Stalin. The young KGB officer often credited with recruiting Blake was Nikolai Loenko. Although he is not named in Blake's autobiography, Loenko would become known within the KGB as 'Blake's godfather'. Based in Vladivostok, he had come to the North Korean prison camp posing as a Soviet army officer. He met all the British prisoners, weighed them up as potential traitors, and latched onto Blake.[48] Loenko died at the age of fifty in 1976 in a car crash, but in 1992 the KGB general K. A. Grigoriev recalled his account of Blake's recruitment. Loenko had said (according to Grigoriev): 'George stood out from the motley crew in the camp; he was intelligent, spellbinding. I knew in my bones that here was an opportunity to do some work. I needed only some kind of pretext to make contact with him.'

Loenko (himself an obese gourmand[49]) had told Grigoriev exactly how he made the conversion: 'I brought him bread, conserves, chocolate. I have been convinced ever since that the way to a spy's heart is through his stomach.' Moreover, Loenko had boasted of charming Blake with intelligent conversation: 'Neither before nor since have I told so many stories. I even had to dig up some I remembered from school. So, word by word, we quietly moved forward, to the serious conversation when the Englishman made his choice.'[50] Loenko then got

Blake to write down everything he knew about SIS's stucture, and compare it with what another traitor, Kim Philby, had told the KGB. The accounts tallied.[51] The Soviets could trust Blake.

In the story of Blake's radicalisation (as we would now call it), Loenko may have applied the final push. However, the KGB man was only the last in a sequence of influences nudging him towards becoming a Soviet double agent: the Wall Street Crash of 1929, which had hit his father's business; the Communist arguments he had heard from his cousin Henri in Cairo; his experience of subterfuge in the Dutch resistance and British intelligence; his wartime separation from his homeland, which had created a space for new loyalties; his Russian studies in Cambridge; the unintentionally persuasive SIS handbook he had read on Communism;[52] the poverty he had seen in Egypt and Korea; his hatred of the South Korean regime; those Flying Fortresses obliterating Korean villages; and his contempt for the 'soft' American PoWs.[53]

In the Second World War Blake had participated in a deadly struggle between good and evil. To him, Communism versus capitalism looked like the sequel. And for a prisoner in North Korea Communism was 'something to give him strength, and fibre, and hope, to keep him alive', as his barrister Jeremy Hutchinson would argue at his trial in London in 1961.[54]

Blake in that North Korean farmhouse was a moralistic twenty-eight-year-old with an abstract cast of mind who needed a new cause. All his old moorings had gone. He was a failed SIS officer, an ex-Dutchman and an ex-Calvinist, a cosmopolitan adrift. He was making up his identity as he went along.

Communism was made for him. He had grown up a Calvinist who believed that everything in life was predestined; it was a small step to believing that history was predestined too. Although he no longer believed that Christ was the son of God, he still thought 'there should be a kingdom of God with justice'.[55] Calvinists disapproved of material display; so did Communists.

In Moscow I put it to him: 'You swapped your religion for Communism.' I expected him to demur, but he said, 'Yes, that's very clear. Religion promises people, let's say, Communism after their death. Because in heaven we are all equal and we live in wonderful circumstances. And Communism promises people a wonderful life here on earth – and nothing came of that either.'

Was his Communism a faith, just as his religion was?

'Yes, I think so,' Blake replied.[56] Of his two faiths, Christianity seems to have left the deeper mark. He never acquired the habit of speaking in Communist jargon. Into old age the Bible and theology came more readily to him. In 1961, in an essay he wrote for the London court explaining his treachery, he described his state of mind in Korean captivity using language that is more spiritual than political:

I had become profoundly aware of the frailty of human life and I had reflected much on what I had done with my life up to that point.

I felt that it had lacked aim and had been filled mostly with the pursuit of pleasure and personal ambitions ... I then decided to devote the rest of my life to what I considered a worthwhile cause.[57]

Like many of today's European jihadis, Blake was a pious young traitor, revolted by western excess (including his own). Like them, he was renouncing a libertine life of 'pleasure' in order to embrace a cause greater than himself. For an ambitious person of his era the KGB had the appeal of an exclusive club that was changing the world. Similarly, today's western recruits to ISIS feel that they are joining 'the small brotherhood of super-heroes', writes Olivier Roy.[58] Another similarity with the jihadis: secrecy was central to Blake's Communism. He never joined the Communist Party in any country. He intended to live his creed only through his spying.[59]

Sir Dick White, who headed both MI5 and MI6, was more scathing about his motives. 'Normal people aren't traitors', was one of White's dictums.[60] He told his biographer Tom Bower: 'Blake felt abandoned, unimportant and wanted to prove himself.'[61] Sean Bourke, who would spring Blake from prison and later become his room-mate in Moscow before turning against him, concurred: 'Without the KGB he was just a weak, insignificant little man. Blake liked to play God. For years he had used the KGB for his own selfish ends. He had used them to enable him to wield the power of life and death over other men.'[62]

I asked Blake whether his knowledge of Stalin's purges – hardly a secret in the West any more by 1951 – hadn't deterred him from going over to the USSR. No, he replied, because Stalin's successor, Nikita Khrushchev, had denounced the purges. 'They were already condemned, and by the Communists themselves,' he said.

Here he was making a rare and telling error of chronology: Khrushchev's denunciation of Stalin came only at the Party Congress in 1956, five years after Blake signed up for the Soviets. Almost all Blake's statements about his life are consistent and stand up to scrutiny. In this case, it seems that his desperation to appear a moral man prevented him from admitting that in 1951 he had joined the side of mass murder. No wonder he was one of the last westerners to sign up for the

KGB for ideological reasons, rather than for money or because of blackmail.[63]

There is an alternative hypothesis about his decision to become a Soviet spy: that he was forced into it. In his autobiography he recounts the night he tried to escape from captivity. He was caught by a North Korean soldier and held prisoner in a cave until morning. He was then brought back to the farmhouse, where a furious North Korean major harangued the prisoners about the crime of escaping, but let Blake rejoin his fellows. Blake suggests the camp leadership hadn't dared take responsibility for executing a British diplomat.[64] Others, though, have suggested that Blake promised to collaborate with the North Koreans in exchange for his life.[65] Philip Deane would remember: 'Blake disappeared for some time. And we were wondering what happened to him. He returned looking better fed than usual [*laughs*], and cleaner, and we wondered where he'd gone. He said he'd tried to escape and got lost, and they caught him.'[66]

We do not know whether Blake was coerced into treachery. There is no known evidence to support this theory. Blake has always denied it, and I think he is telling the truth. His conversion on grounds of principle alone – the story he has told consistently over the decades – makes sense.

Lunchtime Spy

In March 1953 Stalin died. Relations between the Soviet bloc and the West thawed fast,[1] and Blake and his fellow prisoners were soon released. The Communist powers gave them a luxurious journey home, starting with the first staging-post outside North Korea, the Chinese border town of Antung, 'where the former captives revelled in the wonder of a huge communal bath, scrubbing themselves with scented soap and joyfully singing nursery rhymes,' writes Vogel.[2] On 22 April the Britons in their group landed in Abingdon on an RAF plane. The crowd at the airfield sang the hymn 'Now Thank We All Our God'.[3] In Blake's ears, the words 'had an extraordinary irony. For many people, my return would not be a reason to give thanks. I knew: I was no longer the person they were expecting.'[4]

But like the rest of his group, he was greeted as a hero. On the television footage he walks rapidly down the plane stairs smiling, bearded, pointy-chinned and dapper in a smart blazer. He waves, then makes for his waiting mother, and kisses her on each cheek, continental-style.

5. Blake (with pointy beard) and his fellow Britons freed from North Korean captivity return home as heroes in 1953. Little did the crowd know that Blake was no longer on their side.

6. Blake and some of his released fellow prisoners (from left to right) A. C. Cooper, Anglican bishop of Korea; Herbert Lord, commissioner in the Salvation Army; Norman Owen, legation clerk at the British embassy in Seoul; and Thomas Quinlan, Irish missionary priest.

7. Always a mummy's boy: a very dapper Blake, freshly landed
in England after his release from North Korean captivity.

A television interviewer buttonholes him to ask, 'And how
did you find the food out there, Mr Blake?' In a mid-century
Cambridge accent, perhaps put on to sound posh on TV, Blake
replies: 'Well, the food was *edde-quate* but very monotonous.'
The interviewer presses him: were there 'any odd things they
gave you to eat?' Blake straight-bats him: 'No, just rice and
turnips mainly.'[5]

Burgess and Maclean had outed themselves as double
agents just two years before when they defected to the USSR,
yet SIS barely seems to have wondered whether Blake might
have been turned in captivity. The service welcomed him back
after only two days of cursory questioning.[6] He was then given

several months off. In September 1953 he started work at the service's offices at 2 Carlton Gardens, London, a grand stucco mansion that during the First World War had briefly housed Lord Kitchener. It had been badly bombed in the Second World War,[7] but remained an agreeable address for upper-class spies, in a secluded nook overlooking The Mall, yet handy for the clubs and pubs of the West End.

Blake had brought back some distinctly un-British habits from Korea. In captivity he had got used to having an afternoon nap, and he liked to walk around the office barefoot. Cookridge, who presumably had good sources in the SIS of Blake's era, reports: 'He sometimes took off his shoes and socks and picked his toes, which many found "extremely disgusting" and ascribed it to Blake's foreign origin.'[8] Nonetheless, Blake was regarded, in John le Carré's words, as 'the heroic ex-prisoner of North Korea and pride of the British Secret Service'.[9]

But he was also a KGB agent code-named 'Diomid' ('Diamond'). From 1953 onwards he worked hard for two secret services at once. Le Carré calls him 'a most capable field agent in both interests'.[10] Elsewhere, in a passage that immediately follows a riff on Blake, le Carré explains:

> While on one side the secret traitor will be doing his damnedest to frustrate the efforts of his own service, on the other he will be building himself a successful career in it, providing it with the coups and grace-notes that it needs to justify its existence, and generally passing himself off as a capable and trustworthy fellow, a good man on a dark night.[11]

In the phrase of the journalist Clem Cecil, Blake became a 'lunchtime spy'. Whenever he got a moment to himself in

Carlton Gardens, usually when his colleagues went out for lunch, he would pull out his little Minox camera and calmly photograph secret British documents. Years later, asked about the romance of spying as purveyed in James Bond films, he remarked: 'I can assure you that there's nothing romantic about walking around all day with a camera strapped between your legs.'[12]

For the KGB, 'Diomid' was the perfect agent. He was professional, committed and based at the heart of enemy territory. He was doing it for the Communist cause, not for money, so he wasn't tempted to concoct or exaggerate dodgy information in order to have something saleable. A careless SIS seems to have allowed him remarkable access, as witness his later claim to have given away hundreds of the service's agents.

The KGB valued him so highly that it sent an officer to London tasked mainly with handling him. Sergei Kondrashev, who spoke English, German and French, had joined the KGB as an interpreter in 1944. He had told the organisation, truthfully, that his parents were simple Muscovite office clerks, but omitted to mention that some of his forebears had been rich noble landowners. Throughout his KGB career (which would last until 1992) Kondrashev worried that the secret of his origins would come out.

His early work for the KGB had included escorting foreign visitors around the USSR, keeping a cold eye on Soviet writers and interrogating the doomed Swedish war hero Raoul Wallenberg in prison (although Kondrashev only found out much later who he was).[13]

London was his first foreign assignment. Kondrashev prepared by studying maps of the city and immersing himself in Blake's KGB file. To blend in with Britain, or perhaps just because he liked the style, he wore grey flannels and a blue blazer.[14] His cover in London was as the Soviet embassy's first secretary for cultural relations. He accompanied visiting Soviet violinists and chess-players, bought tickets for sports events for Soviet dignitaries and meanwhile dealt with most British double agents of the era.[15] Alister Watson, a Cambridge-educated Communist who at the very least met some KGB agents, recalled: 'I hated that man. He was so bourgeois and had a pet poodle.'[16]

One foggy evening in October 1953, Kondrashev and Blake had their first London meeting. Blake got a fright on his way to the rendezvous in Belsize Park when he spotted a police car waiting at a street corner. He almost turned back, but happily, the police turned out to be hunting a criminal.[17] Blake went on to meet Kondrashev and made the perfect début: he handed over full details of the telephone taps and secret microphones that SIS was using to listen in to Soviet communications in Vienna and around western Europe.[18] Blake noted that Kondrashev 'was of course delighted'. The quality of his revelations almost guaranteed that Blake really was working for the KGB, and wasn't a British plant. 'The English secret services would hardly allow the release of such material.'[19]

Kondrashev later recalled, 'We were astounded at the immense success the British had had in tapping into our secrets.'[20] After the Cold War was over, he told his former CIA opposite number, Tennent 'Pete' Bagley, that Blake had helped the KGB see 'how badly they had underestimated the danger of technical penetration of their official installations abroad, and the secrets such bugs and taps might reveal'. Kondrashev said this inspired the Soviets 'to develop their own capabilities – to dig their own tunnels.'[21]

The relationship between spy and handler is in some ways more intimate than marriage. Kondrashev was the only person

Blake spoke to in those years who knew the truth about him, and the only person to whom he could tell the truth. If Kondrashev ever slipped up, Blake could end up in jail for the rest of his life. Every three weeks or so the two men would rendezvous on London buses and suburban street corners and Blake would pass on his haul.[22] Whenever the latest results of the Vienna taps were sent to British and American institutions, he recalled later, he would give a set of the findings to Kondrashev too, writing on the document, 'A copy for Moscow'.[23]

Blake was constantly running enormous risks. 'The contact', he would tell the Stasi officers, 'is always one of the most dangerous moments in the life of a spy.'[24] The KGB believed (possibly correctly) that a network of taxi drivers and traffic policemen acted as MI6's eyes in London. Once, when Blake wasn't able to turn up to a scheduled meeting with Kondrashev and then missed the agreed alternative meeting too, Kondrashev felt sick with worry the way 'that only a case officer or a parent could understand'. The handler had to wait another month before their final alternative meeting, in specified seats in a London cinema. When Blake appeared, Kondrashev's heart 'leapt with relief', writes Bagley with professional sympathy.[25] Yet Kondrashev always found Blake calm and self-possessed: 'I can't ever recall seeing him under real stress.'[26]

Vasily Dozhdalev, another long-time KGB handler of Blake, would recall a time Blake came up with a piece of news suggesting that a certain Soviet diplomat was about to switch sides. The KGB investigated, and decided that the report was false. In Dozhdalev's telling:

It was obvious that the British side wanted to test Blake. I said to him, 'They want to check whether you're a spy.' He went very quiet, but didn't show any sign of fear. And so quite calmly we planned our future co-operation. A less courageous man would have proposed interrupting or giving up the work. But George went on, fully aware of the danger.[27]

Blake, for his part, admired the professionalism of his KGB handlers. He was impressed that, although SIS owned a property opposite the Soviet embassy in London and photographed everyone who came in and out of the building, the KGB men still managed to get to meetings with him unseen. He also told the Stasi: 'I must say – our Russian friends will forgive me – that though the Russian people aren't known for punctuality, the Soviet comrades of the KGB were always there on the minute.' His German audience roared with laughter.[28]

From 1953 until his unmasking in 1961 Blake gave the KGB every piece of information he could lay his hands on. The CIA said in 1996: 'According to US calculations, he furnished the Soviets with 4,720 pages of documentary material.'[29] A portion of this was material that could be used for blackmail.[30] Some of the documents he passed on may have given the Soviets a preview of British negotiating positions at international summits in the latter 1950s.[31]

Most culpably of all, he gave the KGB the names of hundreds of agents working for British intelligence. Almost every British businessman, tourist, student and journalist (BBC or otherwise) recruited by MI6 to spy on the Soviet bloc had had their identity blown before they even arrived there.[32] Far more dangerously, Moscow also knew about all locally recruited eastern European agents of the British – people risking their lives behind the Iron Curtain. Here is an extract from Blake's interview with Tom Bower of the BBC in 1990:

Bower: How much information did you hand over in that period?

Blake: Well, that I cannot tell you.

Bower: Why not?

Blake: Because it's so much.[33]

No wonder Dick White would assess the damage Blake did as 'much worse than Philby'.[34] Vladimir Kryuchkov, the KGB's chairman until he was arrested for joining the failed Soviet coup in 1991, said: 'You can describe Blake with only one word: unique.'[35]

Meanwhile, Blake had embarked on another major project at Carlton Gardens: he began going out with a young SIS secretary, Gillian Allan. Her father (a colonel, who was a Russian linguist and Soviet specialist) and her older sister also worked for 'The Firm', as SIS was known.[36] 'I liked her a great deal', writes Blake in his autobiography. 'Gillian was ten years younger than I, tall, dark and attractive and would, in every respect, make an ideal wife.' There was just one hitch: as a double agent who expected to get caught one day, he couldn't offer her much of a future.[37]

He also knew from the start that Gillian wouldn't be the type to follow him into exile behind the Iron Curtain. Blake told me: 'She was a real Englishwoman. I remember, we were living in Berlin – in the, er, 1970s?'

'In the 1950s,' I corrected him.

'Fifties, yes,' he continued. 'And there you could get everything, but she only bought clothes in England. Everything that was English was good, but everything that wasn't English wasn't so good, hahaha!'[38]

Nonetheless, Gillian wanted to marry him. He tried to put

her off so as not to drag her into his complicated life, saying he couldn't see himself as a 'respectable householder and family man'. He told her that his desire 'not to clutter up my life' was so strong that he didn't even want to own a car or a record player.[39] His response to Gillian recalls his letter to the Dutch village girl Lous ten years earlier, after his flight from the occupied Netherlands: Lous should not feel bound to him, 'because the entire future is now completely uncertain'. When Gillian asked him point-blank one evening, 'Shall we get married?', he again tried to dissuade her, saying that he didn't want to make her unhappy, and pointing out that he was a foreigner.[40] But she persisted, and in the end he agreed, against his own better judgement.[41] They were married in Marylebone in September 1954. The only people Blake invited to the wedding were relatives; he seems to have been so friendless that his best man was Gillian's brother.[42]

The SIS (which liked to keep romance in-house) and the KGB were both pleased that he had married inside The Firm.[43] If the KGB orchestrated the match, it would imply that the three sons he went on to have with Gillian were a by-product of his intelligence work.

On the sofa, Blake reflected: 'What I shouldn't have done, what I certainly shouldn't have done, what I regret, and they all know that' – he was talking about his sons – 'is I shouldn't have married.'

Ida walked in with more sandwiches. Chewing, Blake went on: 'But it was very difficult to explain that to her [Gillian]. I couldn't tell her. Couldn't.'

I asked whether he might have tried to get out of working for the Soviets.

'Well, it might have been possible. I think so, but I had offered my services myself, and so I felt obliged to keep to my promise.'

Did that promise take precedence over his family?

'You know how it is,' he replied, oddly. 'I thought, "Well, it will all sort itself out." Eh, I have to get out of the sun a bit.'

The midday rays were hitting the conservatory. He raised himself from the sofa with his cane, and we went and sat in the shade. He continued: 'I thought, "I can maybe convince her", although I don't really think that would have been possible, but that's how I thought.' He ummed and awed for a bit, then added: 'I thought, "She is so attached to me, so let's get married and then hope for the best."'[44]

Speaking to the German TV historian Guido Knopp in the 1990s, he had elaborated tellingly on his decision to marry: 'Many soldiers in the Second World War married before they went to the front. I experienced something like that.' He then added, explicitly, 'I was a soldier in the Cold War.'[45]

Western and Soviet civilians in the 1950s may have thought they were living in a time of peace, but Blake did not. He had chosen to risk his life first in the Second World War, again in Korea – where he was one of the very few Europeans to see the Cold War turn bloody – and then for a third time as a Soviet agent. He said of his job in Korea: 'I was a fighter ... I was deployed to fight Communism.'[46] Given his experiences of actual war, he naturally assumed after his return to Europe in 1953 that fighting could break out there at any moment too. As Knopp notes, Blake's self-image as a soldier was crucial. It was the way he justified betraying British agents. If spies on both sides were fighting a new kind of war – on an 'invisible front', as the East Germans liked to call it – then killing was part of the deal.

8

A Mole in Berlin

In April 1955 the newly-wed Blakes took up a new posting, in Berlin. That very month East Germany announced the arrest of '521 agents of western secret services', of whom 105 were thought to be working for the British.[1] But nobody yet suspected Blake. David Woodford, a British military officer in the city, recalled him as

> very popular socially ... He was just a very delightful, charming man. And he used to turn up to all the parties, was very well known, used the officers' club – which was a sort of social centre, I suppose ... Most people knew him. There were a lot of very nice, usually very attractive, girls who worked for 'The Firm'. And you know, it was all part of a very active social scene. That's how he was well known.[2]

Berlin in the 1950s was the epicentre of the Cold War. The new Soviet leader, Nikita Khrushchev, called the city 'the testicles of the West', explaining, 'Every time I want to make the West scream, I squeeze Berlin.'[3]

Blake had landed in the city at a terrifying time. In 1952 the US had tested a hydrogen bomb, that was hundreds of times more powerful than the atomic bombs dropped on Hiroshima and Nagasaki. In 1953 the USSR tested its own. Blake, who at the age of seventeen had witnessed the destruction of his home town, Rotterdam, must have found it possible to imagine the destruction of the world.

The unforeseen Japanese bombing of Pearl Harbor still haunted American minds, including President Eisenhower's. Many senior figures in the US assumed a Soviet offensive was imminent, possibly in Germany.[4] After the Central Intelligence Agency was created in 1947, secretary of state George Marshall said: 'I don't care what it does, all I want from them is twenty-four hours' notice of a Soviet attack.'[5]

But both sides in the 1950s knew little about each other's intentions. The Cold War was being fought in a fog. SIS's great dream, Blake told the Stasi, was to have 'a man in the Kremlin. But I don't think they ever succeeded.'[6] Western spy services had almost no human intelligence of any kind behind the Iron Curtain.

They lived in uncertainty. They had been surprised by the North Korean invasion of the south in 1950, which Stalin had approved.[7] Then, after Stalin died, western spy services had almost no idea whether his successor Khruschev was a warmonger or a peacemaker. Nor did they know much about the USSR's nuclear arsenal. Both Eisenhower and the British prime minister Churchill were dismayed by how little their spies could tell them about the unexpected detonation of the Soviet hydrogen bomb.

After the CIA's director Allen Dulles warned that 'the Russians could launch an atomic attack on the United States tomorrow', Eisenhower recorded in his diary, 'The world is racing toward catastrophe.' In December 1953, he noted that the US should be open to striking first: 'We have come to the conclusion that the atom bomb has to be treated as just another weapon in the arsenal.'[8]

Each side desperately needed to discover the other's intentions, in real time if possible. 'I think it possible that the very life of a nation, perhaps even of western civilisation, could … hang upon minutes and seconds used decisively at top speed or tragically wasted in indecision,' Eisenhower wrote to Churchill in January 1955.[9] Was the enemy planning a nuclear attack like in Hiroshima, or an invasion like in Korea? Or might it blunder into one through a miscalculation? As Blake told me, 'The most important intelligence then was whether the other side would start a war.'[10] On the Communist side the then East German spy chief Markus Wolf would later recall that his main job was 'to prevent surprises, above all military surprises'.[11]

Early warning of a 'surprise' might be the difference between victory and the destruction of one's own civilisation. Consequently, Berlin, a likely venue for the surprise, was teeming with spies.[12] 'Many were agents of multiple services at the same time', Blake recalled in a TV interview with his French cousin, the journalist Sylvie Braibant.[13] The cheaper freelance agents were known as 'Hundert-Mark-Jungen', because 100 Deutschmarks was their going rate for a secret.[14] Some of them just made things up.[15]

Treachery was common. In 1956, for instance, Horst Hesse, a German who had been working for American intelligence in West Germany, defected to the GDR carrying two safes full of agents' index cards. The American embarrassment prompted much laughter in British SIS, Blake reminisced with Hesse when the two men met at a Stasi event in Frankfurt an der Oder twenty years later.[16]

8. The American spy tunnel in Berlin in the mid-1950s, during its productive eleven months of operation. Betraying the tunnel to the Soviets was Blake's biggest feat of espionage. It also might just have helped keep global peace.

If a secret service lost an agent in Berlin, it simply went and found another. Even after Blake's mass betrayals in 1955, writes the historian Paul Maddrell, 'MI6 retained enough [agents] and was sufficiently successful in recruiting new ones that in the years 1958–61 the MfS [the East German ministry for state security] could, thanks again to Blake, arrest about 100 more.'[17] Only after the Berlin Wall went up in 1961 does MI6's recruitment of East Germans seem to have stalled.[18]

Blake, based in the SIS offices attached to Hitler's Olympic Stadium, was supposed to help find out what the Soviets were up to. Part of his mission – oh, the irony – was to recruit Soviet double agents. As he told the Stasi in 1980: 'My task was to penetrate, so to say, the Soviet headquarters in Karlshorst. Well, the day before yesterday I gave a short lecture at the headquarters in Karlshorst, and I believe I can say that I have [carried out] this task ... [*interrupted by guffaws and hand-smacking applause from the agents*].'[19] (He had made exactly the same joke in his speech to the Stasi in 1977.)

He also told the Stasi:

I must say, I did have one success: I actually recruited a Soviet colleague, who told me 'very interesting matters'. I would meet him about once every three weeks in some bar in Berlin. We got on very well, drank a nice bottle of wine. He passed on something to me, and I passed on something to him. [*Laughter from the agents*] So the years in Berlin went by. [*Laughter*][20]

Just before Blake's arrival in Berlin, the British and Americans thought they had pulled off a thrilling intelligence coup: they dug a spy tunnel under the Soviet sector in Berlin to intercept communications. (The story is told in rich detail in Steve Vogel's authoritative 2019 history, *Betrayal in Berlin*.)

The British and American services had each independently come up with the idea for Operation Stopwatch/Gold (as this early instance of 'hacking' was called), but had ended up joining forces. The young CIA was grateful for the SIS's expertise,[21] while the British could never have pulled off the half-mile-long tunnel on their own, because it was to run near the American sector,[22] and would cost several million dollars. Blake recalled that the Americans 'were immediately willing to pay for everything. Because the English are poor, that was of course a very important thing for them.'[23] The tunnel tap – the most direct line the West had ever had into Soviet thinking

– began in May 1955. The whole operation was shrouded in 'cover stories within cover stories', said the CIA's future director Richard Helms. Even many of the agency's own senior people were kept out of the loop.[24]

But Blake had betrayed the tunnel before it was even built. As luck would have it, he had been the secretary at the meeting in London where Stopwatch/Gold was conceived. Given the job of typing up the minutes, he then handed a carbon copy to Kondrashev on the top deck of a London bus.[25] Kondrashev passed the paper on to Moscow, noting, 'The information … is of interest.'[26] It was indeed. Handing over that document was the peak of Blake's KGB career.

When SIS unmasked him in 1961 and discovered his betrayal of Stopwatch/Gold, it assumed that the Soviets must have used the tunnel to pass bogus information, *disinformatsia*, to the West. Bizarrely, however, this does not seem to have happened. Most historians now believe that, although a select group of KGB officials knew about the tunnel all along, these people kept it secret even from other Soviets, including most of their KGB colleagues.[27] In other words, almost none of the Soviet officials speaking or sending messages had any idea the West was listening in. The vast bulk of the conversations overheard through the tunnel taps were genuine.

At a round-table conference in Berlin in 1999, organised jointly by former CIA and KGB officers, ex-Soviet participants confirmed this account of the tunnel.[28] The CIA's historical review came to the same conclusion: 'The intelligence that had been collected was genuine.'[29] Blake told me: 'The Soviets, once they knew what was going on, let it continue even though they could have stopped it.'[30] The KGB defector Oleg Gordievsky and the former East German spy chief Wolf also agree – to a greater or lesser degree – that this is what happened.[31] Wolf wrote in his memoir *Man without a Face*, published in 1997, by which time the GDR and the USSR had disappeared and he was presumably free to speak:

> The Soviets knew about the tunnel from the start, thanks to their brilliant double agent in British intelligence, George Blake. But while this means they protected their own conversations, they never told us anything, leaving us unguarded and exposed. This was lamentably not out of character for the Soviets.[32]

When the East German Politburo found out, it was furious with its Soviet 'friends'.[33] Clearly the East Germans, as a mere satellite people, were beneath the KGB's contempt.

Why didn't the KGB blow the tunnel? The CIA's own secret history of the tunnel, written for internal use in 1967, pronounced itself baffled: 'It is most probable that we will never know the exact rationale behind the Soviet moves.'[34] But since then, historians seem to have worked it out. Blake's revelation of Stopwatch/Gold had plunged the KGB into a quandary typical of the spying game. If the Soviets exposed the tunnel, the British and Americans would try to work out how they had found out about it. In that case British suspicion could easily have fallen on Blake. There were countless western spies in Berlin who might know something that would give him away. The KGB was desperate not to let that happen: over the years it had gone to such lengths to protect 'Diomid' that no more than three people in its Moscow centre knew his true identity.[35]

Alternatively, if the KGB wanted to use the tunnel to spread *disinformatsia*, it would have to let various Soviet and East German institutions in on its discovery – which again risked exposing Blake. The main users of the tapped phone lines were the Red Army and the GRU, Soviet military intelligence. Many in the KGB would rather stiff-arm these rival organisations than endanger their own prized British mole.[36] In Kondrashev's phrase, 'The value of the source outweighed the value of the secrets.'[37] Or, as Blake told the Stasi agents in 1980: 'It showed how highly they valued my broader work.'[38]

While the tunnel was up and running, Blake kept the KGB informed of what the West was discovering. Kondrashev recalled one particular package from the British spy: 'A very voluminous document, about ninety pages long, including only the important information that had been intercepted by the British and Americans.'[39] Meanwhile the KGB did repeatedly suggest to the Soviet military that it ought to improve its telephone security. It even sent indiscreet speakers verbatim transcripts of their conversations.[40]

It should be added that Yevgeny Pitovranov, the KGB's resident in East Berlin in the 1950s, claimed in the 1990s that he had informed Marshall Andrei Grechko, the Soviet commander in East Germany, about the spy tunnel. However, he did so only after the tunnel had already been operating for some months.[41] Pitovranov – who didn't know himself at that point that it was Blake who had revealed the tunnel[42] – recalled the following conversation:

Grechko: Well, listen, what kind of secrets are those? A couple of phone conversations – so what? Mostly they just talk nonsense, maybe a joke, something about work.

Pitovranov: Andrei Antonovich, I'll show you three documents that our agents have fished out of the wastepaper basket of Organisation Gehlen [the West German intelligence service]. Look what kind of information can be provided by chance. And that's just paper. Can you imagine what could be learned from our phone traffic? Even the most disciplined commanders are sometimes careless.

Grechko: Yes. What do you expect from us?

Pitovranov: Not much. Take precautions. Be sure that your people phone with caution, and do not mention the KGB.[43]

But the Soviet military paid little attention to the KGB's warnings.[44] Most military people continued to use the lines blithely unaware that they were being tapped. Soviet communication remained so open that 'one of the messages intercepted in the Berlin tunnel revealed the existence of a Soviet agent working for British intelligence in Berlin', write Christopher Andrew and the KGB defector Vasili Mitrokhin.[45] That agent would be exposed years later as Blake himself.

Chapman Pincher, a British journalist who specialised in espionage, wrote: 'The FBI officer Charles Bates, who was involved in the tunnel operation, told me that to keep the deception going to preserve Blake, the Russians had even allowed the Americans and British to catch an occasional unimportant KGB agent by feeding the necessary information through the tapped cables.'[46] Or possibly the Soviets just gave away these agents through negligence or accident.

The KGB continued to protect Blake and the tunnel long after it was necessary. They could have staged a discovery of the tunnel within weeks of its opening, without drawing suspicion to Blake. By that point, any one of the dozens of western intelligence agents working on the operation could have leaked it. Yet the KGB first developed a plan to uncover the tunnel only in late 1955.[47] It then waited several more months, until April 1956, before arranging for other Soviets to stumble on the tunnel after heavy rains had revealed the cables.[48] When the Americans saw that the tunnel was about to be discovered, they considered blowing it up, but finally decided not to, for fear of killing Soviet soldiers and inadvertently starting the Third World War.[49]

Blake had been nervously awaiting the discovery for over a year. He knew it might alert the British to his treachery. However, the KGB handled things so smoothly that nobody suspected him.[50]

The Soviets then turned the discovery into a propaganda coup. Ivan Kotsyuba, Soviet commander of Berlin, sent his secretary with a bag of 10 pfennig pieces to a phone booth in West Berlin. She rang around journalists in the Western sector and invited them to a very unexpected press conference at Soviet military headquarters in Karlshorst, and then on a tour of the tunnel, where the dastardly deeds of 'the Americans' were exposed. (The Soviets chose not to mention the tunnel's co-creators, the British, whom they were trying to pry loose from their American alliance.[51])

One East German newspaper sneered that the tunnel recalled 'the method of Chicago bank robbers'.[52] Another quoted enraged ordinary East Berliners, such as cemetery superintendent Paul Huhn: 'The extent of US spying is unfathomable. This is a dirty trick for which one cannot find words.'[53] East Germany, at the time, of course, possessed possibly the world's most elaborate surveillance state.

After the tap ended, western intelligence officials chalked up Stopwatch/Gold as a success. They had always expected their luck to run out at some point. Anyway, they already had a new source of intelligence on the Soviets: a week after the tunnel was uncovered, the first American U-2 spy plane arrived in Europe. That summer, U-2s began flying over Communist territory taking photographs[54] (some of which turned out to be fantastically misleading).

So many messages and phone calls had been intercepted during the tunnel's eleven-month life that teams of hundreds of Russian-speakers in London and Washington continued to record and analyse them until 1958. In all, 443,000 conversations were fully transcribed.[55] This itself was only a small selection. Blake estimated, 'To have transcribed one day's worth of conversations would have taken ten years.'[56]

Most of the material obtained was genuine.[57] However, almost all of it was banal. Peter Montagnon, a former British intelligence official, described a tapped Russian conversation on the night the tunnel opened: 'They were discussing sex.'[58] Lots more of that sort of thing followed.[59] Another favourite Soviet topic was the incompetence of their own officers. Even the most innocent conversations were conducted in such profane language that a glossary had to be created for the transcribers in London labelled 'TOP SECRET OBSCENE'.[60]

The taps did reveal what the CIA would later call 'invaluable' information on 'Soviet orders of battle and force dispositions'.[61] Had a conventional war broken out in the mid-1950s, this knowledge might have enabled the West to win it. The CIA listed other important discoveries:

- Early warning of the Soviet's establishment of an East German army
- The poor condition of East German railways
- Resentment between Soviets and East Germans
- Great tension in Poland.[62]

There were also tidbits on Soviet personalities and their rivalries, the names and addresses of Soviet atomic scientists[63] and information on the workings of the KGB and the GRU.[64] Some overheard fragments turned out to be the first tremors from a seismic event: Khrushchev's denunciation of Stalin in February 1956.

Thanks to the KGB's efforts to protect Blake, the western allies almost certainly obtained more intelligence from the tunnel than Blake ever sent to the Soviets. Kondrashev later admitted that the Americans were penetrating more deeply than he had imagined. Blake would write, accurately, in a statement for his lawyers in 1961, after his treachery had been exposed: 'This operation provided the West with more information than a thousand well placed agents could have done.'[65]

But perhaps the most significant information the western spies got from the tunnel was an absence – a dog that didn't bark. At no point did they pick up any signs that the Soviets were planning an invasion. None of the overheard conversations suggested unusual movements of men or materials. In other words, the very banality of the intercepted communications was immensely reassuring. In the words of historian David Stafford, 'No news was good news.'[66]

Blake and others have even gone so far as to argue that the KGB had deliberately engineered this channel of genuine information. If true, that would help explain why the Soviets let the tunnel operate for as long as eleven months.[67] Blake told me: 'They let it [the communications] continue not just for my safety, but also because they thought it was very good that the other side could see and understand that the Soviet Union wasn't planning to start a war.'

I said, 'So you see your role in the matter as good, too?'

'As productive, yes,' he replied.[68]

He was claiming that his treachery had helped keep the peace. Of course this sounds awfully like retrospective self-justification. Certainly the KGB was not an instinctive champion of openness. Nor did any Soviets claim later that this is why they let the West's tap continue.[69] Openness was almost certainly just an accidental side-effect of their efforts to protect Blake. Still, it is very possible that the tunnel, despite its betrayal by Blake, ended up being a net benefit to humanity.

The Game Is Up

In 1959 SIS transferred Blake back from Berlin to London. It may well be that by this point he was already under suspicion, and that the service wanted to keep an eye on him at head-quarters.[1] A year later it assigned him to a language school in Lebanon to learn Arabic. By then he was almost certainly under suspicion. SIS was sending him to a place where he would have no access to intelligence secrets.[2]

Decades later he admitted to the Stasi: 'I must honestly say I was pleased by this [move to Lebanon], because the pressure – though one gets used to it – of illegal work in the long term is quite hard. To lead a double life isn't easy, of course. To study Arabic for a year would be a form of relaxation for me.'[3]

At his trial in London in 1961 Blake said that, when he went to Lebanon, he had been hoping to quit his double agent's existence, 'possibly by trying to get, through my knowledge of Arabic, a good job in an oil company'.[4] His barrister Jeremy Hutchinson would even tell the London court that his client, through spending some of the 1950s in Britain, had begun to move away from Communism: 'He begins to understand, become more normal, to see life as it is led here, and he begins to realise how mistaken he was in many ways.'[5] That is possible, even if in his Moscow exile, a ward of the KGB, Blake never said anything of the kind.

By the spring of 1961 he was studying at the little Arabic-language school MECAS, which was housed in an old silk factory at Shemlan, in the hills outside Beirut. ('The biggest espionage centre in the Near East', grumbled the Lebanese magazine *Hawadith* in February 1961, voicing a widespread local suspicion for which at that moment there seemed to be no evidence.[6])

It was an idyllic place and time. 'Lebanon in 1960 was another world,' recalled David Gladstone, a British diplomat-in-training who was on Blake's course. 'There was a fully functional social scene, people with money throwing parties, a casino down the road. Above all I enjoyed it because I had a fast car and we could travel around the Middle East.'[7] There was skiing in the mountains, 'sea bathing' in Beirut, tennis and squash. Prospective students were told: 'Amateurs should bring their rackets etc.'[8]

Some Arabists scoffed that MECAS 'taught a version of Arabic that only MECAS alumni could understand'.[9] Nonetheless, the school's influence would survive far beyond its closure in 1978. 'In the mid-1990s, the Permanent Undersecretary, the Political Director and the Chief Clerk at the FCO, as well as the Head of MI6 and the Director General of the British Council were all graduates from MECAS', writes Juliette Desplat of the UK National Archives.[10]

Blake was the star of his course. Much of his early acquaintance with Arabic in Cairo seems to have stuck with him.[11] He loved the language's 'beautiful, logical, almost mathematical construction'.[12] Away from school, too, life seemed good. He had a happy marriage, two young sons and a third on the way. On the surface he must have seemed beyond suspicion. As the British historian Hugh Thomas later noted: 'Blake lived an impeccably dull life, had no amusing friends to drag down to perdition with him, seemed (even to his wife) an ordinary family man, and had no vices apart from treachery.'[13] Nonetheless, back in Europe, SIS was getting ready to rumble him. His life and his young family's were about to change for ever – and his fall would mark British society too.

Blake's unravelling had been set in motion in 1958, when a letter written in fluent German reached Henry J. Taylor, the American ambassador to Switzerland. Taylor passed it on to the embassy's CIA station chief.

The letter-writer identified himself only as 'Heckenschütze' ('Sniper', in German). He claimed to be a senior intelligence officer in a Communist country, but didn't say which one. He offered to help identify Soviet moles who were working for western spy services.

Heckenschütze's first reports quickly identified seven Soviet spies working in the US, Britain and Israel. But he also sent a list of twenty-six Polish officials whom British agents in Warsaw were hoping to recruit as double agents. He said he had obtained the list from the KGB. The CIA quickly deduced that the KGB had got the list from a mole in the British secret service. The Brits angrily denied it. They said Heckenschütze's list was fabricated – even that the names on it could have come from the Warsaw telephone directory.

Then came the breakthrough. 'To everyone's astonishment,' writes the American investigative journalist Edward Jay Epstein, 'a researcher in the CIA's Eastern European Division discovered that British intelligence had sent essentially the same list to the CIA a year or so earlier.'

The CIA now knew that the Soviets must have got the list from the files of British intelligence.[14] The KGB later worked out what had gone wrong: an over-diligent KGB adviser had passed the list to Polish intelligence, ignoring the order that any material coming from 'Diomid' had to be cleared with his superiors first.[15]

MI6 now knew it had a mole, but didn't know who he was. It also knew that he had passed on two other secret British documents to Moscow. Only ten officers, including Blake, had had access to all three documents. An investigation was held, and it exonerated all ten. British counter-intelligence continued to presume that gentlemen wouldn't be so caddish as to spy for the Russians. It seems to have concluded that the KGB had got hold of the documents through a burglary of an MI6 safe in Brussels.[16]

But MI6 did realise that there was a mole who was doing damage. British secret agents were disappearing, not turning up to meetings or supplying less and worse information than before. One British agent had even been executed, according to a defector's report.[17]

Then, in January 1961, 'Heckenschütze' defected to West Berlin with his East German mistress, who knew neither his real name nor his line of work.[18] He turned out to be Michael Goleniewski, a senior Polish counter-intelligence officer with a handlebar moustache (who in later years in western exile would insist that he was the last of the Romanovs, Grand Duke Alexey, son of the murdered Tsar Nicholas II). MI6 sent an officer to interrogate him. Goleniewski, terrified that the interrogator might himself be the British mole intent on killing him, 'insisted on being in one room while the MI6 man was in another, with an interpreter running between them', writes Chapman Pincher.[19]

Goleniewski's testimony, when combined with an accusation by Horst Eitner, an unmasked Berlin double agent who
had worked with Blake, was damning for Agent Diomid.[20] A
CIA historical review mentions yet another informant: the
Polish chief of secret police, 'Col. Alster, a Jew, who defected
to the West after learning in late 1960 that the Soviets were
planning secret anti-Semitic measures. Among the Soviet spies
Alster identified was George Blake.'[21] The SIS officer Harry
Shergold was now confident that Blake was the Soviet mole.[22]

In March 1961 the service informed Nicholas Elliott, its
station chief in Beirut, of its discovery. Elliott then engineered
an apparently casual encounter with Blake during a showing
of *Charley's Aunt* at a local theatre. He mentioned that head
office in London wanted to see Blake 'in connection with a new
appointment', and suggested he fly home a few days later, that
Easter Monday.[23] Elliott was deliberately encouraging, telling
Blake it was a good sign that the personnel department was
taking his next job seriously. An intelligence officer who spoke
German, Dutch, Russian and Arabic was a rarity, he said.

Still, as Elliott would admit in his final interview before his
death decades later, he said goodbye to Blake unsure whether
the traitor had walked into the trap.[24] SIS was worried that
Blake would 'do a fade' from Lebanon to the USSR. Blake did
indeed suspect that the British had unmasked him. 'I thought
there was something going on,' he told me, 'but I didn't con-
cretely know what was wrong.'[25]

Anxious, he arranged to meet his Soviet handler on an
empty Lebanese beach. The handler checked back with
Moscow, and days later reassured Blake that he needn't worry:
London didn't suspect him. Blake's trust in the KGB's judge-
ment after ten years in their service must have been great.
The Soviets had even managed to 'discover' the Berlin tunnel

without endangering him. Crucially, too, the handler's reassurance was exactly what he wanted to hear: it spared him the torment of having to break the news to Gillian that he was a KGB agent and then flee to Syria, probably without her and the children.[26] 'I would have to leave her or take her with me, and I don't think she would have come with me.'[27] On the other hand, if he flew to London, he thought he would probably be fine. Nearly twenty years later, he still claimed to be pleased he hadn't done a bunk: 'Otherwise I would always afterwards have felt that I had fled for nothing and that there had been no reason to do it. So I was very happy that I could travel to London.'[28]

When I asked him what he felt the moment he arrived at the SIS's personnel department on Petty France, near St James's Park, he replied in English: 'The game is up.'[29] He told the Stasi men in 1980: 'I was immediately arrested. I will tell you that this arrest happened in an English way. It may be interesting to you to hear how that works.'[30]

At Petty France, recalled Blake, a friendly Shergold 'said he wanted to discuss certain questions which had arisen in connection with my work in Berlin'. Blake assumed the conversation would take place at head office in Broadway. But instead, 'Shergy' (as he was known inside SIS) walked him across St James's Park to Blake's old office, the stucco mansion in Carlton Gardens – the best venue, Blake later realised, to record an interrogation.[31] The moment had come that Blake, as a self-described 'realist', had been expecting for years.[32] Given the quantity of information he had betrayed, it was probably inevitable.

At Carlton Gardens two other colleagues 'in the Soviet field' greeted him cordially.[33] Here was his final showdown, and he was to have it with fellow members of a close-knit club, a small group of men 'whom I knew very well, with one of whom I even had very good personal relations'.[34]

For the first two-and-a-half days of questioning Blake revealed nothing. In the evenings the suspected KGB agent was allowed to return to his mother's house in Radlett in Hertfordshire, although SIS did take the precaution of having someone tail him there.[35] Blake recalled: 'Knowing that I was in serious danger, that, whatever happened, life would never be the same again for any of us, I had to pretend to my mother that all was well.'[36]

He knew he was poorly prepared for an interrogation. In the past he had occasionally asked his first KGB handler, Nikolai Rodin, known as 'Korovin' – an intelligence legend who had also handled the Cambridge spies – what to do if he was unmasked. Should he try to turn his trial into a political demonstration?[37] Korovin always refused to discuss the issue. He argued that in a perfect system nothing could go wrong, and that to talk about failure was itself a sign of weakness.[38] In his colleague Kondrashev's view, Korovin suffered from 'arrogance, overconfidence, and indifference to others' views and problems'.[39]

Now, under interrogation, Blake was left cursing Korovin. The only strategy left to him was the simple one that Philby once counselled to East German spies: if caught, 'Deny everything!'[40] When one of the SIS interrogators suggested Blake had spied for the USSR, he erupted, 'Absolutely untrue!'[41] Had he stuck with denial, he might have got away with it: SIS probably had no evidence against him that could have stood up in court.[42] Dick White, then head ('C') of SIS, said that if Blake did not confess, 'we'll invite him to fly to Moscow'.

Blake's early biographer H. Montgomery Hyde, who had worked for MI6 during the war and retained friendly sources in the service, writes that at one point during the interrogation

Blake left the building for lunch and was trailed by two Special Branch policemen. Hyde says they

> watched Blake approaching a telephone kiosk as if to make a call and then suddenly changing his mind. He appeared to be in some distress since he repeated the performance, the assumption being that he thought of telephoning his local Soviet contact for advice but could not make up his mind.

When the interrogations resumed, writes Hyde, Blake was challenged about his planned phone call.[43] It's impossible to know whether or not this particular episode happened.

Chapman Pincher describes one interrogator, Terence Lecky, trying to intimidate Blake by casting 'menacing glances … at an imposing pile of files, seemingly full of evidence'.[44] However, by the third morning, it seemed that Blake's denials might get him off the hook. MI6 would never again have trusted him, but he might have been allowed to disappear into a kind of purdah, like Philby, who after resigning from the service as a suspected double agent had found a niche as a foreign correspondent in Beirut. Shergold, the chief interrogator, said later: 'After another half hour, Blake might have been free.'[45]

Then, suddenly, Blake cracked.[46] It happened when Shergold suggested to him that his treachery was understandable, almost excusable: he had been forced into it through torture and blackmail in the North Korean camp. Blake, by his own account, burst out: 'No, nobody tortured me! No, nobody blackmailed me! I myself approached the Soviets and offered my services to them of my own accord.'[47]

In 1990 Bower asked him, 'What was the look on their [the interrogators'] faces?'

Blake replied: 'Of great amazement.'

When a Dutch friend of mine versed in wartime history read this passage, she was reminded of Protestant resistance fighters in the northern Netherlands who, when captured by the Germans, revealed all their group's secrets because their faith would not allow them to lie.

Blake must have found it oddly tempting, after keeping his secret for all these years, to unburden himself at last, especially to such an understanding set of listeners. He later devoted a lot of thought to trying to grasp why he had confessed. In 1980 he told the Stasi: 'Really it was as simple as when one says to a small boy, "You stole the plums", and he says, "No", and one says, "I know you stole the plums", and he says, "Yes, I stole them."'[48] In 1999 he reflected again: 'I don't know what it was that suddenly made me say it. I wanted them to know why I had done it.'[49]

His one vulnerability under interrogation was his pride in himself as a man of conviction. Probably more than the thrill-seeking Burgess or Philby, this unbending Calvinist was an ideological spy –'a phenomenon such as had hardly appeared in these islands for some four hundred years', noted Prime Minister Harold Macmillan.[50] So keen was Blake to spell this out to his long-standing colleagues that he sacrificed his hopes of freedom. He insisted (the SIS files record) that he had spied 'for purely ideological motives, although he was on many occasions offered large sums of money'.[51]

Having confessed, a savvier spy would then have asked for an immunity deal before agreeing to reveal more. Blake did not.[52] Once he had begun spilling the beans, he just kept on spilling, perhaps hoping for clemency in return. Later in jail he told a fellow prisoner that 'he was still unable to understand why he had received such a long sentence; he had co-operated with the authorities after his arrest'.[53]

At one point during his outpourings he asked his interrogators, 'Am I boring you?' 'Not at all,' one of them replied. Bower, whose book *The Perfect English Spy* gives the fullest description of the interrogation, recounts another gem:

> Blake: Perhaps you should give me a revolver and leave me alone in the room?
>
> A voice: Oh no, it's not as serious as that![54]

The interrogators remained polite, soothing and genial, hoping to get this oddly naive traitor to reveal as much as possible. Blake did so. Afterwards he confessed to the police too.[55] White was disdainful: 'No backbone and unstable. Having taken a high-minded line, he's just crumpled up. He's a Walter Mitty character. He even believes that he deserves punishment.'[56]

The self-confessed Soviet spy was then allowed to spend another night at his mother's home in Radlett. She was his closest confidante, but he was under orders not to tell her anything.[57] Afterwards Blake and his interrogators proceeded to Hampshire, where he poured out more confessions during a surreal weekend at Shergold's country cottage. At one point Blake joined Shergold's mother-in-law in the kitchen to make pancakes for the SIS men. (He always prided himself on his talents as a pancake chef.) Blake found the scene 'endearingly English'.[59] But it wasn't as endearing as it looked. According to Michael Randle and Pat Pottle, the peace activists who would eventually help him escape from Britain, Blake had been told that the authorities were trying to work out whether to bump him off rather than put him on trial.[59]

When the staff at SIS were informed that Blake was a mole, some refused to believe it. Others cried.[60] David Cornwell (aka John le Carré) had then just finished his SIS training course, having learned 'skills I never needed and quickly forgot'.[61] On the day of his group's initiation, Robin Hooper, the pink-faced head of training, broke the news to them that a traitor had been discovered named George Blake. 'Then he wept', writes le Carré's biographer Adam Sisman, 'and sent them home while it was determined whether they had been blown, or whether they were still employable under cover.'[62] John de St Jorre, who was an MI6 officer at the time, recalls:

The internal investigation, done by the counter-intelligence people back in head office, came up with a classification code called 'Cruet'. As far as I know all officers in the service were assigned a colour: Cruet Red for the fully compromised; Cruet Amber for those in doubt; and Cruet Green for those who were clean of any Blake contamination. I am pretty sure that I was Cruet Green.[63]

Le Carré, looking back decades later, would reflect that Blake had given away 'the entire breakdown of MI6's personnel, safe houses, order of battle and outstations across the globe'.[64] Still, the shock of betrayal inside the service was less than it would be in 1963, when Philby defected to Moscow. Philby, after all, was a very senior official and 'one of us', whereas Blake had always been something of a foreigner.[65] And although Blake had worked for SIS for seventeen years, few of his colleagues knew him more than superficially.[66] After his exposure, MI6 became hesitant to recruit foreign staff for fear that they might prove disloyal.[67]

Le Carré, who never met either Philby or Blake, said he felt 'a quite particular dislike for Philby' because 'he had so many of my attributes', and 'an unnatural sympathy' for Blake, because he was half a Dutchman and half a Jew, and in both capacities a most unlikely recruit to the secret ranks of the British establishment. Where Philby had been born inside the fortress and spent his life burrowing beneath its ramparts, Blake had been born in the wastes of foreign and ethnic disadvantage, and had gone to great lengths to gain acceptance by those who secretly despised him: his employers.[68]

Le Carré later elaborated: 'Well, Blake was a better writer. And somehow the absolutism of his conversion, and his enormous physical courage and endurance, impressed me. I think it's really only by contrast with Philby that I've found some admiration for Blake.'[69] Le Carré also diagnosed in both traitors 'a predisposition to deceive', adding: 'History delivered for both of them a seemingly noble motive.'[70]

In Lebanon the heavily pregnant Gillian Blake was told that her husband was a KGB agent, and instantly believed it. 'I didn't say, "You must have got hold of the wrong man, it can't be true." As I thought back to George's background and to the six-and-a-half years of our very happy life, it all fitted in somehow.'[71] Trying to explain his actions, she pointed out his 'lack of the substantial background that people have, of family and schools and all that sort of thing'.[72] The Dutchman Louis Wesseling, a fellow student of Blake's on the Arabic course, said later: 'It was my Eureka moment: that's it! That's why he is so reserved, wants to be open but cannot be fully open, holds something back from me, is a friend but not a total friend – that's it.'[73] As Gillian commented, 'He really had no friends, though he knew a lot of people and liked a lot of people.'[74]

* * *

In the spring of 1961, when Blake was unmasked, the British public was just entering the grip of a 'spy craze'.[75] The spy-fi television series *The Avengers* had been launched on ITV that January. Le Carré's first novel, *Call for the Dead*, would appear that summer. Len Deighton made his début the following year. The James Bond books were just becoming best-sellers, thanks partly to the revelation in March 1961 that President Kennedy was a fan.[76] On 20 June 1961 the United Artists studio in New York needed only forty minutes to agree a deal to make the first six Bond films.[77]

The source of the fascination was real life. That March, a month before Blake's arrest, a set of traitors known as the Portland spy ring had been jailed in Britain amid huge public interest. Two clerks at the Admiralty Underwater Weapons Establishment in Portland, Dorset, had photographed a large amount of classified information and passed it on to the KGB. Like Blake, they had been unmasked by Goleniewski.[78] Their story seemed made for the tabloid press:

> The clerks, a shambolic alcoholic and his middle-aged mistress, sold the secrets to a man posing as a Canadian (and apparently in the business of selling bubble-gum dispensers and jukeboxes), but who was in fact a Russian member of the KGB. The secrets would then be transmitted to Moscow by two American Communists living under false names in an unassuming villa in Ruislip and posing as antiquarian booksellers.[79]

After the Portland ring had been jailed, the *Daily Mail* noted: 'There will undoubtedly be repercussions on Anglo-American relations. It is only recently that the Americans have got over their mistrust of British security caused by the Fuchs case, the Pontecorvo case, and Burgess and Maclean.'[80] In the US, Senator Joseph McCarthy had created national hysteria about reds under every bed; in Britain, it seemed that they really were under every bed, even in Ruislip. Blake's arrest was just the latest in a sequence of British spy scandals.

Luckily, when SIS broke the news about Blake, the most senior Americans weren't as angry as they might have been. James Angleton, head of the CIA, reassured Dick White, 'It can happen to anyone.'[81] J. Edgar Hoover, director of the FBI, reflected sympathetically: 'Christ Himself found a traitor in His small team of twelve.'[82] Meanwhile President Kennedy was distracted by an intelligence fiasco of his own: the Bay of Pigs happened barely a fortnight after Blake's arrest. The failed American-sponsored invasion of Cuba by a ragtag mob of exiles left the US in no position to lecture the UK on intelligence blunders. When Allen Dulles retired from the CIA in September 1961, having been discredited by the Cuban misadventure, White told him that his generosity was 'never more manifest than in your recent handling of the Blake case'.[83]

Still, some in American intelligence did feel the British should have used polygraph lie-detector tests on Blake.[84] ('They regarded the polygraph as ungentlemanly', one American 'security expert' complained.[85]) This umpteenth British fiasco would leave the CIA wary of working with MI6 for decades to come.[86]

Harold Macmillan, who hated each of his many espionage embarrassments and referred disparagingly to the 'so-called Security Service',[87] responded to Blake's unmasking characteristically: 'The government could fall on this.'[88] His biggest worry was how the British public would react. Many Britons had already begun to suspect that a cabinet of ageing and incompetent public schoolboys was leading a fading empire into decay.

The prime minister did score a small victory in the Commons when he was asked why the Foreign Office had hired Blake even though he didn't have two British parents. Strict application of that rule, Macmillan pointed out, would have ruled out himself and also Winston Churchill, both sons of American mothers.[89]

The prime minister was so keen to keep the excruciating story quiet that he wanted to offer Blake immunity. He had never liked prosecutions of traitors. As he once explained, 'When my gamekeeper shoots a fox, he doesn't go and hang it up outside the Master of Foxhounds' drawing room; he buries it out of sight.'[90] In the British tradition an intelligence service was meant to be invisible. The very existence of MI6 was still officially denied at the time.[91] The organisation was referred to in Whitehall only with the euphemism 'the friends'.[92] Macmillan ordered a letter to be sent to the British press asking them not to mention that Blake had worked for MI6, nor that MI6 was overseen by the Foreign Office. When the latter fact came out, Macmillan (according to Pincher) called it 'the most damaging admission' of his political career.[93]

No SIS officer had ever been prosecuted for espionage.[94] However, Dick White insisted that Blake be the first.[95] Blake later reflected, 'Maybe it's better for me that they decided to take me to court.'[96]

The newspapers identified him only as 'George Blake, a government official, of no fixed address', charged with three offences under the Official Secrets Act.[97] The public would not learn anything about his betrayal of the Berlin tunnel, or much about Blake himself. The press, starved of information, inevitably tended to reimagine this dutiful father with theological leanings as a sort of real-life Bond.[98] And the writer Rebecca West commented: 'At first it looked as if the moral of this case was that we could trust nobody. For George Blake was an attractive man.'[99]

Much of the trial at the Old Bailey on 3 May 1961 was conducted in 'closed session'. Officially this was done to prevent British intelligence secrets from being exposed (insofar as any still remained). More likely, the aim was to limit the government's embarrassment.[100]

The establishment chose its A-team to punish Blake: the attorney-general, Sir Reginald Manningham-Buller, prosecuted the case, and the most senior English judge, Lord Chief Justice Parker, presided. Manningham-Buller (a faintly monstrous fat man nicknamed 'Bullying Manner') found the world of espionage seedy. During spy trials, hordes of journalists would camp out on his family's doorstep. The fuss intrigued his teenage daughter Eliza,[101] who, perhaps not coincidentally, ended up as director-general of MI5 from 2002 to 2007.

Blake's barrister, Jeremy Hutchinson, was a witty and hyper-articulate product of the Bloomsbury Group into which he had been born in 1915. His mother was the model for Virginia Woolf's Mrs Dalloway. Aged fourteen, he had his first bow tie tied for him by Lytton Strachey. Hutchinson the barrister– with his habit of referring to the judge as 'that poor old darling on the bench' – would become one of the models for John Mortimer's fictional hero Rumpole. Six months before trying to defend Blake, Hutchinson had made a name for himself defending Penguin Books in the famous Chatterley trial.[102] But at this point in his career, he had little of Manningham-Buller's weight.

Manningham-Buller worried that Blake would withdraw his confession in court, claiming that it had been obtained under duress.[103] Had Blake done so, then, given the secrecy of SIS, the prosecution might not have been able to produce any witnesses.[104] In that case Blake might have been acquitted. Blake himself only realised this too late. He told the Stasi in 1980: 'Maybe, although the service [SIS] had evidence that I had worked for the Soviet service, it wasn't the same as that a court would have convicted me. Those are two different things.'[105]

But, as he admitted to the Stasi, he blamed himself for having come to court unprepared: 'I hadn't occupied myself at all with English law on this subject. England, as you know, is a country where the law is very precisely observed, where you have to know exactly what rights you have and what rights you don't.'[106] And so, in court, he let his previous confession stand. Maybe in any case he was too principled to contest it. By 11.30 a.m. both lawyers had said what they had to say.[107]

Parker struck Blake as 'a friendly old man with a white wig and a red gown'.[108] But in his summing up, the judge described the case 'one of the worst that can be envisaged in times of peace'. Blake recalled, 'I was prepared for him to condemn me to death, but because I didn't know the law, I didn't know he couldn't do that ... He would gladly have done it, of that I am convinced.'[109]

Instead Parker sentenced him to three terms of fourteen years, to be served one after the other. A confused Blake didn't immediately grasp what this meant,[110] but Macmillan in his diary phrased it bluntly: 'A savage sentence – 42 years!'[111] Hutchinson would reflect wryly in the House of Lords in 1996: 'I appeared for Mr Blake at his trial in a professional capacity and secured for him the longest term of imprisonment that has ever been handed down by a British court.'[112] Cookridge called the forty-two years a 'kind of liquidation'.[113] If Blake served the full term, he would walk out of jail in 2003, aged eighty. The sentence was meant to be the end of him.

'Anyway, the British have guts!',[114] rejoiced Hoover in the US. But White was shocked by Parker's harshness (as was Philby, watching anxiously from Beirut). Some in MI5 and MI6 considered the long sentence counter-productive, believing that it would dissuade any mole from ever confessing again, reported Chapman Pincher.[115] Fourteen years – often significantly shortened for good behaviour – was a price that many double agents might be willing to pay to escape their entanglements. Even the physicist Klaus Fuchs, who had handed the Soviet Union the knowledge to build an atomic bomb, had only been sentenced to fourteen years in 1950 and was released after nine.

Macmillan clearly hoped that the Blake problem would now fade away, like the prisoner himself in his jail cell. The day after the trial, he told his cabinet that he proposed to resist any calls in parliament for an inquiry. 'It was also suggested,' the cabinet minutes say, 'that the anxiety aroused by this case might provide an opportunity for taking fresh measures to restrict the leakage of official information to the Press.'[116]

Hutchinson would always believe that Lord Chief Justice Parker's motives were political: that the forty-two-year sentence was meant to show the American authorities and the British public that Britain was serious about traitors. Indeed, in 2015 the hundred-year-old Hutchinson received a remarkable letter from the barrister Benet Hytner. In it Hytner described a conversation between himself, some other young barristers and Parker at a dinner in Manchester soon after Blake's trial. Parker had told them that before pronouncing sentence he had phoned Macmillan to ask how much damage Blake had done to Britain. Hytner wrote: 'I have a fairly clear recollection, but not an absolutely certain one, that he said that this call took place the night before the day of sentencing.' English judges are not supposed to discuss their cases in private, and certainly not with the prime minister.[117] If Parker's decision was influenced by unofficial information procured out of court and concealed from Blake's counsel, then the sentence was 'a miscarriage of justice', writes Hutchinson's biographer Thomas Grant, himself a barrister.[118] (Hutchinson died in 2017, aged 102.)

Even the mammoth sentence could not assuage Macmillan's humiliation. Blake's sentencing was followed the next year by the unmasking of John Vassall (a former cipher clerk at the embassy in Moscow who was spying for the USSR), and then in 1963 by Philby's flight to Moscow and the Profumo affair (a sex scandal masquerading as a security scandal).[119] The sequence of embarrassments eventually pushed the prime minister to resign in October 1963.[120] With hindsight, some in the establishment may have regretted the decision not to quietly bump off Blake. In Graham Greene's 1978 novel *The Human Factor* – inspired by the Philby and Blake cases, and by Greene's own dealings with the security services – an MI6 doctor kills a wrongly suspected office mole by poisoning.

In court, Hutchinson had pleaded 'mitigating circumstances'. I asked Blake what those circumstances might be.

Blake: I don't really know that myself [*laughs*]. In my eyes, from an English point of view there were no mitigating circumstances. The only thing – which the judge said too – was that I didn't do it for money, that I didn't get any advantages from it. But I don't know if you can call that a mitigating circumstance. That's the only one I can think of.

Me: So you regard the trial as having been fair, honest?

Blake: Honest?

Me: Just.

Blake: Yes, I think so.

Me: A difficult question, but would you have done it all again?

Blake: Huh?

Me: Would you have done it all again?

Blake: Well, that's a question one can't really answer, because life builds itself up from one situation to the next, the one flows as it were from the previous one, and you yourself don't know which way it's going. So I, eh, yes that, that question, I don't ask myself. 'Would I this or would I that?'[121]

10

The Human Cost

Until his death, aged a hundred, in 2014, the journalist Chapman Pincher spent much of his life covering espionage. So good were his sources that Harold Wilson, prime minister for much of the period from 1964 to 1976, developed an obsession with leaks to Pincher.[1]

A few weeks after Blake's trial, on 20 June 1961, Pincher published a front-page story in the *Daily Express* claiming that the forty-two-year sentence represented one year for each agent's life lost.[2] The alcoholic Labour minister George Brown – 'always an easy oyster to open', as Pincher reminisced much later[3] – had released the information almost the moment the two men sat down to an expensive lunch, on the very day that Blake's appeal was heard.[4]

Hutchinson would later dismiss the story of a year's sentence per agent's life as 'absolute rubbish'.[5] Blake, too, expressed disbelief, saying, 'It would really be an insult to British justice, it seems to me, that a judge would evaluate the life of an agent at one year.' But in fact, Pincher seems to have got it right. Tom Bower, who for his biography of Dick White was granted

New shock over spy Blake

By CHAPMAN PINCHER

GEORGE BLAKE, the Secret Service agent who spied for Russia, betrayed the names of at least 40 other British agents to the Communists, I understand. My investigations over the last 12 weeks also reveal that many of these agents have disappeared and several are believed to have been executed.

9. The *Daily Express*'s famous front page of 20 June 1961, which first gave the British public an inkling of what Blake had done. However, the number 'forty' is used incorrectly in the headline. He had in fact betrayed hundreds of agents; forty was just the approximate number he had sent to their deaths.

a series of interviews with White and other SIS officials, wrote that in the weeks before the trial 'SIS officers had contacted agents and sources throughout the satellite countries [of the Soviet bloc] and had concluded that Blake's treachery had cost at least forty lives, among them a Red Army technical expert whom Blake had personally known. That information was discreetly passed by Manningham-Buller to Lord Parker.'[6]

The *Express* story finally gave the British public some indication of Blake's crimes. However, the article's headline – '40 Agents Betrayed', beneath a drawing of forty stick men in black trenchcoats, a gimmick that Pincher's editor had long been wanting to use[7] – was inaccurate. Blake had betrayed many times that number. To quote that BBC interview from 1990:

Bower: You gave away the identity of every agent?

Blake: Any agent, yes.

Bower: Operating on behalf of MI6?

Blake: Yes.

Bower: How many is that?

Blake: I can't say but it must have been – oh, I don't know – but maybe 500, 600.[8]

Le Carré commented: 'He now claims hundreds, and who is to deny the wretched man his boast? His cause, like his victims, is dead.'[9] But Alexander Sokolov, a retired KGB counter-intelligence officer, provided a rare specific piece of corroboration from the Soviet side:

I think his most important work for Soviet intelligence, from the strategic point of view, was Blake's information on British agents who were sent to Balkan countries and the Soviet Union after the Second World War, in the 1950s and the beginning of the 1960s. Several hundred agents were arrested thanks to Blake's information.[10]

Blake once told a journalist that he had no idea how many agents he gave away: 'I never added them up.'[11] He always claimed to have no compunction about having betrayed them. He said he was surprised to find how well he could do it.[12] I don't think this is because he was a psychopath. Rather, for him, betrayal was part of the spying game. After all, spying on one's own country was fairly routine in his business. For much of Blake's time at SIS, he was tasked with persuading Soviets and East Germans to work against their states. 'This was my life work and it is bound to affect the way one looks upon betrayal,' he said.[13] Le Carré thought that British outrage at double agents was hypocritical: 'If your mission in life is to win over traitors to your cause, you can hardly complain when one of your own ... turns out to have been obtained by someone else.'[14]

Having your identity betrayed was part of the spying game too. In 1992, wheeled out by the KGB to address a press conference for western journalists, Blake said he hoped the agents he had given away didn't hold it against him.[15] He explained:

Those people who were betrayed were not innocent people. They were no better or worse than I am. It's all part of the intelligence world. If the man who turned me in came to my house today, I'd invite him to sit down and have a cup of tea.[16]

Asked once whether he was sorry about the betrayed agents, he replied: 'No, because they knew what their risk was. We were soldiers in the Cold War.' He admitted in his autobiography that a spy often did dirty work, everything from eavesdropping to blackmail to organising people's assassinations. 'One would never dream of doing any of these things as a private individual in pursuit of one's own personal interests', he added. But Blake was willing to do them for a cause. 'Perhaps I possess this ability to distinguish and separate the personal from the official to a high degree and it was this that enabled me to do my work as a Soviet agent.'[17] Blake could morally compartmentalise.

Nonetheless, he always denied that his victims had been killed. That was just 'an invention of the press', he claimed.[18] He liked to point out that, even at the closed sessions of his trial, he was never accused of causing any deaths.[19] However, that may simply be because SIS didn't have irrefutable evidence that agents had been killed, and would have been reluctant to produce witnesses or reveal secrets even before a closed British court.

Blake often said the KGB promised him that none of the agents he betrayed would be killed. He once went so far as to claim that the combined total of jail time his victims had served was less than the forty-two years he himself had been given.[20] In a handwritten document appealing against his sentence in 1961, he said he had 'stipulated ... and repeated' to the Russians 'that these agents should not be arrested', and 'that the only use the Russians should make of the information was to protect themselves'.[21]

He probably did stipulate all this. But his KGB spymasters – who were hardly the Sisters of Mercy – probably didn't listen to him. He should have known they wouldn't. Alan Judd, a British writer on espionage, asks: 'What did he think happened to Soviet spies caught in the deep Cold War – community service?'[22] Blake himself admitted to a journalist in 1990 that he couldn't be sure that these people had been spared.[23]

In any case, the Soviets had negotiated a get-out clause with Blake: if the Stasi found out about any agents through its own efforts, the Soviets couldn't stop it taking action. So whenever the Stasi did catch an agent, even if it was thanks to Blake's information passed on by the Soviets, the KGB could tell a wilfully credulous Blake that the agent's punishment had nothing to do with him.[24]

Blake never tried to check whether the KGB had kept its word about protecting the agents, probably because he was afraid to find out, notes Knopp.[25] Oleg Kalugin, the KGB's head of counter-intelligence, who had learned good English after the KGB managed to inveigle him into Columbia University in New York in 1958, and who would later become friendly with Blake in Moscow, shielded him from the truth: 'I didn't have the heart to tell him that his work led directly to the deaths of dozens of agents behind the Iron Curtain.' Blake

was a gentle, well-meaning, peace-loving man who probably
became a *de facto* serial killer. Rebecca West likens his role to
those of the First, Second and Third Murderers in *Macbeth*.[26]

Blake did have stronger moral compunctions than certain
other spies, notes Kalugin: 'Philby, on the other hand, knew
that his spying and tips to the KGB had doomed many men,
but he wrote them off as casualties of the Cold War.'[27] Kalugin
himself freely recounted having supervised the murder of the
Bulgarian dissident Georgi Markov, who was stabbed with
the infamous poison-tipped umbrella in London in 1978.[28] In
Kalugin's analysis,

> George Blake had that innocent mind … He is still a very
> naive man. He didn't want to know that many people he
> betrayed were executed. And I think we even discussed
> this subject at one point, and he wouldn't believe it. He
> would say, 'Well, I was told that this would not happen.'
> It did happen; he was not told.[29]

It seems almost certain that some of the agents Blake
betrayed were executed. But for decades we had no evidence
of what happened to these '500, 600' people, or even who they
were. Almost no details were revealed at Blake's trial, not even
in the closed sessions.[30] As late as 1996 a historical review by
the CIA named only one dead victim of Blake's: 'General
Robert Bialek, the Inspector General of the People's Police in
East Germany'.[31]

Bialek had been an anti-Nazi resistant who spent six years
imprisoned by the Gestapo. After the war he became a senior
Communist. However, he was a man of principle who actually
believed the 'workers' state' rhetoric, and he made the mistake
of starting a feud with a rising figure in the East German

security forces, Erich Mielke. After Bialek defected to the West in 1953, he began broadcasting on BBC radio to East Germany. This annoyed the regime.

The CIA's historical review says: 'His apartment in West Berlin was only a block from Blake's. In February 1956, acting on information from Blake, the East Germans under Soviet control kidnapped General Bialek and brought him back to East Germany.'[32] More precisely, Bialek had been invited to a fictitious birthday party in West Berlin, where two East German Stasi agents put a knock-out drug in his beer. Germany's *Der Spiegel* magazine recounted in 2010:

> Bialek realised what was happening, and hauled himself to the toilet, where he fell unconscious. There he was found by someone who thought he was simply drunk. The two agents quickly called a taxi and took the supposed drunk to East Berlin.

Bialek was probably extensively tortured over several months.[33] The CIA concludes, 'He died in a Soviet prison.'[34] Blake says in his autobiography: 'Whatever the truth about this kidnapping, I can only repeat that I had nothing to do with it.'[35]

The CIA's historical review also attributed the deaths of some unnamed victims to Blake:

> He was present at joint planning sessions concerning the activity of the anti-Soviet Russian émigré organization known as NTS. Four NTS leaders, who had previously entered and left the USSR, were caught on their next trip as a result of Blake's information, and were never heard from again.[36]

The MI6 officer Frank Bicknell noticed that the operations he arranged into Russia invariably failed, killing young agents. He later discovered that details of these operations, down to specific codenames, had been published in the Soviet press – presumably placed there by the KGB, which was using files passed on by Blake.[37]

The well-briefed Pincher named two SIS spies in Cairo, James Zarb and James Swinburn, as having been betrayed by Blake.[38] Both men were imprisoned in 1956, the year of the Suez crisis, when Britain was trying to depose Egypt's nationalist President Nasser. Swinburn, the Cairo business manager of the Arab News Agency, was released in 1959, and Zarb, a Maltese businessman, two years later.

It remains unclear whether Blake also had a hand in betraying two double agents in the GRU, Soviet military intelligence: Pyotr Popov, a lieutenant-colonel who was the CIA's first major source within the Soviet state,[39] and Oleg Penkovsky, a colonel who worked as a double agent for both the US and the UK.

The Soviets executed Popov in 1960.[40] When Blake was jailed in 1961, Penkovsky was still free, although possibly already under Soviet surveillance. 'KGB officers were stationed in apartments above and across the river from Penkovksy's home', wrote the CIA in a 'historical document' published in 2010. Before and during the Cuban missile crisis of October 1962 Penkovsky passed the Kennedy administration information about the Soviet missiles on Cuba. The CIA wrote: 'Because of Penkovsky, Kennedy knew that he had three days before the Soviet missiles were fully functional to negotiate a diplomatic solution. For this reason Penkovsky is credited with altering the course of the Cold War.' On the afternoon of 22 October 1962, in the middle of the Cuban crisis, the KGB seized him on a Moscow street. He was executed the following

May.[41] Blake told the Stasi in 1980 that he had worked for the SIS department that handled Penkovsky.[42] While in Berlin he had also known Ruari and Janet Chisholm, the MI6 couple who went on to handle Penkovsky in Moscow. Janet Chisholm, writes Phillip Knightley,

> would take her young children for a walk in a park. Penkovsky would wander by, stop to admire the youngest child and slip a box of sweets into its pram. The box contained film of secret Soviet papers that Penkovsky had copied with his Minox camera.[43]

It seems that that the KGB was watching these transactions. As Blake admitted to SIS under interrogation in April 1961, he had told the Soviets that Ruari Chisholm was an intelligence agent. Yet even after that SIS seems to have gambled that the KGB would ignore Chisholm's wife.[44]

On the other hand, Kondrashev told the CIA's Bagley after the Cold War that Blake hadn't helped the KGB unmask any significant enemy agents. Whatever spies Blake did expose, said Kondrashev, were mostly among the Russian émigré community and already known through the KGB's 'very adequate' penetration of that milieu.[45]

East Germany's Stasi did undoubtedly benefit from Blake's betrayals. A document in the Stasi's archives provides evidence of the fates of a few SIS agents based in the GDR. The document's anonymous author crows that 'the Soviet informant in the British secret service George Blake' gave the Stasi the names 'of about 100 spies in the years 1958–1961'.[46] There follows a list of the names and occupations of the six people whom the Stasi considered the most important British agents. They included a 'Stenographer in the Ministerial Council of the

GDR', a 'Colonel in the National People's Army', a 'Department Leader in the Ministry for Foreign Trade' and so on.

Five of the six names on the document have been redacted, to protect the privacy of the agents and their children. However, the film-maker George Carey saw an unredacted version while making his BBC documentary on Blake. A German researcher hired by Carey then found the court records for these six agents. Three had received life sentences in the GDR. Yet all but one of the imprisoned agents had been released by the end of the 1960s.[47]

At that point only Hans Möhring, who had been a senior official in East Germany's state planning commission, and had reportedly spied for Britain out of idealism,[48] was still in jail. Möhring would serve sixteen years of his sentence before West Germany finally bought him out in 1976.[49] He may well have 'held it against' Blake.

At least Möhring lived. That is telling. If the GDR didn't execute the most important spies, then it probably didn't kill the smaller fish either. Communist regimes had moderated their bloodlust after Stalin's death. However, no court records were found for one of the six names on Carey's list, the army colonel. The suspicion is that this man was handed to the Soviets and executed. As Kalugin implies, the KGB probably treated western agents more brutally than the Stasi did.

The East Germans did not forget their debt to Blake. The Stasi officer responsible for countering infiltration of the GDR by western spies in the 1950s was Bialek's old enemy Mielke.[50] Thirty years later, as head of the Stasi and the GDR's minister of interior – effectively the country's chief jailer – Mielke acted as a sort of luxury travel agent for his old British accomplice. Blake told me, discreetly:

It was possible for me and Ida and my son Mischa ... to go to the GDR. The minister of interior – Mielke, he was called – was very fond of me for one reason or another. And he did everything for our holiday in Germany on the Baltic Sea. They had a big sanatorium there, and we were very well received. When my mother turned ninety, we went there too; she celebrated her birthday in that sanatorium.[51]

In other words, betraying agents had its perks.

Mielke, at a meeting with visiting Soviet intelligence officers in November 1985, boasted about his own generosity to Blake, and specifically the hosting of Catharine's birthday in East Germany. He said it was a model for how a secret police force should treat its informers:

I always meet Blake, when he's in the GDR. I have absolutely no relations with him. But these are human relations. It gets talked about everywhere ... I wrote the mother a message of greeting. The most important sentence was, 'I congratulate the mother who has given birth to such a wonderful, heroic son, who has devoted his life to peace and progress.' In addition, I sent a present. Gen. Honecker [Erich Honecker, East Germany's leader] also sent flowers and a small token of appreciation from Meissen [the ancient German porcelain town]. The mother, of course, doesn't take the message of greeting with her. Blake takes it with him. Isn't this an inspiring example of party work?

In the past one barely acknowledged connections to these people [double agents]. Today the enemy names examples of when we let them down. The relationships with informants are a criterion of party work. Whoever leads this kind of agency has to be responsible until the end of life.[52]

* * *

Blake was responsible for an unknown number of agents' deaths. Without being specific, I asked him if there was anything he regretted.

He replied, in Dutch: '*Ik heb spijt van alles.*' This literally means, 'I regret everything.' But taken in the context of our whole conversation that day, I don't think that is what Blake meant. He had already said he didn't regret working for the USSR. Rather, I think what he wanted to say was: '*Ik heb spijt van van alles.*' The clumsy-sounding addition of the second '*van*' ('of') would change the meaning to, 'I regret all sorts of things'. That appears to have been Blake's meaning, because he then continued: 'I'm sorry about the suffering that I caused to people in one way or another and also in my own circle, because of course I would rather not have done that, but well, I – there's nothing to be done about that any more.'

Me: Do you still often think about that?

Blake: Yes, I think about everything. When you're as old as I am, you think about everything, and then everything goes through your head again and you see all those images from past times, and I often dream about police and things, but eh – so that is really the position.

Me: Images go through your head. What kind of images?

Blake [*laughs*]: I think back to everything. From let's say the Calvé Delft [food] factory in Rotterdam to what I have experienced here in the last few years.

Me: Do you have traumas?

Blake: What do you mean?

Me: Well, a trauma – something that really gets to you, something you have trouble dealing with.

Blake: No, I don't have that. I am a very satisfied man, who feels that in his life he has had an enormous amount of *geluk* [the Dutch word for both 'luck' and 'happiness'].

Me: You do look happy, I have to say.

Blake: Yes, ha ha ha ha! Yes.[53]

Perhaps he really was as cheerful as he appeared, or perhaps life had taught him to internalise his fear. From 1940 to 1961 Blake had lived almost continuously in dangerous environments. Even during quieter phases he can't have encountered much tolerance for fear or for post-traumatic stress disorder in MI6, Wormwood Scrubs or the Soviet Union. He had learned to grin and bear it.

Yet despite everything, he wasn't cold-hearted. At one point in our conversation, while we sat in the garden being eaten by mosquitoes, he began musing about the Russian Tsar Peter the Great:

Blake: The method by which he tried to modernise the country through violence, I didn't think that was very – I don't like violence. I think violence prompts counter-violence, and that remains an endless cycle of …

Me: But have you never used violence in your –

Blake: In my life? No, never. Physical violence, you mean?

Me: You never shot at anyone?

Blake: No. There was never a reason to [*laughs*]. I never had weapons. I have a gas pistol, but that's for self-defence if necessary, as it were. Otherwise I've never had the need to use violence. I must be honest, I have always tried to avoid it. I never put myself in a position that, eh, eh, must almost inevitably lead to violence.[54]

I think he was being sincere. Blake, raised in the pacific Dutch political tradition, was peaceable by instinct. He even avoided verbal aggression – as I found in our conversation, he was skilled at deflecting it amiably. Nobody who knew him seems to have recalled arguing with him.

Gerald Lamarque, a fellow prisoner during Blake's time in Wormwood Scrubs, a right-wing former army officer and a murderer who became a prison librarian, observed under his pen-name, Zeno: 'He abhorred anything that approached physical violence.'[55] That was why Blake had to spin himself a fantasy that the agents he had betrayed were not harmed. He chose to live in denial.

11

Espionage, Balls and Rackets

All these betrayals and deaths may have been pointless. That begs the great question about spying: how useful is it?

Two of the Cambridge spies, John Cairncross and Donald Maclean, arguably helped alter the course of history. Cairncross, the 'fifth man' in the Cambridge spy ring, may have secured victory for the Red Army in the Battle of Kursk, the biggest tank battle in history. From 1942 to 1943, while working at the British code-breaking centre Bletchley Park, he gave the KGB secret British decryptions of German messages. This informed the Soviets about the armouring of the new German 'Tiger' tank; confirmed that the Germans had discovered the position of Soviet regiments, prompting the Red Army to move them; and revealed the location of Luftwaffe squadrons, enabling the Soviets to destroy about 500 German aircraft before the battle.[1]

Maclean, as a diplomat in Washington from 1945 to 1948, passed on some of the West's biggest secrets to Moscow: the use of uranium in atomic bombs, the content of wartime discussions between Churchill and Roosevelt, Anglo-American negotiating positions for the Yalta conference of February 1945, the size of the American atomic arsenal, and the negotiations to create NATO. The Soviets appear to have used much of this information. Maclean's biographer Roland Philipps calls him 'the most influential spy of the century'.[2]

But Cairncross and Maclean were exceptional. Almost all other spies of their generation were much less consequential. Even their fellow double agents Philby and Burgess, who passed on a large share of their country's secrets, ended up complaining that the Soviets did nothing with the material. Many of the British documents that Burgess handed to the KGB were never even translated into Russian.[3] The same is probably true of most of the thousands of documents passed on by the Cambridge spies. Maclean's early Soviet handlers sometimes complained that they didn't have time even to photograph all the material he brought them.[4] After those handlers disappeared – probably in the purges of the late 1930s – there was, for at least some months in the run-up to world war, no Soviet agent in London to receive the Cambridge Five's intelligence. The British spies were again abandoned for six months early in the war.[5]

When Blake was working for Moscow in the 1950s, the KGB protected his identity by severely restricting the use of the information he sent. Arseny Tishkov, a senior KGB officer, wrote to department chiefs in April 1954: 'Proposals for dealing with this material are to be reported to me, and all measures on this question will be implemented only with my permission.'[6] One wonders how much of Blake's material – beyond the names of the agents he betrayed – was ever used by Moscow.

One problem with espionage is that paranoia about one's own colleagues often exceeds paranoia about the enemy. You might be able to recruit a traitor, but how could you trust him?

The KGB was always suspecting a golden double agent like Philby of being a British plant. When he or another British traitor passed on information that seemed too good and ample to be true, and didn't get caught doing it, the Soviets often assumed the material was western disinformation, perhaps part of some brilliant double-cross. Christopher Andrew writes of the five Cambridge spies recruited by the USSR in the 1930s: 'The KGB later concluded that they were the ablest group of foreign agents in its history.' And yet, Andrew adds:

> In October 1943 the [KGB's] Centre informed its London
> residency that it was now clear that all along the Five had
> been double agents, working on the instructions of SIS
> and MI5. There were few more farcical moments in the
> history of Soviet intelligence than the Centre's decision
> to despatch to London an eight-man surveillance team,
> none of whom spoke English, to trail the Five and other
> supposedly bogus agents in the hope of discovering their
> meetings with their non-existent MI5 case officers.[7]

Even when the Soviets believed a spy's piece of information, it had a tendency to get lost. Sometimes the suitcases full of British secrets were overwhelming. Sometimes intelligence got fragmented, distorted or discarded as it was passed up the KGB's hierarchy. Blake – certainly once he had spent some time in Moscow – came to understand this problem. In 1999 he told the Dutch journalist Hans Olink about an unnamed book he had read, written by senior CIA officers with a KGB officer. The book (probably *Battleground Berlin*, by David E. Murphy, Blake's old minder Kondrashev and George Bailey) had concluded that the Soviets knew much more than the western powers about the other side's doings. However, Blake added:

The only thing is that they often didn't manage to use that good information, because due to their own – how shall I say this? – narrow-minded view, they didn't want to believe what was in there … They only wanted to see what they wanted to see. If the information didn't match their ideas, they didn't want to use it.[8]

He blamed this kind of thinking on the Soviet system itself:

The Russians here have a lot of esteem for their boss, and the higher he is, the more esteem and fear. And if the intelligence service gave information that didn't match the boss's view, then either that information wasn't passed on, or it was changed so that it did match the boss's view. So he was never correctly informed … It worked like that throughout the whole system: don't give information that isn't pleasing to your superiors … That was a mirror of the whole society.[9]

This Soviet tendency helps explain why Stalin ignored possibly the most valuable single item of intelligence of the Second World War. In 1941, Maclean in London and Richard Sorge, a Soviet agent in Tokyo, were among several sources warning the Kremlin that Germany would soon invade the Soviet Union. 'The Weekly Political Intelligence Summary compiled by the [British] Foreign Office had been flagging up the [German] offensive for two months before it happened,' writes Roland Philipps. 'When Stalin had heard that the German ambassador to Moscow was hinting at the invasion a few weeks before, on top of the warnings from both overt and covert channels for months, he said, "Now disinformation has reached ambassadorial level!"'[10]

On 15 May, Sorge specifically predicted that the invasion would come between 20 to 22 June. But Sorge's information didn't match the boss's view: Stalin was then still in alliance with Germany. Famously, Hitler was said to be the only person he trusted. After one of Sorge's warnings, Stalin dismissed the spy as 'a little shit who has set himself up with some small factories and brothels in Japan'.[11] On 21 June Stafford Cripps, the British ambassador to Moscow, warned that the invasion would come the next day[12], yet when it did, the USSR was taken by surprise. Had Stalin believed the intelligence, millions of Soviet citizens might have lived.

As Blake recognised, Stalin's successors continued to ignore the USSR's vast foreign espionage apparatus. 'Intelligence had little influence on Khrushchev's basic views towards the United States', writes the former US ambassador Raymond Garthoff. Khrushchev didn't bother to find out how the Americans might react before he tried to cut off West Berlin in 1958, or before he sent nuclear missiles to Cuba in 1962.[13]

Under Khrushchev's successor Brezhnev, 'the opinion of Intelligence was usually ignored or not even seen by political leaders deciding most important foreign policy questions', writes Oleg Kalugin.[14] Just to be on the safe side, anything that might 'upset Leonid Ilyich [Brezhnev]' was removed from reports, admitted the KGB foreign intelligence officer Vadim Kirpichenko.[15]

Sir Richard Dearlove, former head of MI6, summed it up in 2017: 'If you look at the history of Soviet intelligence ... they're massively successful at collecting intelligence. But relating intelligence production to making policy was a real weakness in the Soviet system.'[16] Of course, western systems had their own shortcomings. While Dearlove was running MI6, American and British intelligence reports assured George

Bush and Tony Blair that Saddam Hussein had weapons of mass destruction.

The secrets that Blake and the other British spies passed on to Moscow were often ignored. Yet even the ones that were believed rarely shaped Soviet policy, let alone changed the course of history. We are conditioned to think of the world of espionage as a treasure chest of great secrets. In fact, it is more like a junk shop whose proprietor has lost track of his stock. Spies, said le Carré, 'provide second-rate intelligence whose lure lies in the gothic secrecy of its procurement, rather than its intrinsic worth'.[17]

The left-wing journalist Paul Foot wrote of Blake's 'dreary cycle of finding things out for Britain, photographing them and handing them over to Russia':

> None of this made the slightest difference to the plight of humanity. A Communist Party branch in Clapham would have done ten times as much, even if it had encouraged only one group of workers to form a union, or helped save only one tenant from eviction.[18]

Blake himself understood the limits of espionage. Asked in 1992 about the damage he had done to western intelligence, he replied: 'I don't want to overrate my own importance, but certainly I did damage. It cannot be otherwise. But … we must not overstate the importance of intelligence services. You see, the Cold War was fought to a large extent by the various rival intelligence services. But if we look at what actually decided the issue, it wasn't the intelligence service, it was the economy, the success of the economy. Whether the CIA had been stronger or whether the KGB had been stronger, or the British intelligence service, wouldn't have made any difference. What made a difference was which of the two economies was the most successful.'[19]

Spying in the Cold War wasn't primarily a means of uncovering vital information. Rather, it was an internal game between western and eastern spy services. In the words of the journalist Geoffrey Wheatcroft, 'Spies spy on spies spying on spies.'[20] Blake reportedly once remarked in Moscow, 'In London we used to call our office the Wimbledon Club, because it was all balls and rackets.'[21]

In the spying game you scored points by foiling your opponents' espionage plots or unmasking their spies. To the people involved, these could be matters of life and death; to the rest of the world, they scarcely mattered. Perhaps readers and viewers enjoy the very inconsequentiality of the Cold War spying game: it is almost light relief from the worst horrors of the twentieth century.

At Blake's trial in London in 1961 his barrister Hutchinson plausibly presented his client's work as fairly inconsequential. Blake, he said, had never 'given information which in his view could be used against this country in the sense of doing military damage or anything like that'. All that Blake had intended, argued Hutchinson, was 'the disruption of the Intelligence Service'.[22]

In truth Blake had intended more. However, the worst damage he did to Britain was caused not by any piece of information he handed over, but by the very fact of his unmasking. Every time a senior British official was exposed as a Soviet spy – a regular, almost ritualised event in the period from 1946 to 1963 – Britons' trust in their own society crumbled a little bit more. People in MI6 began to look at each other and wonder, 'Are you a KGB agent?' After Blake and Philby were exposed, SIS created a Directorate of Counter Intelligence and Security to sniff out traitors.[23] The service's anxiety eventually spiralled into the paranoid mole-hunting by 'Spycatcher' Peter Wright, which almost tore the intelligence services apart in the 1960s and 1970s. Wright got it into his head that Sir Roger Hollis, head of MI5, was a Soviet agent. And the paranoia stretched into politics too. The popular story that the security services suspected Prime Minister Harold Wilson of being a Soviet agent probably isn't true,[24] but the rising Labour MP Bernard Floud did commit suicide in 1967, months after being grilled by Wright on his supposed Soviet ties.[25] Blake helped create paranoid dysfunction inside the British state – not by all his hours of diligent photographing but by the unintentional act of getting caught.

The worst damage that Blake could do to Britain was by being unmasked. Yet the KGB never seems to have grasped this. It spent a decade going to enormous lengths to prevent his unmasking. The KGB valued him above all as a spy passing on intelligence, when in fact that was probably the least important thing he did. Even after his exposure the Soviets did little to milk it as a propaganda coup. Then for years after his escape from the Scrubs, MI6 waited in vain for him to pop up triumphantly on Soviet TV to tell his story.

The great majority of double agents such as Blake, who must have fancied themselves serious historical actors, have ended up in the dustbin of history, their treasonous slog almost pointless. They had barely any effect on geopolitics. What they did no longer matters much, except to their victims.

Yet who they were still fascinates. Their tangled human stories continue to inspire books and movies. In part it's because the double agent embodies the popular fantasy of living a double life: *I might look like a pen-pusher in a suit, but secretly I'm doing dastardly deeds for an enemy nation.* The feckless young loser who becomes a jihadi must experience the same thrill.

Foreign Traitor

Blake has gone down in British history as a traitor. This raises the question of whether – quite apart from his Communist beliefs – he felt any hostility to Britain itself. One theory is that he turned against the country because the British establishment excluded him as a part-Jewish foreigner. In Dick White's words, 'Blake was partially motivated by his feeling that he would never be accepted as a social equal by his colleagues because he was foreign born.'[1] This theory mirrors one about the Cambridge spies Burgess and Anthony Blunt, who supposedly became traitors because the establishment excluded them as open homosexuals. (The British upper class at the time accepted that young males would have gay experiences, but expected them to give it all up after university. Blunt and Burgess did not.) The literary critic George Steiner wrote: 'The homoerotic ethos may have persuaded men such as Blunt and Burgess that the official society around them, whatever prizes it might bestow on their talents, was in essence hostile and hypocritical. It was, consequently, ripe for just overthrow.'[2] But does British snobbery really explain George Blake's treachery?

The belief that social exclusion produced traitors was popular around the time of Blake's arrest. Today only the upper-class British traitors of the 1950s and 1960s are widely remembered. However, the nation's 'other ranks' generated a few too, and each time one of them was exposed, the standard explanation was that he had betrayed Britain as a reaction to snobbery. For instance, after a former telegraphist at the British embassy in Moscow named William Marshall was outed as a low-level spy in 1952, he complained: 'I was a misfit at the embassy from the start. The people there were not in my class of people.' He added that, when his bus-driver father had been disabled by a wartime bomb, higher-ups had worried only about his bus.[3]

In 1962, a year after Blake's imprisonment, it was the turn of John Vassall, a clergyman's son who had worked as a cipher clerk at the embassy in Moscow. Vassall had attended a boarding school so minor that it had run out of money and turned into a grammar soon after his time there. After being exposed as a Soviet spy, he cited snubs from the ambassador and other British diplomats in Moscow: 'They branded me as a social climber.' Vassall's excuses delighted popular newspapers during the Macmillan boom, a time when Britain's class system was coming under pressure.[4]

Blake certainly experienced some exclusion by the establishment. Elizabeth Hill, his beloved Cambridge professor, would later recall: 'I never for one single moment thought that he was anything but British – though there was a slight greasy look about him, which gave me the idea that he might have some perhaps Jewish blood in him, or perhaps something oriental, tinge of oriental somewhere.'[5] Blake says in his autobiography that Britain, even more than other western European countries, suffers from 'exaggerated class-consciousness ...

which often degenerates into sheer snobbishness'.[6] He saw 'something fundamentally wrong, something decidedly un-Christian, in judging people by what class they belonged to'.[7]

After his exposure the standard explanation was parroted: British snobbery had pushed him into treachery. Those who believe this have pointed to the end of his post-Liberation relationship with Iris Peake, a woman so much posher than Blake that she later became lady-in-waiting to Princess Margaret. It sounds like just the kind of snub that could drive a man into the arms of the Soviet Union. Certainly Blake's first wife, Gillian, believed it was significant.[8]

But Blake himself dismissed this interpretation as 'just thought up'. He described Peake as a 'girlfriend' but added: 'It was a friendship which was normal at that time of life – and it came to a natural end. I don't think she ever wanted to marry me and I don't think I ever wanted to marry her.'[9] The story that her snobbish rejection broke his heart may have stemmed from the cack-handed intervention of her father, Sir Osbert Peake. When Blake visited the family mansion in Yorkshire soon after the war, the Tory MP took it upon himself to tell him there was no chance of a marriage, even though the young people probably weren't contemplating one.[10]

What did bother Blake (he says in his autobiography) was that the British authorities gave him forty-two years in jail while letting off Philby and Blunt scot-free. Blunt even got to keep his knighthood and his job as Surveyor of the Queen's Pictures after his confession in 1964. He lost the knighthood only in 1979, when Prime Minister Margaret Thatcher publicly denounced him.

The contrast between Blake's treatment and Philby's was particularly blatant. Macmillan and Dick White agreed in 1963 to offer Philby 'immunity from prosecution in return for

a full confession and complete cooperation', writes Ben Macintyre, who adds: 'No such deal had been offered to George
Blake; but then Blake, a foreigner, was not a gentleman.'[11]
In the event things unfolded differently, but still to Philby's
advantage. In 1961 Nicholas Elliott had lured Blake back from
Lebanon to Britain to be caught and then jailed. Two years
later, back in Lebanon to deal with another traitor, Elliott
seems to have tacitly encouraged his old wartime pal Philby to
flee to the USSR.[12] (It must be added that Philby, having seen
how Blake had been gulled, wasn't about to step onto a plane
to London.[13])

Blake might also have noted that Cairncross was never
prosecuted despite making a full confession to MI5's investigative officer Arthur Martin in 1964, and another to a journalist
in 1979. The Scot spent a comfortable old age in Italy and the
south of France, before returning to Britain to die in a Here-
fordshire village in 1995, aged eighty-two.[14]

Unequal treatment must have seemed particularly unfair to
a Calvinist from the egalitarian Netherlands. Blake grumbled
that Philby and Blunt were spared partly because they

> were both English and, what is more, members of the
> establishment – though that, it would seem, should have
> made what they did more and not less reprehensible in
> British eyes. I, on the other hand, did not belong to the
> establishment, was of foreign origin and could, therefore,
> safely be made an example of.[15]

Admittedly, he omits a crucial point: he made a full confession
to the police, something Philby was too cunning to do. 'Blake
lost his nerve', commented Elliott.[16] That made it easier for
the British to prosecute him. But Philby did make a partial

confession to Elliott, admitting to having spied for Moscow for a limited period. The last time the two friends saw each other, over dinner at Chez Temporel in Beirut, they went to the restaurant urinals together, where Philby handed Elliott several typewritten pages enumerating selected misdeeds.[17] Nonetheless, Elliott gave Philby the chance to flee.

Blunt and Cairncross weren't prosecuted either after confessing. It is possible that they did less damage than Blake, but that should have been for a court to decide. It does seem that the establishment – and specifically White, who insisted on putting Blake on trial – was tougher on the Dutch-Egyptian half-Jew than on upper-class British traitors. Pincher writes: 'Officers of both MI5 and MI6 ... have told me that he [Blake] was "a real outsider, greatly disliked by his colleagues", and that this was the reason why there were no internal moves to save him from prosecution.'[18]

No doubt Blake *was* resentful about Britain's class system. But this resentment isn't what turned him into a Soviet spy. It simply didn't play much of a role in his life up to the point in 1951 when he decided to become a KGB agent. Until then his relationship with Britain had been distant but pleasant. 'The precepts of my father had filled me with deep respect and admiration' for Britain, he wrote. He had admired British fortitude in the Second World War, and later appreciated Cambridge. He probably enjoyed the game of adopting a posh accent, and grooming the lower slopes of the British establishment for SIS. In Korea he got on well with his British fellow captives. Indeed, three unwitting mentors in his conversion to Communism were conservative members of the British establishment: Elizabeth Hill at Cambridge, Vyvyan Holt in the North Korean farmhouse and Carew Hunt, the SIS theoretician whose handbook 'Theory and Practice of Communism' jolted Blake's views.

Blake was fond of Britain, despite its snobbery. However, his feelings for the place didn't go deeper than fondness. He never became a British patriot. He had grown up a Rotterdam Calvinist devoted to his Dutch mother and to Queen Wilhelmina. He was already fourteen when he first set foot in Britain, on a stopover during a sea journey from Cairo to Rotterdam.[19] Before joining the permanent staff of SIS, he had lived in the UK 'for a year, or a year and a half altogether out of his life so far', pointed out Hutchinson at his trial. Blake, continued Hutchinson (who was trying to explain and thereby mitigate his treachery), was 'without attachment to this country by birth, by growing up, by tradition, by education'.[20] The patriot Donald Maclean was tormented by guilt for spying on Britain.[21] Blake wasn't. One mark of his foreignness was that all his life he said 'English' instead of 'British'. The only completely British thing about him was the name he had assumed in his twenties.

In sum, the British establishment probably did exclude Blake, but then he wasn't very interested in joining it. On the sofa in the dacha I asked whether his lack of British patriotism had made it easier for him to betray Britain. 'I think so, yes,' he replied.[22]

Would he have been able to betray the Netherlands? 'I don't know,' he said, 'but I don't think so. I was very Orange-minded.'[23]

Had his sons ever been made to suffer in Britain for their father's treachery? 'No,' Blake said,

That hasn't affected them at all. And when they've been here [in Moscow], they are never questioned about what they did here, and how I am. In that regard of course the English are very special: that they don't treat children as guilty for what their father did. And my mother, too, was never given any trouble.

Blake considered this British fair play. 'That's an English quality. Certainly. And one that I appreciate.'[24]

Later in our conversation, he returned from a visit to the bathroom with a new thought:

Blake: Yes, that's it, I want to say it: the strange thing about my life is that I owe everything, well not everything but a lot, to English people. English people arrested and sentenced me, and eh, as I said, eh, rightly. And English people helped me escape from jail and otherwise arranged my life, to a certain degree. And that's very peculiar, if you think about it.

Me: So you don't look back in anger at England?

Blake: Not at all! To the contrary. I'm a great admirer of England and all that is English.

Me: But a distant admirer. You don't feel any love for the country.

Blake: Love?

Me: Sentiment.

Blake: That's true. It's more, eh – yes, but a very large admiration. Love is something different.[25]

By law Blake was a traitor to Britain. At heart, he wasn't. To quote from Le Carré's novel *A Perfect Spy*: 'Love is whatever you can still betray ... Betrayal can only happen if you love.'[26] Or in Blake's words: 'To betray you first have to belong. I never belonged.'[27] He didn't feel British enough to betray Britain, and that must be why his treachery has attracted relatively little interest from Britons. Compare the thin trail of British writings about him with the fascination inspired by the Cambridge Five. Their stories mix the ancient themes of treachery, drink, sex and exile with the peculiarly British themes of eccentricity and class. Philby, in particular – the establishment's favourite son turned traitor – has prompted a whole genre of novels, films and biographies. Writings on him display an 'anti-hero worship' that is absent from the literature on Blake, notes the political sociologist Philip Davies.[28]

Christopher Andrew has pointed out that the British public isn't very interested in spying itself, which is why memoirs by former KGB agents hardly sell in the UK. Rather, the British public is interested in upper-class British spies, from Philby to James Bond.[29] Blake's story was different: he was a Dutch cosmopolitan who lost his faith, and filled the hole with Communism.

13

Headstands in Jail

In 1961 Blake entered Wormwood Scrubs prison ('the very name inspires sympathy for the inmates', wrote the *Times Literary Supplement*[1]). He would stay there for five peaceful years, the longest period he ever spent in Britain.

He went to jail in anguish over his abandoned family. His exposure and arrest had come as 'a terrible shock' to his wife and his mother, he wrote in his autobiography. 'For a long time I could hardly bear to think about the suffering I had caused them. It was too painful.'[2] (In this passage he doesn't mention the suffering he caused his three small sons, possibly because that remained too painful to express nearly thirty years later.)

Being jailed also meant a radical shift in his social status. 'Imagine,' he recounted to the Stasi officers,

I had been a civil servant, with a good position, who moved in good circles. And suddenly I found myself a state criminal, in jail, surrounded by all kinds of criminals and murderers ... You have to adjust to that a bit.

> Also, outwardly I had been a somewhat conserva-
> tively oriented civil servant, and now I had to appear
> before the whole world – before my fellow prisoners, the
> judge, everyone – as an open Communist.[3]

After twenty years of subterfuge, he suddenly had to learn how to live as himself.

Happily, there was another Soviet spy in the Scrubs to cheer him up. Gordon Lonsdale had been born in the USSR in 1922 as Konon Molody. At the age of ten he moved to California to live with an aunt, apparently with the blessing of the Soviet spy services. He learned perfect English, returned to the USSR in 1938, spent the war in Soviet intelligence and in 1954 moved to Canada and took the name Gordon Lonsdale. He later went to Britain as a KGB spy.[4] But his cover – as 'the director of several companies operating juke boxes, vending machines and one-arm bandits'[5] – wasn't mere cover. Lonsdale turned out to be a natural businessman, even if his subsequent claims to have 'become the KGB's first multi-millionaire illegal resident' were overblown.[6]

He was jailed for twenty-five years for masterminding the Portland spy ring. Against all regulations, because of an administrative mix-up he and Blake were briefly thrown together in the Scrubs. Lonsdale exuded good cheer despite the circumstances. One day he told Blake: 'Well, I don't know what is going to happen but of one thing I am certain. You and I are going to be on Red Square for the big parade on the fiftieth anniversary of the October Revolution [in 1967].' Blake was saddened when, a few days after this pronouncement, Lonsdale was suddenly moved to another prison.[7]

In 1963 Blake would become chummy with another imprisoned Soviet spy, the clergyman's son John Vassall. The two

Communists bonded over a shared interest in Christianity. Vassall lent Blake a book on the lives of the Catholic saints, and later recalled: 'He was cultured, with impeccable manners and an open heart.'[8]

A rare inmate of the Scrubs who claimed to have got a glimpse of Blake's inner turmoil was Michael Hollingshead. A dealer in the newly fashionable drug LSD, he had reputedly given the hippie guru Timothy Leary and more than one Beatle their first trip. As Hollingshead told it, he had been jailed on drugs charges after unwisely trying to conduct his own defence while high on LSD.[9] In jail he met Blake, who decided after some discussion that he would like to be 'turned on'. The idea probably appealed to his spiritual side. Hollingshead later recounted:

> Nothing much happened for the first hour. But as the session developed, Blake became quite tense, a nervous strain verging on complete paranoia, and seemed to believe that I was a Secret Service agent who had administered him a truth serum. He told me that I'd be killed within the next twenty-four hours, and made other similar threats. I felt quite baffled as to what to do, so I did nothing, merely listened as he went through his flip-out, and tried to reassure him by means of treating the whole affair as if it were all somehow something quite ordinary ...
>
> He finally settled down, however, and the last couple of hours were spent in deep thought and quiet reflection concerning his future existence, and he said he might not be able to stand up to many more years of incarceration.[10]

Sadly, in the absence of supporting evidence, Hollinghead's

biographer Andy Roberts suspects the story was probably made up.[11]

Blake had spilled lots of beans to his SIS interrogators before going to jail. During his first six months in the Scrubs he spilled more. Indeed, he was put in the west London prison partly so that SIS (as well as his remarkably forgiving wife) would have easy access to him.[12] 'He cooperated to the full', according to Nigel West.[13] SIS questioned him forty-two times in prison; MI5 also kept him busy,[14] and, if we can believe Blake's early biographer Cookridge, the CIA interrogated him too.[15] In the Scrubs, Blake reconstructed for SIS 'each meeting he had held with the KGB and identified his three case officers' from MI5 surveillance photographs, writes West. Naturally there isn't a word about this in Blake's autobiography, written in Moscow under the KGB's eye, but while in jail he must have thought that by co-operating he could get his sentence reduced.

He was in every way an unusual prisoner. A yoga devotee, he was known among his fellow convicts for standing on his head for fifteen minutes every morning and evening.[16] He spoke a 'stilted, colonial English'.[17] He dutifully sewed mail bags,[18] but otherwise used his time in prison to study a range of subjects (and got a degree in Arabic). He taught Arabic, French and German to uneducated fellow prisoners, helped them write petitions to the Home Office and dispensed advice on personal problems.[19] He joined a writers' group that met with a prison visitor named Alan Maclean – whose brother, the Soviet spy Donald, would one day become Blake's best friend in Moscow.[20]

Zeno, the murderer-turned-man-of-letters, wrote:

Sometimes when I go to his cell I am greeted by cockney voices holding an animated conversation in French, or

reading to each other from French newspapers or peri-
odicals ... I may find him alone, standing as he sometimes
does, and reading the Koran, which rests on a lectern
made for him by one of his pupils ... Or again he may be
lying on his bed reading a tale in Arabic from The Thousand and One Nights. Whatever he may be doing, if he is
alone I am greeted with a charming smile of welcome, an
offer to seat myself, and if the time is right an invitation
to take a mug of tea.[21]

Zeno admitted to having spent years in jail looking for a model
of humility – a quality he himself lacked. After getting to know
Blake, he wrote: 'I have found the model, and when I am in his
company I am conscious that he has the humility I seek.'[22] As
late as 1997–8, when the former MI6 officer Richard Tomlinson was in Belmarsh Prison for having written a book about
the service, he claims to have met an elderly prisoner who said
he had known Blake in Wormwood Scrubs and remembered
him as 'a cracking fellow'.[23]

In the Scrubs, Blake also became friendly with the peace
activists Michael Randle and Pat Pottle. The duo had been
jailed in 1962 for demonstrating at the US Air Force base at
Wethersfield. Both had a lot in common with Blake. Like him,
they had been prosecuted by Manningham-Buller. (Randle
claimed that it was he and his co-defendants who first came up
with the enduring nickname 'Bullying Manner'.) Like Blake,
the two peace activists considered themselves 'political prisoners'.[24] Like him, they were educated and principled men who
belonged to the intellectual élite of Wormwood Scrubs. And,
like almost everyone else in the Scrubs, they fell for Blake.
Randle recalled that Blake was known in jail for his 'extraordinary composure':[25]

He was very quiet, didn't say much. In fact some of the prison officers used to point to him as an example of how to 'do your bird', as it were, say, 'Look at that man over there. He's serving forty-two years. Now what are you worried about?[26]

By contrast, short-term prisoners like Randle and Pottle were used to being greeted with a mocking, 'Eighteen months! That's just long enough for a shit and a shave!'[27]

Only politics separated Blake from the peacenik duo. Randle and Pottle disapproved of both Communism and spying. Randle recalls at one point showing Blake an article in *Peace News*, headlined 'The Stinking Net of Espionage'. Spying, said the article, was 'nauseating', undemocratic and mostly pointless: 'Even after the most elaborate sifting of recruits and the elimination of "security risks", the small minority who are base enough to be employed as spies are usually immature, unbalanced, untrustworthy, unscrupulous and addicted to double-crossing.' When Randle asked Blake later what he thought of the piece, Blake replied, 'I agree with every word of it.' However, he added, 'Unfortunately, as long as the world is divided into nation-states, I suppose it is inevitable that espionage will continue.'[28]

Much as Randle and Pottle disagreed with Blake ideologically, they felt for him as a human being, on the principle of 'A man's a man for a' that'.[29] Randle said, 'It seemed to me hypocritical to send a man to jail for 42 years for doing for the Soviet side what he had been trained to do for the British side.'[30] Pottle wondered, 'What would he be thinking about lying alone in his cell? The future – there was no future. His family? – he had destroyed his family.' Even with full remission for good behaviour, Blake would be in jail until 1989.[31]

He did indeed look to be settling into the Scrubs for the long haul. His biographer Roger Hermiston writes: 'Blake's cell room took on all the appearance and function of a Cambridge don's tutorial room: book-lined, with an expensive Bokhara rug on the floor, and a medieval print of St Paul on the wall.'[32]

Yet this air of resignation was only a façade. In fact, Blake had been planning his escape from the day he entered jail. He would tell the Soviet newspaper *Izvestia* years later: 'After I was imprisoned, my mother had my suits dry-cleaned, and hung them in the closet. She often told friends, "These things can wait for their wearer, George will return to freedom!"'[33]

Being a British citizen, he knew he would never be traded to the USSR in a spy deal, as Lonsdale was. Blake would have to get out 'on my own strength'.[34] Everything he did in the Scrubs, even yoga, was in part, a strategy: he was a middle-aged man, and if he wanted to escape, he would have to be fit. He imposed a much tougher discipline on himself than the prison did.[35] And he looked around ceaselessly for potential accomplices. No doubt Blake genuinely liked Randle and Pottle. But with hindsight we can also see that he was cultivating them: he had identified them as reliable, morally upstanding people who would run personal risks to set him free. Importantly, too, they had connections to moneyed activists, who might be able to finance his escape. And because he didn't spend much time with the two men while they were in jail, the authorities wouldn't suspect them after he escaped.[36]

Acting the model prisoner was, in part, a strategy too: it would gradually persuade the authorities to let their guard down. When the newspaper *The People* reported a foiled plot to spring him from jail, Blake tried to get the Home Office to demand a retraction.[37] (The story came from a mentally disturbed Old Etonian ex-prisoner named Sacheverell de Houghton, who had told the Scrubs's governor that a helicopter with the word 'Police' painted on the sides was to land in the prison yard and whisk Blake off to East Germany.[38])

Blake's outward docility in prison had some effect. Six months after he entered the Scrubs, the prison authorities removed him from the 'escape list' of prisoners thought most likely to make a run for it. Nearly four years into his sentence, he was allowed a prison visitor. Roger Falk visited Blake fifty times from April 1965 until his escape, and recalled decades later: 'We had nearly two years of fascinating conversation. I used to take him on each visit a small packet of Bournville plain chocolate, and this modest if illegal offering (he didn't smoke) seemed to trigger off dialogues of – at least to me – far-ranging interest.'[39]

Lord Mountbatten, who in 1966 would write a report on prison escapes prompted by Blake's, noted that the authorities had assumed that 'he had settled down to prison life and showed no particular intention of escaping'. After all, wrote Mountbatten, 'from the outset he gave every appearance of being a cooperative prisoner'.[40]

Nonetheless, the authorities weren't entirely naive. They continued to keep a close eye on Blake. Fears that he would escape never went away, especially as ex-inmates of the Scrubs 'sometimes managed to sell plausible "rescue plans" to Fleet Street journalists', writes Nigel West.[41] Even after Blake was taken off the escape list, notes Mountbatten, 'the [prison] Governor also said that he should never be put in a situation in which trust was placed in him'. Visits from Gillian and Blake's mother (nobody else came to see him except intelligence officers) were held in a separate room, with a prison officer listening in. Conversation had to be in English, even though Blake and his mother habitually spoke Dutch together.[42] In 1964 the home secretary, Lord Brooke, noted that a Blake escape 'would be as disastrous as if another of the train robbers were to get out'.[43] But Sir Roger Hollis, the hapless head of MI5, reassured the government that it couldn't happen: Blake was too closely watched.

He was nonetheless quietly scheming. One day, some time after Pottle had offered his help in escaping, Blake pushed a note into his hand in the urinals. It was wrapped in half a bar of chocolate, which Pottle ate – guiltily, because he thought that maybe he was supposed to return it to Blake. The note said:

> If you feel you can help me on your release, go to the Russian embassy, introduce yourself and say, 'I bring you greetings from Louise'.
>
> Between 10 and 11 o'clock we exercise in the yard outside D Hall. If a rope ladder is thrown over the wall at the spot I have marked X [a sketch was enclosed] as near to 10.30 as possible, I will be ready.

If the Soviets agreed, they were to put an ad in the personal column of the *Sunday Times* saying, 'LOUISE LONGING TO SEE YOU', and the break-out would be scheduled for the next Sunday. But Pottle refused to co-operate: 'I had no intention of getting mixed up with anyone's secret services, and certainly not with the KGB.'[44] Blake later told him, 'I doubt anyway if the embassy would have been willing to help.'[45] He continued to look for accomplices. In 1964 a freshly released prisoner from the Scrubs, who had bonded with Blake as a fellow Dutch-speaker, told police that Blake had asked him to act as his contact 'on the outside'. The man had given Blake two phone numbers and an address, but Blake seems not to have tried to get in touch afterwards.[46]

Blake didn't yet know to which country he would escape, but wherever it was, he hoped that his wife and children would join him there. However, one day Gillian visited him in jail with big news. Blake told me:

> She had met someone who, eh, had fallen in love with her and wanted to marry her, and that was very dramatic in the sense that my escape plans were ready ... But of course I couldn't tell her, so when she said she wanted to divorce, I said, 'Well, I have nothing against that, you are practically a widow, so if you want to marry that's good, you should. I'll do everything to make sure it happens as quickly as possible.'[47]

According to the Irish journalist Kevin O'Connor, who interviewed Blake several times in Moscow, Gillian's new man was himself an SIS officer.[48]

Straight Out of Hitchcock

There are rumours to this day that it was the KGB that got Blake out of Wormwood Scrubs. The former KGB officer Victor Cherkashin would claim fifty years later that in 1963 he was meant to be sent to the UK with a range of assignments including 'the task of devising a plan to spring George Blake from prison. Once in Britain, I'd contact locals who'd pass the information to him ... Familiar with the intelligence Blake had provided us, I knew how seriously the KGB leadership took his case.'

Cherkashin's cover was to be as a representative of Sovexportfilm (which, yes, sold Soviet films abroad). But then KGB policy shifted: the decision was made that Sovexportfilm should earn some hard currency by actually selling films, so Cherkashin never went to Britain. Still, he says, 'In the end, a KGB plan accomplished his escape, though I don't know how many of my ideas, if any, were included.'[1]

It is more likely that Blake got out of jail without help from his employers. After Randle and Pottle were released, he knew he had people on the outside willing to assist him once he had escaped. Now all he needed was an accomplice to spring him from the Scrubs. He told the Stasi: 'I needed a man who first of all would do something like that, who secondly had the opportunity, who wasn't stupid, and who thirdly didn't have much more time in jail. I managed to find a young Irishman. He was a man with a great deal of initiative.'[2]

Sean Bourke was a bright, talkative, erratic drunk from Limerick – almost 'a stage Irishman'.[3] Born in 1934 into a poor family, one of seven brothers, he spent much of his adolescence in a reformatory at a time when Ireland routinely incarcerated its people in institutions. He was first sentenced aged twelve for stealing bananas from a lorry.[4] Later he worked as a tailor, printer, actor and writer.[5] He landed in the Scrubs after sending a home-made bomb to a policeman who had accused him of molesting a boy. (The bomb exploded, but the policeman survived.[6])

Crucially, Blake told the Stasi, Bourke 'had no connection to the people of whom I hoped they would help me.'[7] This wasn't entirely accurate: Bourke did know the peaceniks, from the same literature course on which he had met Blake, but he hadn't been close to them.[8]

Shortly before the Irishman was to be released, Blake asked him for his help in an escape attempt. Bourke agreed – apparently because he liked Blake, liked adventure and disliked authority. He later explained: 'You couldn't help liking him. Virtually everyone at the prison, both inmates and authorities, were deeply impressed by Blake's charm and good manner and by his humanitarian concern for the well-being of his fellow men.'[9]

A fellow prisoner, the upper-class far-right fraudster Kenneth de Courcy, who got on well with Blake in jail, and kept his escape plan secret after accidentally finding out about it,[10] observed that Bourke is a natural good friend in need and Blake was more than lucky to meet him; he was a far better friend than Blake is ever likely to prove. That is not to say that I in any way dislike Blake. But I regard him as a man devoid of mercy.[11]

In November 1965 Bourke was released from prison. Acting on Blake's instructions, he then asked Blake's mother and sister Adele for £700 to fund the escape. As Bourke tells it, the women considered it, and Mrs Blake surreptitiously discussed the matter with her son in Dutch on prison visits. (If so, she broke the English-only rule.) However, Catharine and Adele eventually decided it was too risky.[12]

Nonetheless, the men continued planning the jailbreak. Bourke contacted Randle and Pottle, who agreed to help. Randle borrowed money to buy walkie-talkies and materials for a rope-ladder.[13] Bourke then smuggled a walkie-talkie into the jail, so that he and Blake could communicate. He also recorded some of their conversations, storing up proof of his role in the escape. Heard today, the recordings give a sense of the awkward alliance between flamboyant Irish performer and experienced KGB agent:

Bourke: I hope that in four days' time it will be just like the words of the old Irish song, [*warbles*]

> 'I'll look into your eyes and hold your hand
> I'll walk beside you through the golden land.'

Blake: Yes, lovely, and I'm looking very much forward to hearing you singing it very soon directly.[14]

Bourke, Blake, Randle and Pottle had agreed that the

10. The getaway car: the beaten-up Humber in which
Sean Bourke drove Blake to the safety of his bedsit. Eager
to claim credit for the escape, Bourke later told police
where they could find the abandoned vehicle.

escape would be effected unarmed.[15] On the evening of 22
October 1966 the Irishman parked his old Humber car beside
Wormwood Scrubs. He held a pot of pink chrysanthemums in
which he had hidden his walkie-talkie. Any passer-by would
have taken him for a visitor to the neighbouring Hammersmith
Hospital. But he also had with him a rope-ladder made of knit-
ting needles.[16]

The time of the break-out had been set for 6.15 p.m. By
then Blake had climbed out of a prison window, the bars having
been broken beforehand by a fellow prisoner who was, in
Blake's words, 'a good burglar'.[17] Meanwhile, though, Bourke
on the other side of the wall had unwelcome company. First,

a man who seemed to be a security officer came to stare at his car, forcing him to drive off for a few minutes. Then a courting couple parked beside him. Now it was Bourke's turn to stand beside their car staring at them, until they in turn drove off.

All this time Blake had been waiting anxiously inside the prison wall for Bourke to throw him the ladder. As time passed he began to give up hope. He claims to have waited 'a whole hour, which turned into an eternity'.[18] He later recalled thinking: 'Now he's gone away. I couldn't go back, but I also couldn't go over the wall.'[19] At this point, it seemed probable that he would be caught and spend the rest of his life in prison.

Then, suddenly, he heard Bourke's voice coming through again.[20] But by this time people were parking in the street for visiting hour at the hospital, and Bourke had to resume his wait. Time was ticking away. Blake knew that, when the prisoners were returned to their cells at 7 p.m., the wardens would discover that he was gone.[21] It was about 6.55 p.m. when Bourke finally threw the ladder over the wall.[22] Blake climbed up it. When he reached the top, he realised that Bourke had forgotten to affix a metal hook to the ladder so that it could be attached to the wall. Blake jumped 20 feet, broke his wrist and cut his forehead, but Bourke picked him up and bundled him into the car. In Simon Gray's play *Cell Mates*, when a minor character is told about the escape, he responds: 'But that's – that's – (*Laughing.*) It's like something out of a – a comic book!' Within twenty minutes Blake and Bourke were safe inside the bedsit that the Irishman had rented just a few hundred yards from the prison, at 28 Highlever Road. Soon afterwards, a prison officer found the rope-ladder and Bourke's chrysanthemums, still wrapped in florist's paper. Only about forty-five minutes after the breakout did the prison authorities alert the police.[23]

News of the escape delighted the prisoners.[24] The *Observer*

11. The exterior wall of Wormwood Scrubs prison a month after Blake's escape. It was a long way for a forty-three-year-old to drop.

quoted one prisoner as saying the atmosphere in the Scrubs was 'like Christmas Day after Father Christmas has been'.[25] In Zeno's telling, even the prison wardens seemed happy that Blake was free.[26] Meanwhile, at Highlever Road, Blake and Bourke watched TV news report the escape, and raised a glass.[27]

Some people on the outside were pleased too. 'Flags went up on my house,' Jeremy Hutchinson said half a century later.[28] The prime minister, Harold Wilson, reportedly remarked in private: 'That will do our Home Secretary [Roy Jenkins] a great deal of good. He was getting too complacent and he needs taking down a peg.'[29] Jenkins hadn't even known that Blake was in Wormwood Scrubs.[30]

The British prison system was starting to look as error-prone as the British intelligence services. A couple of dozen prisoners had escaped in the previous two years, including the Great Train Robbers Charlie Wilson and Ronnie Biggs, and six men from Blake's own wing of Wormwood Scrubs on 5 June 1966. Ten more prisoners would get out in December 1966, including the 'Mad Axeman' Frank Mitchell, who once at liberty began writing letters to the newspapers.[31] 'Over Christmas,' wrote the *New Yorker* magazine in early 1967, 'the breaks were such almost daily occurrences that some of the more sporting-minded newspapers took to facetiously reporting the figures in handy tables, like football-league results or horse-race prices.'[32]

Yet none of the other escapes was as embarrassing as Blake's. Tory MPs in the House of Commons bayed 'What about Blake?', but Jenkins silenced what he called their 'tribal bleating'. He pointed out that, if the spy shouldn't have been in porous Wormwood Scrubs, it was the previous Tory government that had put him there. Cheered on by Labour MPs,[33] Jenkins landed the Tories with much of the blame for lax prison security. The *Daily Mirror* credited him with 'a Commons victory unequalled by a minister since Labour returned to power [in 1964]'.[34]

The Scrubs immediately tightened up its controls, removing some of the prisoners' privileges. The inmates were furious. One evening eight days after Blake's escape, about 150 of them refused to return to their cells after dinner, and sat at their canteen tables chanting, 'Blake, Blake, Blake!'[35]

Soon afterwards, Mountbatten's report concluded mournfully: 'Wormwood Scrubs Prison as constructed and administered had little chance of holding him once he had determined to go.'[36] The Home Office belatedly set about improving security across the country. The net effect of Blake's escape on British prisons would be to make them tighter, nastier places, more concerned with containing prisoners than rehabilitating them.[37] Blake could have foreseen this. Zeno, who saw the changes in the Scrubs, wrote: 'It would upset George to know that he, who while he was here had a greater concern for others than any man I have ever met, was responsible for this.'[38] Blake himself admitted it, writing in his autobiography: 'I am deeply sorry about this.' However, he hadn't let his altruism deter his escape.[39]

* * *

Alfred Hitchcock was captivated by Blake's escape. 'The details of that are incredible', he marvelled later.

> They sound as though they came straight out of a movie. Bourke and Blake communicated by a walkie-talkie that had been smuggled into the prison. Hammersmith hospital is right next to the prison, and Bourke used to stand outside it on visiting days with a bunch of flowers wired for sound, into which he would talk to Blake. They finally got him over the wall one night when there was a film show in the prison, with all kinds of delays, and then hid him three minutes away until the fuss had died down.[40]

Hitchcock planned to base his fifty-fourth and final film on Blake's escape. He bought the rights to Bourke's 1969 memoir *The Springing of George Blake* and to Ronald Kirkbride's 1968 novel *The Short Night,* which is based on Blake's story.[41] In 1970 Hitchcock approached Walter Matthau and Catherine Deneuve to play the leads,[42] although the promotional poster designed years later starred Sean Connery and Liv Ullmann.[43]

Hitchcock spent much of his final decade scouting locations for the film (provisionally titled *The Short Night*), and putting together a script. Blake's politics didn't interest him. What did was the jailbreak, and the human story of a fugitive leaving behind his wife and children, recounts David Freeman, the young screenwriter who worked on the final version of the script with Hitchcock in 1978 and 1979.

The problem was that Hitchcock, by then nearly eighty, was arthritic, losing his memory and generally falling apart. 'Let's play with my pacemaker,' he would say to Freeman, and he'd attach the thing to his electric typewriter. He would repeatedly ask his assistant Peggy Robertson, 'When do you think I'll go? When?'[44]

He coped by drinking, often brandy, which he hid from his nurses in a brown paper bag in his office bathroom.[45] One last high was his knighthood, after which he started calling himself 'The short knight'. He then accepted his decline, and told a relieved Universal Studios he was quitting.[46] He died in April 1980, but still managed to play one final Hitchcockian joke: there was no coffin at his funeral. He had quietly arranged to have himself cremated beforehand.[47]

All that remains of *The Short Night* is the script. 'EXT LONDON – ARTILLERY ROAD – 6.45PM,' it begins. 'A drizzly London evening in the fall. Wormwood Scrubs prison and Hammersmith Hospital sit side by side. Artillery Road, hardly more than a service lane, runs between them.'[48]

There's a moment in the script when the hero, the American spy-hunter Joe, sighs: 'Spying and espionage. Everybody suffers from it. The gains are vague and abstract. The losses are all personal.' Freeman comments: 'If there is a psychological-political-cultural meaning in this melodrama, this is it.'[49] That was Hitchcock's take on Blake's profession. The script ends with the Blake character's sons watching as the train carrying their father disappears into the Soviet Union.[50] Here is a film just waiting to be made.

* * *

Blake spent the first few weeks after his escape hiding in London. It was an anxious time. A discreet doctor had to be found to mend his wrist, Bourke seemed to have made almost no plans for getting Blake out of the country, and Bourke and Blake kept having to find new hiding places. Blake reflected later:

> It's one thing to get out of jail, that's maybe not so ter-
> ribly difficult in England, but it's very difficult to get out
> of England, because England is an island. That's why the
> English prison authorities generally don't worry much
> when somebody escapes; they know that sooner or later
> he'll swim back into the net. But of course, in my case
> they did worry a bit more.[51]

Randle and Pottle proved a devoted support team. However, harbouring Britain's most wanted man stretched their amateur capacities. As Randle's wife, Anne, asked: 'What do we do now?'[52] They had only one concrete plan: to use the drug meladi-nine to dye Blake's skin, and then smuggle him out of the country as a black man.[53] Blake, who never much liked the idea, once sug-gested an adaptation: 'I think I could be rather more convincing as an Arab,' he said, then wrapped a towel around his head, bowed and intoned, '*Salaam Aleikum*'. His accomplices imme-diately resolved to dye him only light brown, and fly him to an Arab country.[54] But eventually the idea was binned. Blake wasn't keen to risk becoming 'a half-caste for the rest of my life'.[55]

Meanwhile the British public had become obsessed with the jailbreak. Conspiracy theories abounded. One of the most popular held that the UK's intelligence services had sprung Blake or let him escape: otherwise, people argued, he could never have got out so easily.[56] Another theory was that he hadn't been in Wormwood Scrubs in the first place.[57] When Randle asked his anarchist friend Alex Comfort (later the author of The Joy of Sex) to help with the escape, Comfort countered with a conspiracy theory of his own: what if MI6 had turned Blake, as part of some intricate plot against either the KGB or anti-nuclear campaigners? Comfort recalled telling Randle, 'It sounds a damn silly idea to me, because you have no idea about which side Blake is on or who he's been talking to, or even whether this is being planted on you.' Long afterwards Comfort reflected, sadly: 'But they didn't have the brains to see that … They wouldn't see an intelligence stunt coming if it had a label on it.'[58]

The British secret services were equally misguided. They seem to have suspected until the late 1980s that Blake's escape was a KGB plot, albeit with Bourke as a freelance operative.[59] Perhaps that just sounded better than admitting that (in Pottle's phrase) 'two peaceniks and an Irish petty criminal' had liberated Britain's most notorious traitor.[60]

Days after the escape, Blake and Bourke moved into the maisonette of the anti-nuclear clergyman John Papworth and his wife, Marcelle, in Earls Court. However, the Papworths weren't happy to find out that they were housing George Blake. The outlaws had only been in the house one day when Papworth walked into their bedroom to have a conversation along these lines:

Papworth: My wife is undergoing a course of analysis.

This requires her to be absolutely frank with her analyst and not to conceal anything from him.

Blake: Are you saying that she has told him about us?

Papworth: Everything. There's no point in it if she isn't completely frank. You must understand, of course, that what she says to him is in the strictest confidence.

Blake: And what did the analyst say when she told him?

Papworth: Oh, he said that she was imagining it, and that it was because there had been so much publicity about the escape of George Blake.

Blake: In view of what you have told us, I think it would be advisable if we left immediately and went back to our previous address.[61]

In 1997, when Papworth publicly admitted his role in the escape, he said he had done it strictly as a matter of principle: 'I took an instant dislike to Blake. He was a dyed-in-the-wool Marxist and he had an absolutely closed mind, but that was not the point.'[62]

Blake and Bourke finally found relatively tranquil medium-term lodgings at Pottle's flat in Hampstead.[63] (Pottle's role in the escape may explain why his father-in-law, Harold Abrahams, the Olympic sprinter and hero of *Chariots of Fire*, never received a knighthood.[64]) There were dinners, with time for political debate. Randle and Pottle challenged Blake about Soviet acts of terror, such as the Stalinist purges of the 1930s. 'As far as any of us can recall,' they write, 'George never explicitly defended these policies.'[65]

Helpfully, the authorities were meanwhile still exploring the theory that Blake had already got to either Ireland or Eastern

12. Pat Pottle in 1961. Five years later, the anti-bomb campaigner hid his old prison pal Blake and the maddening Bourke in his Hampstead flat.

Europe. When Roy Jenkins later discovered that Blake had hidden in London after the escape, he grumbled: 'I consider that MI5 and the Special Branch contributed little skill to the attempt to find him.'[66] The press had got the wrong end of the stick too. The *Express* suggested Blake might have escaped on a fishing boat straight after getting out of jail.[67] A front-page story in the *Evening Standard* on 21 November laid out exactly how he had fled to Frankfurt on the night of the jailbreak, and revealed that he was now in East Berlin. Pottle, reading the paper on the London Underground, thought confusedly, 'But he can't be. He was at home with me this morning!'[68]

Blake seems to have been an exemplary house guest, doing

the washing up, making puddings and entertaining himself with the beautiful edition of the Koran that the Randles had bought him for his birthday.[69] Bourke was more trying. 'Many times during this period,' Pottle admitted, 'I came the closest a pacifist has ever come to committing murder.'[70] Bourke wanted glory. From early in the planning stage he had viewed Blake's escape as a sort of real-life work of art, and he was determined to be recognised as the creator. To do this, theorises Randle, he needed the police to name him as a suspect. Bourke accordingly maddened his co-conspirators by constantly dangling pieces of evidence before the authorities. For instance, a few days after the escape he called the police to explain where they could find the Humber he had used as the getaway car.[71] Blake, who had only known Bourke in an alcohol-free prison, was appalled to discover how much he drank outside.[72]

Bourke, Pottle and Randle would later all recall that Blake wanted to go to neutral Egypt rather than the USSR. 'He offered no explanation for this,' wrote Bourke, 'but I suspected that he felt unsure of the sort of reception that might be awaiting him in Russia. The spying game was a treacherous business in which no one could ever be sure who his friends were.' Blake must have worried that if the Soviets found out about his full confession to SIS, they wouldn't be impressed.

However, smuggling him all the way to North Africa would have been 'a nightmare', wrote Randle.[73] Instead, Randle and Pottle suggested taking him on the shorter journey to Eastern Europe. Blake then suggested East Berlin, a city where he knew the set-up of the security services.[74]

It was agreed that Bourke would follow him behind the Iron Curtain for a while. The Irishman had no desire to go, but Blake, Pottle and Randle encouraged him to leave Britain because they were worried about his propensity to blab.[75]

The peaceniks' altruism seems to have genuinely moved Blake. Shortly before leaving Britain for ever, writes Randle,

> George commented on how difficult it would be to explain to the East Germans and Russians the motivation of the people who had helped him.
>
> 'I shall have to explain to them that this is England, and that really what has happened could only happen here.'
>
> … Ironically, he was more Anglophile than any of us.

Blake told Randle that he hoped one day to be able to visit Britain again. Randle replied, 'If you are so attached to this country, why did you spy against it for the Russians? Blake, 'nonplussed', explained he had acted not out of hatred for Britain, but from a desire to protect the USSR.[76]

A week before Christmas 1966 the Randles took a very big risk: they packed Blake and their toddler sons into a Dormobile camper van, and set off on the journey from London to East Berlin. The van had been paid for by an anonymous socialist who had recently inherited some money, but who didn't believe in inheritance.[77] Randle and a friend had spent weeks constructing a secret compartment underneath one of the seats.[78] Blake was hidden in it, with a hot-water bottle to pee into. With the Randles' two small boys coming along for the ride, the whole thing looked like a family holiday. But if the Randles were caught, Anne and Michael could have faced many years in jail, while Blake would almost certainly have died behind bars. Blake anguished over the fact that Randle was 'risking his whole family'.[79]

The most dangerous leg of the journey went without a hitch: the Randles drove to Dover, got onto the car ferry

13. Michael Randle and his wife Anne during his trial in 1962; he was jailed for having demonstrated at an US air force base. Blake would forever remain grateful to the couple who changed his life.

14. The Randles' son, Gavin, lending a holiday air to the Dormobile van. He is sitting on top of the secret compartment in which Blake was smuggled to East Berlin.

with only minutes to spare, and safely crossed the Channel to Ostend without anyone checking the van. Once they were driving through Belgium in the dark, they finally dared to pull up by the side of the road to check whether Blake – who had been hidden away soundlessly for eight and a half hours – was still alive. He was, and proved it by climbing out to take a long pee by the roadside. 'What did you think of during all those hours?' the Randles asked him. 'Well,' he replied, 'I've had some experience of being on my own in a confined space. It was a chance to do some meditation.'[80]

From then on, as the van drove unchallenged through Belgium and West Germany, Blake was sometimes allowed to sit on the back seat. It was a game for the children, Randle would recall: sometimes the strange man was gone, and sometimes he'd reappear again on the back seat, joining in the games of 'I Spy'. The kids never got to see him transition from one state to the other.[81] When the windscreen wipers broke down in pouring rain in Germany, Blake used his linguistic skills to negotiate with some local car mechanics. Randle writes that he came away saying 'he would give one Englishman for ten Germans any time. He remained a firm Anglophile to the end.'[82]

Even on the final leg of the escape, as the van approached East Berlin, Blake was relaxed enough to ask the Randles whether they thought he would look better with a beard. But Randle, who hadn't slept for thirty-six hours, had become distracted by an awful new thought: perhaps the western secret services knew about their mission and were planning to stop the family on the way back.[83]

On arrival in Berlin, Blake climbed carefully over the sleeping children, thanked his saviours and said he hoped to celebrate with them over champagne one day.[84] Then the slight figure in the borrowed trilby and oversized coat disappeared into the cold night. He walked up to an East German border guard and said, 'I am an Englishman. I would like to speak with a Soviet officer.'[85] The guard, Blake later recalled, 'didn't want that at first. He wanted to know why, what, who I was. But I told him nothing.' Blake was given a bed. 'I slept well. I was very tired.'[86]

By chance, his former handler Kondrashev happened to be visiting East Berlin. The KGB man had just fallen asleep that night when a colleague came into his bedroom and said, 'Some Englishman at the border is asking to meet a Soviet official. Maybe it's him!' 'Him', of course, meant Blake. Kondrashev got dressed and was taken to the border crossing, where he found Blake. 'You? Here?' asked the amazed Blake.[87] The double agent and his former handler would remain friends until 2007, when Blake attended Kondrashev's funeral in Moscow.[88]

Just around the time that Blake arrived in Berlin, the FBI surmised that he was living in the south of France. An ITN programme on the escape, broadcast on New Year's Day 1967, suggested, 'He might even be watching this programme here at the Russian embassy' – a line followed by a long, meaningful close-up of an embassy window in Kensington.[89] However, an MI5 report on 13 January 1967 got it right:

> An extremely delicate source has indicated that shortly before Christmas an unnamed man arrived in East Berlin who was considered important enough to be met by the deputy head of the KGB. This individual possessed only the clothes he stood up in. The possibility that this man was Blake cannot be discounted.[90]

For the second time in his life, with no institutional backup, he had escaped across Europe's most heavily guarded borders.

15

Someone Who Adjusts Easily

In the spring of 1967 Blake sent his mother at least four letters, each of them posted to a different address in England. The one sent to her home bore an Egyptian postmark. She was tearful with joy to hear from him, and happily passed on the letter to Scotland Yard, which, she remarked, had always been good to her. Blake's ex-wife, Gillian, freshly remarried, commented that she was very pleased to hear that he was doing well.[1]

In the letter Blake expressed his distress about his divorce and his anxiety over his sons' future, and sent greetings to his sister and brother-in-law in Margate.[2] He assured his mother:

> I am well and in complete safety so that you need not worry about me any more. I would have written much earlier but in the very special circumstances that I found myself it was impossible to get in touch, longing though I was to do so. Even now, for reasons over which I have no control, I cannot tell you where I am.[3]

He was in Moscow.

His arrival there, recalls the KGB officer Sokolov, 'was naturally a day of joy for everyone in intelligence'[4] – except perhaps for Blake himself. For anyone suffering from an infatuation with Communism, the quickest cure was a visit to the USSR. Guy Burgess described his first Soviet experience as 'like Glasgow on a Saturday night in the nineteenth century'.[5] Most western double agents who arrived in grey, hungry, repressive Cold War-era Moscow realised almost at once: Communism doesn't work, I've sacrificed everything for a mirage, and now I can never go home. Back in London, the spy chief Dick White always enjoyed hearing about disillusioned British traitors.[6]

Blake found life in the Soviet Union not very different from Wormwood Scrubbs.[7] He once told his Dutch Muscovite friend Sauer, with a guffaw: 'After a week in Moscow I knew that communism was the biggest disappointment of my life.'[8] He recounted his first impressions of Moscow to the Dutch journalist Hans Olink: 'A bit ramshackle, a bit old, a bit decrepit, the paint had come off. I myself had a nice warm flat and warm clothes. But of course I felt quite lonely … It was a difficult moment.'[9]

The city seemed full of shambling drunks. Shopping for the simplest item took for ever.[10] When the Soviet authorities gave him a Volga car, he planned to drive it across the country, until he discovered the state of Russian roads.[11] Occasionally in these early days he managed to persuade himself that the USSR was moving forward.[12] However, he soon realised that Soviet propaganda had lied, and that Soviet citizens weren't 'new people' at all, but just like people in the capitalist world. He later said, 'If in Britain or America there were lawsuits between husbands and wives involving large property and jewellery and yachts, here there was the same bitter enmity, only over a television set or an old car or a room which had to be divided in two halves.'[13] (Of course, Blake was speaking as a man with an apartment on a quiet tree-lined street in central Moscow plus a dacha outside town – material luxuries that not every Russian enjoyed.) When he told Russians that he had dedicated his life to building Communism, 'they couldn't really understand it'.[14] Many of them were pleased that the Soviet Union was a superpower, but very few were interested in international social justice.[15]

He also had to come to terms with the end of his spying career. The western secret services now knew everything about him, while the KGB was obliged to suspect him as a potential triple agent. Like many ordinary Britons, the Soviets wondered whether MI6 had facilitated his remarkably easy escape from the Scrubs.[16] No matter how reliable Blake had proven himself during eight years as a Soviet spy, his masters no longer trusted him. So he lost his vocation. In Bourke's words, 'He had been deprived of his reason for living.'[17]

Blake found himself hanging around Moscow inactive, unable to start his new life. When he asked his KGB contacts about finding work, they urged him to rest. Blake later recalled thinking, 'I have rested for six years, and I don't want to rest now.'[18] He eventually found a boring and solitary job as a Dutch translator for a Soviet publisher.

I pressed him repeatedly on how he had coped with his encounter with Soviet reality:

Me: You were forty-three when you fled from jail. You left three small children behind in the West. I'm now forty-two, I also have three small children, and if I had had to live behind the Iron Curtain without my family I might have drunk myself to death like Burgess.

Blake: Well, eh, I never had that temptation because I

15. The first picture of George Blake's life in the USSR, taken on 28 September 1967. Here Blake proudly shows off his diligently exercised body; the Soviets hadn't given him much else to do.

don't like strong drink much ... I only drink vodka when I'm having stomach troubles or something. I know vodka is a good medicine, but I drink it as a medicine and not because I enjoy it ... So I never had that temptation, that's very lucky. But you can't do anything about that.

Me: But didn't you get depressed? Maybe in the beginning?

Blake: No, I have never suffered a depression [*laughs*].[19]

At another point I pressed him on the subject:

Me: But wasn't it a terrific disillusionment for a convinced Communist to arrive here in the Brezhnev era and see that the system didn't work?

Blake: Yes of course it was a disillusionment, but with Donald Maclean we got through it together. And we agreed with each other completely that [the system] shouldn't be like it was – to the contrary, in fact. For instance, I think that the Stalin period did a lot of harm, not only in itself but also harm to the image of Communism. People – the working class in Europe and the whole world – couldn't possibly identify with the system that had been built up here.

Me: But you had taken so many risks, you had given up your family for Communism, and then you come here and it's a let-down. How did you deal with that?

Blake: Well, I must tell you that I'm someone who – and I'm very pleased about that – I'm someone who adjusts easily –

Me: Yes, so it appears.

Blake: – Adjusts easily and always tries to see the positive in life, hopes for the best, shall I say. And that attitude has always helped me a lot in life, and I inherited it from my mother.

Me: So that's how you could cope with situations like being imprisoned in Korea and –

Blake: Yes, all those situations I could somehow adjust to and could hope that it would all end well. And I must say honestly: it has all ended well [*laughs*]. Maybe I didn't deserve that, but it really has all ended well.[20]

While trying to settle in Moscow, he was made miserable by British news reports that Gillian had been granted a divorce from him.[21] When he heard later that she was pregnant by her new husband,[22] it was a 'very bitter blow'. Blake had been hoping that she and the boys would follow him to Moscow, even though he knew 'what I had inflicted: the effects of my jailing on her father, who was in the Service – it caused a rift between them – the upset of her own family life and her relationship with former colleagues in SIS – and then the further blow of my escape'.[23]

But with hindsight, Blake told me, he was grateful that his family hadn't joined him in Moscow.

> When I arrived safely here – and you'll have read about that and so on – I thought, 'Well, maybe she'll come here like Maclean's wife did.' But by then she had already married that man, or was going to marry. Anyway she didn't come here and of course that was very sensible because it would have been a great tragedy if she had. It could never have gone well. And for Maclean's wife it was a very difficult time adjusting here ... Of course, I didn't know that then, but later when I knew them and we were very good friends, I understood that it was a great blessing that my plans weren't realised. And my mother played a big role in that, because she was a very sensible, sober woman. She saw the situation as it was, and she, eh – let's say explained to me [laughs] – that nothing would come of those dreams of mine.[24]

Blake's mother must have known that her daughter-in-law and grandsons wouldn't thrive in the USSR. Few of the western double agents and their families did. For Melinda Maclean and her children, or for Burgess, who refused to learn Russian,[25] Moscow was exile. Vladimir Putin must have been thinking about people like Burgess when he remarked in 2010, 'Traitors always end badly. They finish up as drunks, addicts, on the street.'[26]

But for the cosmopolitan Blake there was no such thing as exile. Although alone and bereft in Moscow, he was perfectly equipped to start a new life there – his eighth or ninth. He had been trained in adjusting to new places since the day he boarded the boat to Cairo in 1936. He had fallen in love with Russian at Cambridge. And he had long experience in transforming himself. When 'Poek' Behar had arrived in London in 1943, he had become George Blake. In Moscow he dropped the Christian name he had always disliked and became Gyorgi Ivanovich Bekhter – a Russian approximation of his original surname, Behar.[27] From the start, he accepted Moscow as his fate.

Initially he shared his flat with his rescuer, Bourke. The Irishman had travelled to the Eastern bloc via Paris and West Berlin, using Pat Pottle's passport with his own photograph inserted.[28] However, Bourke and Blake were not ideal roommates.[29] The Irishman could not adapt to Soviet life or KGB scrutiny. An impulsive drunk who spoke no Russian, he was in every way the opposite of Blake. Living in each other's pockets, isolated in Moscow, the two men fell out fast. In Blake's telling,

Both of us were in the apartment for long periods and we got on each other's nerves. I found I was doing all the housework and washing up – I am by nature a tidy person, whereas Sean was the opposite, and soon I began to resent him. I thought at least he should do some housework.[30]

Bourke, for his part, was always quick to find enemies.[31] The Blake he had got to know in Wormwood Scrubs had been a kindly prison professor. But now he found his housemate

16. Sean Bourke (*c.* 1965): he had great charm and talent but ended up destroying himself. The springing of Blake, and the self-expressive book he wrote about it, proved his main creative legacy.

'sullen, intolerant, arrogant, and pompous'. Bourke wrote: 'Blake spent most of his long day writing memoranda for the KGB ... giving the KGB every scrap of information he had been unable to pass on before his arrest, as well as details of the methods employed by the British to investigate and interrogate him.'

Bourke soon decided that the charm he had shown in the Scrubs had been just an act.[32] In fact, he wrote, in Moscow Blake revealed himself as 'a narcissist':

In his determination to preserve his schoolboy figure he devoted at least one hour a day to physical exercises, which he performed completely stripped in front of a full-length mirror. Several times I found him dancing by himself. When the dance step required him to turn his back on the mirror he would look over his shoulder and admire himself from behind, so reluctant was he to lose sight of his body ...[33]

Bourke believed Blake was spying on him, which was almost certainly true.[34] He also came to believe that Blake wanted the KGB to kill him, which is at least possible.[35] Blake knew that Bourke was writing a book about his experiences. It was to be the Irishman's *magnum opus*, his expressive autobiography as well as the story of the escape. In the Moscow flat Bourke witnessed more of the workings of the KGB than almost any other western outsider. He was bound to reveal sensitive information. Blake must have feared being blamed by the KGB. In addition, Bourke's book might point the British police towards Randle and Pottle.[36]

When Bourke's twin brother, Kevin, tried to smuggle the manuscript out of the USSR, the KGB seized it. Bourke reports subsequent conversations with KGB officers who didn't mind his critical passages about Soviet society, but 'were concerned solely about my attitude to Blake'.[37] If the book tarnished Blake's image, that would reflect badly on the KGB. In addition, as the fictional Blake tells the fictional Bourke in *Cell Mates*: 'Well, it does make us seem absurdly incompetent – that the KGB couldn't do what you did. A single Irish fella. With his rope ladder and the Dormobile.'[38]

After two Soviet years Bourke returned to Ireland in 1968, against Blake's wishes. On arrival he told the Irish press that he had come because he was homesick.[39] The police swiftly arrested him, and a Dublin judge ordered that he be handed over to Britain. Bourke appealed against extradition.[40] The crucial issue at his hearing in Dublin was why he had helped Blake – for political reasons, or otherwise? If his motives had been political, Ireland would not extradite him.

> State Counsel: Are you capable of a deep and burning hatred?
>
> Bourke: Very capable.
>
> State Counsel: Do you have a deep and burning hatred for the British police?
>
> Bourke: I do.
>
> State Counsel: Does your deep and burning hatred extend to the British establishment?
>
> Bourke: It does indeed.[41]

In the end the judge refused to send him across the Irish Sea. Bourke walked out of the court into the Dublin sunshine and told journalists that he had no plans to visit Britain, but would consider it if the UK's attorney-general 'were to give a guarantee that he will not charge me with anything at all, and for good measure throw in an OBE'.[42]

Meanwhile Bourke had been sending letters to the KGB asking for the return of his manuscript. One day 'a tattered parcel' arrived at his solicitor's offices in Dublin:

> It contained my original manuscript, from which had been removed the entire final section, which deals with my experiences in Moscow. The rest of the book had been heavily censored by another hand, which I am sure was that of George Blake himself.[43]

Blake (who was indeed almost certainly the censor) had cut out sections identifying Randle and Pottle.[44] Randle wrote: 'Neither Blake nor the KGB stood to gain anything from the removal of our names, or details about us, and our judgment is that George was genuinely concerned to prevent us being arrested and imprisoned.'[45] However, Bourke reinstated the sections, thinly disguising the two men as Michael Reynolds and Pat Porter. When his engaging memoir *The Springing of George Blake* was published in 1969, the British security services rapidly worked out who 'Reynolds' and 'Porter' were, but decided for the moment against prosecuting the 'little fish' when the big ones had got away.[46] Randle and Pottle were free to continue working for peace. Randle writes that a few years after he had taken Blake to East Berlin, they used 'camper vans modified in the same way to smuggle books, pamphlets and duplicating machines to human rights activists in Eastern Europe'.[47]

Bourke's book contains some fictionalised detail but remains the most detailed account of Blake by anyone who knew him well. The British Special Branch officer Rollo Watts judged it 'ninety-nine per cent' authentic,[48] although that is probably a tad generous. The book royalties and Hitchcock's payment for the film rights made Bourke rich.[49] But Randle, who met him again in Ireland later, suspected that at times he 'felt deeply ashamed at having helped Blake escape'.[50]

From Ireland, Bourke got into the habit of phoning Scotland Yard's man in charge of the Blake escape file for long chats.[51] The British remained keen to nab him. When Prime Minister Edward Heath heard in 1972 that Bourke had been spotted in Belfast, he ordered, 'Get him.'[52] In the end, the Soviets may have got him instead. Oleg Kalugin recounts that one day, going through KGB dossiers on Blake's escape, he opened a sealed envelope marked, 'Never to be opened without permission'. Inside was a murder plot:

> Alexander Sakharovsky, chief of intelligence, said the KGB feared that Burke [sic] would describe to British intelligence how he and Blake were smuggled into the USSR and would divulge Blake's whereabouts in Moscow, thus making him vulnerable to assassination. Sakharovsky therefore ordered that Burke be given a drug that would mimic a stroke and produce damage to his brain. The drug was administered, and Burke returned to Ireland in a debilitated condition. A few years later, he died, apparently a result of the KGB's drugging and his alcoholism.[53]

Perhaps the KGB had not quite perfected its long-term stroke-inducing drugs, because people who knew Bourke in Ireland believed that alcohol alone was quite enough to kill him. In his final years he drank and gave away a fortune.[54] He died of a heart attack in 1982, in a borrowed caravan in a small town on the west coast of Ireland, aged forty-seven.[55] The doctors who treated him as he died would later dismiss any suggestion of foul play.[56] Blake said, 'I was very sorry to hear of his death, because I owe him everything … so I cannot think badly of him. He gave me life.'[57]

* * *

After Bourke had left the Moscow flat, Blake quickly found the perfect housemate: his seventy-five-year-old mother, Catharine. 'I would like to live with my son in Russia', she told a Dutch newspaper in 1967. 'I am starting to get older and I hope to stay with him for a long time. He has a flat in Moscow

17. The company of his mother – here in the Carpathian
Mountains in September 1967 – helped ease Blake's
difficult early days in the Soviet Union.

with two bedrooms, and one of them is for me.'[58] For a while
she divided her time between Britain, the Netherlands and the
Soviet capital.[59] She brought Blake his English suits from SIS
days,[60] and cooked him Dutch meals in Moscow.[61] For Blake, if
home meant anything, it meant his mother,[62] 'my closest and
dearest friend'.[63]

Soon after arriving in Moscow, Blake met his old Soviet-
Canadian friend from the Scrubs, Gordon Lonsdale. Blake
enjoyed reminding him 'of his extraordinary prediction' that
they would see each other again in Red Square in 1967. The
two men became expat buddies, meeting over lunch to reminisce 'about life in England and our days in the Scrubs', wrote
Blake. But Soviet life frustrated Lonsdale's instinctive capitalism. In 1970 he died suddenly of a heart attack while picking
mushrooms in the woods with his family.[64]

In 1968, on a cruise on the River Volga, Blake met Ida, a French translator with a background in mathematics.[65] She took up with the foreigner, at the risk of being branded a spy herself.[66] Blake told me, 'She had lots of friends and acquaintances and family and that filled my life completely, enough really.'[67] When he told her friends that he was a 'political immigrant' to the USSR, they guffawed; most of them wanted to emigrate.[68]

Blake's other companion in Moscow was, still, God. The walls of his study at home were hung with medieval religious icons and Russian Orthodox tabernacles.[69] He liked to think that the first Christians and later monastic communities had been Communist. Kalugin, whose family socialised with Blake's, said:

> We discovered, through electronic surveillance of his apartment, that Blake also was a religious man who enjoyed reading the Bible, particularly the gospel of John. I later talked to him about his belief and asked whether he thought it contradicted his Communist faith. 'What's wrong with it?' he replied. 'Communism is the same as Christianity, only put on a scientific basis.'[70]

Blake found himself just as much an outsider in the KGB as he had been in SIS. The Soviet service didn't employ many Calvinist-Jewish intellectuals with an aversion to violence. Kalugin writes that, although he 'essentially trusted Blake', 'we considered him less reliable than Philby'. One episode in particular gave the spooks cause for doubt. The KGB had found out that a British intelligence officer was visiting Moscow under diplomatic cover. Both Blake and Philby knew the man, but as Philby was 'ailing', Blake was asked to recruit the officer.

However, Blake demurred, saying, 'Oh no, Oleg, I'm not a recruiter.'

Kalugin told him, 'You don't have to go in for the kill. Just scare him. Make him vulnerable. See how he reacts.' It was finally agreed that Blake would bump into the officer in a Moscow hotel as if by accident. The Briton refused to speak to him, so nothing came of it. Still, writes Kalugin, 'Blake's resistance to the recruitment made some people suspicious, and the electronic eavesdropping in his apartment was continued.'[71]

In these early years in Moscow, Blake was a non-person rather than a hero. Philby had been greeted with a 'Hello, Mr Philby' headline in the *Izvestia* newspaper mere months after arriving in Moscow.[72] But Blake had to wait three years, until 1970, before *Izvestia* unveiled him to the Soviet public.[73] In an interview Blake introduced himself to readers and divulged some of the grubby specifics of western spycraft. He revealed, for instance, that there was a bugged room in the luxurious Hotel Astoria in Brussels that was always given to guests from Soviet-bloc countries. *Izvestia* and Blake also pulled the mean trick of naming in print his long-time boss at MI6, Peter Lunn. The biggest scoop was the revelation that Blake had blown the Berlin tunnel.[74]

Izvestia's interview was proudly relayed around the Communist world, and picked up in the West. On 25 February 1970 President Nixon was informed in his 'daily brief' from the CIA that the USSR had timed Blake's coming out to counter a wave of 'bad press' for the KGB: in the previous year there had been over fifty 'public exposures of Soviet intelligence officers in various countries'.[75] But this was a very rare public appearance for Blake in the Soviet era. The MI6 agent Tim Milne marvelled at how little the USSR did to exploit Blake's propaganda value.[76]

Instead Blake lived quietly in Moscow, becoming a model immigrant. He received the Order of Lenin, socialised in the KGB Club,[77] was made a colonel in the KGB,[78] and never once in Soviet times seems to have made a public statement against the regime. He came to consider himself 'a foreign-made car that has adapted very well to Russian roads'.[79]

The KGB eventually even began to use him as a sort of counsellor to other traitors in exile. This was a reversal of policy: at first his masters had tried to limit his meetings with fellow defectors. In 1971, in Moscow, Blake had run into Morris Cohen, an American traitor from the Portland spy ring. They expressed 'genuine joy' at seeing each other, exchanged phone numbers and agreed to meet again soon, according to the KGB's report.[80] But the KGB ordered them to break off contact. 'Cohen telephoned Blake to say that he and his wife Lona were about to go on holiday and could not meet anytime soon; Blake replied that he too was going out of town, and a meeting was out of the question.'[81] Some years later the KGB's policy changed. When the Cohens went through a hard time in Moscow, Blake's employers encouraged him to befriend the couple.[82]

Another needy traitor was Kim Philby, a man utterly unsuited to Soviet life. In the late 1960s he had tried to kill himself by slashing his wrist.[83] Blake said, 'He found it very difficult and spoke almost no Russian.'[84]

Blake and Philby seem never to have encountered each other before Moscow.[85] They finally met in 1970 and got to know each other about as well as each man's natural secrecy per-mitted. During one of the Englishman's hard-drinking phases, when the KGB decided he needed a woman to look after him, the Blakes introduced him to a friend of Ida's, Rufina, at an ice-dancing show in Moscow.[86]

Philby asked her in his rudimentary Russian: 'Please take

off your glasses, I would like to see your eyes.'[87] Rufina was not instantly charmed. Ida had briefed her on Philby's drinking, and 'a middle-aged man with a puffy face was hardly the hero of my dreams'.[88] But the Blakes organised a follow-up encounter at their dacha. Philby cooked a dinner of coq au vin with copious alcohol, and late that night wandered into Rufina's room, so drunk that he could only say, 'I am an Englishman'. Rufina deflected him with, 'Tomorrow, tomorrow'. He returned two or three times that night with the same chat-up line. The next day he had forgotten the whole incident.[89]

Philby continued to proposition Rufina, in Russian so bad that it made her laugh, but as she was thirty-eight and keen to marry, she finally agreed to become his fourth wife. The marriage lasted the last eighteen years of Philby's life and, by Rufina's account, was wonderful, even if she had to give up her job to be with him because he was incapable of being alone.[90] Blake concluded that Philby 'was not the womaniser he was portrayed to be. You see, he married all the women.'[91]

Rufina writes that when she and Philby were first married, 'the Blakes were the only people with whom we socialised'.[92] There were 'parties at Blake's dacha and Philby had taken an avuncular interest in Blake's son by Ida, Misha', says Philby's biographer Phillip Knightley.[93] Philby and Blake's mother enjoyed drinking martinis together in the evening.[94] Philby grew 'rather fond' of Blake, writes Rufina.[95]

However, the two traitors were very different men. Blake told me he found Philby

a real Englishman. He read *The Times*, it would arrive later [i.e., well after its publication in the UK], and he laid them out by date so that one day he could do the one crossword and the next day the next ...

18. Blake with his Russian second family, wife Ida
and son Misha. At this point, in 1975, he had lost
contact with the sons he had with his first wife.

Me: And he followed the cricket, and –

Blake: Yes, yes! Of course, he was very interested in everything that had to do with England. And he found it very difficult to adjust here. What happened was, he was a journalist by trade, and a very good journalist, and when he came here he got work at the APN, the Russian news agency. One time he wrote an article about a certain issue in the Middle East, he was a great expert on the Middle East because of his father. Anyway, he gave that article to the person who was supposed to print it, and that person made all sorts of changes to it, and he [Philby] was simply furious, because he couldn't imagine that anyone would dare change or improve what he had written. Then he walked out of there and he didn't want to work with them again …

19. Kim Philby and Blake, the Englishman and the
cosmopolitan, never got on well. Blake was scornful
of Philby's failure to adapt to Soviet life.

Me: He didn't understand that the Russians used
censorship.

Blake: Yes! ... So that was the end of his work [*laughs*].[96]

Still, Blake and Philby continued to do odd chores for Soviet
intelligence. The KGB officer Mikhail Lyubimov remembers
taking them to the noted Soviet-era restaurant Aragvi in 1974.
'My task was to restore the work of our British station and I
needed some consultations,' Lyubimov reminisced in 2016. 'I
remember the excellent fried suluguni cheese – my mouth is
watering just to think of it.'[97]

But mostly Philby spent his Soviet years in grouchy

20. Kim Philby and Blake with their Russian wives, Rufina and Ida. These photos – taken by Philby's son John in the garden of the Blakes' dacha in 1975 – prompted the final rupture between Blake and Philby.

obsolescence. In Britain he had been the insider and Blake the outsider. In Moscow, perhaps gratifyingly for Blake, their roles were reversed. The two traitors must also have felt some professional rivalry. Philby remarked that Blake's escape might have been arranged by SIS; 'pure spite', retorted Blake. Philby regarded Blake as a 'young upstart', and, writes Tom Bower, 'bickered over their status when Blake received the Order of Lenin before he did'.[98] A handwritten note beneath Blake's official biography in the Stasi files reads: 'According to western accounts, he betrayed Philby.'[99] Blake almost certainly didn't, but Philby may at times have suspected him of giving his MI6 interrogators some supplementary information. The East German spy chief Wolf, well placed to judge both men, thought Blake 'a good intelligence officer, fearless and enterprising, though not as intellectual and analytical as Philby'.[100]

The two traitors fell out in 1975. One day Philby's British son John joined the two couples at Blake's dacha and took some photographs. Rufina said she witnessed Philby asking Blake, 'Do you mind if John tries to make something out of our photos?', and that Blake replied, 'Of course not'. But a few days later Ida rang the Philbys asking them not to publish the pictures, adding that the Blakes had never wanted them to do so. This didn't go down well. Rufina writes, 'Kim felt it was a matter of principle, having always abided by the rule that "Your word is your bond"' (not a principle for which Philby is remembered in MI6). The two Philby men ignored the Blakes' request, whereupon 'George immediately reported the matter "to the appropriate quarters"', writes Rufina. The pictures ended up in the *Observer*. John was handsomely paid.[101]

Blake, who had tried so hard over the years to protect Gillian and his sons from publicity, was furious with Philby:

> He could have apologised or maybe explained that it was out of his control, but he wasn't that kind of man. Never apologise, never explain – he was an English individualist and apologising did not come into his way of living. So I did not see him again, until his funeral [in 1988], when I went to pay my respects.[102]

* * *

Blake's best friend in Moscow was another of the Cambridge spies. Donald Maclean, the son of a Liberal cabinet minister, had been recruited by the Soviets as an openly Marxist undergraduate in the 1930s. He joined the British Foreign Office at the KGB's urging, and served the Soviets brilliantly throughout the Second World War and the early Cold War. In 1951, just as he was about to be unmasked, he disappeared behind the Iron Curtain with Burgess.[103] When he arrived in the USSR, he took on the pseudonym Mark Petrovitch Frazer,[104] but eventually became the bemedalled old Soviet hand Donald Donaldovich Maclean. He worked as an expert on British foreign policy at the grandly named though rather pointless Institute of World Economics and International Relations (IMEMO), a research centre.[105]

When Kalugin met Maclean in the 1970s, he found him 'a bitter, acid-tongued man battling alcoholism, personal demons, and disillusionment with life in the Soviet Union'. After Melinda Maclean left him in 1965 to have a relationship with Philby that lasted several years, the two British traitors 'never spoke to one another again'. (Once Melinda and Philby broke up, she moved back in with her estranged husband for two years, perhaps partly impelled by Moscow's housing shortage.[106])

Maclean was politically naive. When Kalugin first visited his large apartment in central Moscow, the Briton launched into a rant against Brezhnev and the USSR, while Kalugin – who knew that the flat was bugged – tried in vain to shut him up.[107] 'His disillusionment with our way of life knew no bounds', writes Kalugin.[108]

But Blake adored Maclean, who, he said, 'gave me much good advice and helped me come to terms with my life here'.[109] Blake remarked, 'There was a strong Calvinistic streak in him, inherited from his Scottish ancestors and this gave us something in common.'[110] (In fact, Maclean's upbringing was Presbyterian,[111] though he had once thought of writing a PhD involving a Marxist analysis of Calvin, before ditching the idea to infiltrate the Foreign Office instead.)[112]

The two men were made for each other. Both men were intellectuals. Both instinctively kept others at a distance: when Maclean's tutor at Cambridge remarked that his student had 'no friends, although he had many acquaintances,'[113] it pre-figured almost word for word Gillian's description of Blake. Each man's unmasking had cut him off from a beloved mother, a wife, two small sons and a third child on the way. Both had made spectacular escapes from the UK. Both made new lives in the Soviet Union, instead of pining for home. And both saw themselves as principled traitors who had gone into a dirty business only out of idealism. Maclean once described spying on his own country as 'like being a lavatory attendant; it stinks but someone has to do it.'[114]

'He never liked spying,' Blake recalled approvingly. 'Philby and Burgess were attracted to the adventure and the secrecy of belonging to a small group of people with inside knowledge, and they enjoyed the small amount of danger. Maclean didn't like that, but he felt he should do it as that was how he was of most use.'[115]

Blake told me:

Maclean adapted very well here, to some degree maybe even better than me ... He was a convinced communist and ... he wanted to participate fully in life in the Soviet Union. He'd been a member, and in his mind he still was a member of the English Communist Party ... In our insti-tute, to which I am still attached and where he played a very leading role, he was also a member of the local party committee. He spoke very good Russian, but of course with an English accent. And he wrote very well in Russian too.[116]

In fact, Maclean never joined the British party.[117] Blake, for his part, refused his friend's entreaties to join the Russian party, reasoning, 'They'll manage with me'.[118] Maclean got Blake hired at the IMEMO institute, as an expert on the Middle East.[119] Blake told the Stasi it was the topic he had 'always wanted to' work on.[120] A colleague at the institute, Piotr Cherkasov, recalled Gyorgi Ivanovich Bekhter's arrival: 'He was very dashing, so he didn't look like a Soviet.' Cherkasov and Bekhter/Blake sat near each other, and had many frank, irreverent un-Soviet conversations. During one of them, said Cherkasov, 'we heard someone knocking on the wall from the other side of the plug socket. So we said, "Comrade Major, we are joking!"' The incident made Blake chuckle, but it was a reminder of just how close Big Brother was.[121]

Blake's job at IMEMO proved satisfying and lasting. He told me: 'Since I arrived here I have had quite a quiet life, but an interesting life because I was at the institute, and that institute is one of the elite ones in the Russian system.'[122] He enjoyed the company of his colleagues, who were sophisticated, multilingual and (by Soviet standards) well travelled.[123] Quite a few were former or current intelligence officers.[124] With some he formed decades-long friendships. In Moscow, where he no longer had to dissemble, Blake seems to have dropped his former reserve and become a warm and charming companion. In 2002 a staff member named V. Vladimiroff, who was considered IMEMO's house poet, produced a commemoration for Blake's eightieth birthday:

His entire life is a constellation of mysteries
But the greatest mystery still hasn't been revealed:
How, having survived the crash of two empires,
Has he managed to stay for ever young?[125]

IMEMO had one great shortcoming, Blake told Olink, one that it shared with the Soviet system as a whole: 'Very little work was done.' People went into the institute three days a week. There were also two so-called 'library days', intended for work-related reading, 'but of course that didn't happen', he said. Much of the official work week was spent in 'endless conversations, about politics, about life. That is very Russian.' People were always loafing in the corridors smoking. Whenever a child was born or there was anything else to celebrate, the vodka would come out.

So little got done that Blake tells the possibly apocryphal story of a visiting Japanese delegation saying, 'We are very sorry that we as foreigners cannot participate in your strike.' Soviet workers skived off because they knew they couldn't be sacked. 'That was one of the reasons why the system fell behind: people just didn't work hard enough,' Blake admitted.[126]

He was privately critical of the USSR, but he was not free to speak out. He bravely registered his disapproval of the Soviet war in Afghanistan in internal IMEMO documents, but not in official publications. His writing on the Middle East was too free for the tastes of Soviet journals. Cherkasov said, 'Blake learned Russian but he couldn't learn the propaganda language of the Soviet press.'[127]

In private, Blake and Maclean often discussed their shared fantasy of Communism with a human face. Blake told me that Maclean 'had his own idea of Communism. It wasn't the Communism that was here, because he didn't really agree with that at all. He was an idealistic Communist.' Then Blake added:

I'm convinced to this day that the Communist system is better for everyone, but that system mustn't be made reality by violence and firing squads. I think the majority of people must themselves come to the conviction that the Communist system is more just and also more effective.

I still think that, but then they say, 'Well, that's utopia, that's impossible'. But I'm convinced – I don't know how many generations it will take – that people, most people anyway, will decide that it's a better system. And those who don't want it must be left free, they mustn't be forced or shot dead.[128]

When Andropov succeeded Brezhnev as Soviet leader in 1982, Maclean hoped that 'the old gentleman' would pursue 'more realistic politics, more in line with the true Communist ideals,' Blake told me. 'Of course, nothing came of that, but he didn't live to see that. He died before Gorbachev's big changes. He was a really committed Communist and he dedicated his whole life to it.'[129]

Maclean died bereft of family, as Melinda and their children had returned to the West. Blake recalled:

In his last days I visited him almost daily. The day before he died he could still get up, and he was writing a big piece of work. On 6 March 1983 he felt really unwell and we called the ambulance … They received him at the hospital and put him in a room and I went home, having promised that I would come and visit on 8 March. When I arrived at hospital reception, it turned out there was no pass issued under my name. I had to go home. I later found out that he had died on 7 March.[130] On the last day he lost consciousness, and no one was there with him except the doctors.[131]

Along with Maclean's library, Blake inherited his friend's old tweed cap. It was something of a holy relic: Blake had come to regard Maclean as 'saintly'.[132] At Maclean's funeral he recounted – perhaps to the befuddlement of the elite Communist congregation – the biblical parable of the forty just men. Maclean, he told the assembled, was one of those rare just men 'for whose sake mankind would be preserved'.[133] After Elizabeth Hill and Vyvyan Holt, Blake had lost his last mentor from the British establishment.

Henri Curiel, A Parallel Life

Blake is often discussed as a sort of offshoot of the Cambridge Five. I have done it myself at times in this book. That is a consequence of seeing him above all in a British context. The comparison encourages us to group him with Philby, Burgess and Maclean.

However, that can be misleading. Blake made the same choice as they did, but he was propelled by very different influences. In fact, his path is much more like that of another clandestine Communist activist: his Egyptian cousin Henri Curiel.

The point is not that Blake tried to emulate his older cousin. As Blake said, Curiel didn't convert him to Communism. After Blake sailed out of Cairo in 1939, the two men never saw each other again (although when Curiel heard of Blake's escape from Wormwood Scrubs, he told friends, 'One is proud to have a cousin like that!'). But the cousins were shaped by many of the same forces, starting with their shared Jewishness and their encounter with extreme poverty in 1930s' Egypt. They ended up living parallel lives.

Like Blake, Curiel converted to militant Soviet Communism in his late twenties. By his own account, on 22 June 1941 he was on an Egyptian train reading a book that described how the Soviet Union was eradicating illiteracy, training engineers and giving the people culture. None of this was happening in Curiel's Egypt. This, he thought, was a model for a poor country. When the train arrived at Cairo station, he heard that Germany had invaded the USSR, and his conversion was complete.[1]

No matter how it really happened, he became a devout Communist, writes his French biographer (and occasional hagiographer) Gilles Perrault. All his life Curiel would tell people, '*Je suis un communiste orthodoxe*', sometimes followed by the precision 'I am what one generally calls a Stalinist.'[2]

He could easily have ended up a Soviet agent like Blake. He visited the Soviet embassy in Cairo several times, but it dismissed his offers to collaborate.[3] In any case, he had decided early that the Egyptian people wanted liberation from British rule first. Communism could wait. So he learned Arabic, became an Egyptian citizen and tried to encourage Arab Egyptians to join clandestine groups in which almost all the members – Curiel, his friends and his lovers – were Jewish salon Communists. During the Second World War, while Jews in Europe were being massacred, Jews in Cairo were leading tiny Marxist movements.

Blake lost his fatherland when he left the Netherlands for Britain in 1943; Curiel lost his five years later with the first Israeli–Arab war. Suddenly Egyptian Jews, some of whose families had lived in Egypt since ancient times, were treated as a potential fifth column.[4] Immediately after the 1948 war, Egypt's monarchy imprisoned Curiel as a Zionist agent. In fact, he had always supported separate states for Israelis and

Palestinians, but that didn't help him: he lost out to the Arab nationalism of the period. The regime was keen to depict Egyptian Communism as the brainchild of a rich Jew in silly shorts. In 1950 Curiel was stripped of his Egyptian citizenship and deported from his beloved homeland.[5] He entered France on a false Austrian passport,[6] and spent almost all the rest of his life in Paris without ever obtaining French citizenship. In his memoirs he called himself 'an old man who was torn up from his own roots by a complicated series of events'.[7] Like Blake, he became a global soul.

In Paris, as in Cairo, the Communists rejected this *communiste orthodoxe*. They literally wouldn't go near him. 'A communist cousin of his, also living in Paris, ignored him on the street', writes the American journalist Adam Shatz. The French Communist Party (PCF) even tried to stop Curiel meeting his illegitimate son, the journalist and (for a while) Communist Alain Gresh (who was the spitting image of Curiel).[8] Shatz explains:

> Curiel had run afoul of the Russians because, as a young man in Cairo, he had once hosted André Marty, a Communist falsely accused of being a police spy – and, in 1952, expelled – by the French Communist Party. The Marty affair was one of the more notorious purges inside the PCF, and Curiel's reputation in Communist circles never recovered.

Curiel was bursting with political energy – like Blake, he was more interested in action than theory[9] – and he had to create his own outlet for it. Many of his Communist Jewish friends from Cairo had also landed up in Paris, and they remained keen to follow their handsome, charismatic leader, so he turned them into an underground network that tried to help colonies gain independence. One of his Arab followers, Sherif Hetata, said: 'He lost his *watan* [homeland], therefore he chose the whole world as his *watan*.'[10] The same was arguably true of Blake.

Curiel's group began in 1957 by smuggling money for the Algerian liberation movement FLN, which was fighting for independence from France. After his parents died, he and his brother Raoul donated the Villa Curiel in Cairo to the FLN. Today the mansion where the adolescent Blake once lived is the Algerian embassy.[11]

In October 1960, six months before the British arrested Blake, the French caught Curiel and jailed him at Fresnes. There is a possibly apocryphal account of his responses on the prison's admissions form:

Nationality: None
Religion: None
Profession: None
Address: None[12]

Like Blake, Curiel was imprisoned in multiple countries. Like Blake, he seemed to thrive in captivity. Raymond Stambouli, who had been jailed with Curiel in Egypt, said, 'He felt happier in jail than at liberty, because he said, "In prison you have already experienced the worst. So what can happen that's worse?"'[13]

Like his cousin across the Channel in Wormwood Scrubs, Curiel in Fresnes followed a spartan lifestyle of study and physical exercise. One of the first practitioners of yoga in France, he would sometimes interrupt a prison conversation to stand on his head without using his arms.[14] Like Blake, Curiel lived in a book-lined cell. His fellow prisoner Etienne Bolo recalled (in an uncanny echo of Zeno's description of Blake's cell in the Scrubs): 'He would receive you in his cell like in a salon, offer you a coffee, smiling and polite as if nothing had happened ... He would go to teach in a cell as if he was at the Sorbonne.'[15]

Like Blake, Curiel was a prison professor. In jail in Egypt, as Perrault tells it, he had transformed three German former Nazis into such enthusiastic Communists that each morning they would 'march around the prison yard behind a red flag singing the Internationale in German'.[16] In Fresnes he taught his fellow inmates classes in history, yoga, French and basic Italian.[17]

Curiel was released in 1962 after the Algerian war ended. Over the following decades his network – called MAF, and later Solidarité – would aid national liberation and anti-fascist movements from Vietnam to Chile to the ANC in South Africa. Viewed psychologically, Curiel's anti-colonial work looks like a long attempt to gain acceptance from the Third World that had expelled him from the land of his birth.

His group forged passports for foreign militants and offered them courses on everything from making explosives to writing in invisible ink. Curiel taught a course on how to cope in jail. He recommended prison as an excellent opportunity for political and cultural growth, advised militants to do yoga to keep fit inside and gave them tips on how to escape.[18] 'Getting someone out of prison was his obsession', a fellow militant recalled.[19]

Curiel's anti-colonial network came to include clergymen as well as Communists.[20] Like Blake, he seems to have got on better with Christians than with Communists, perhaps because of his Jesuit education. One of his nicknames was 'The Bishop',[21] and a French militant would recall '*son aspect clergyman*', with his roll-neck sweaters and dark-grey suits.[22]

But in 1972 many of the Christians and other anti-Communists in Solidarité were furious to discover that Curiel, without telling anybody else, had written to Moscow asking for Soviet co-operation. 'Very dear and very honoured comrades', the letter began.[23] Moscow never replied.[24]

Curiel maintained his one-sided love affair with the USSR to the end. If friends criticised the country, he threw tantrums.[25] He didn't like hearing about gulags or seeing Soviet dissidents on TV.[26] A pastor named Rognon, a fellow member of Solidarité, would explain that for Curiel the Soviet Union

> was his only fatherland. An imaginary fatherland, certainly, but the only one that couldn't renounce him, as all the others had, precisely because it was imaginary. The fact is that he never set foot there, nor in any other socialist country ... Henri, who was the internationalist par excellence, a man of the whole world, helped me understand that each of us needs a fatherland. He chose the Soviet Union.[27]

So did Blake.

Both cousins devoted the last stage of their careers to the same insoluble problem: the Israeli–Palestinian question. Both had witnessed Arab–Jewish cohabitation in pre-1948 Cairo and could identify with both sides in the conflict. Blake in Wormwood Scrubs studied the Koran; Curiel in jail observed Ramadan in solidarity with Muslim prisoners.[28] For Curiel the Arab–Jewish split had an additional personal poignancy: it had forced him into exile.

Both cousins in later life wrote frequently on the Israeli–Palestinian question.[29] Both favoured talk over violence. Curiel's mission was a two-state solution, and he spent years setting up back-channel Palestinian–Israeli meetings. (Several of the Palestinian participants were later murdered by extremists.[30]) Blake urged the Soviet Union to build good relations with Israel as well as with Arab countries.[31]

Curiel's friend Uri Avnery, an Israeli peace activist, argues that Curiel's work helped lead to the Israeli–Palestinian Oslo Accords of 1994.[32] That seems charitable, even disregarding the fact that the Oslo deal did not hold. In sum, the anti-colonialist Curiel may have devoted most of his life to a cause without making very much difference. The historian Joel Beinin concludes that he was 'perhaps, ultimately, not ... especially effective'.[33] That was also probably true of Blake.

Curiel and Blake didn't merely work for similar ends; they also worked with similar means. Both spent their careers in subterfuge. They seem to have felt most at ease backstage. Hannah Arendt has explained that this is a classically Jewish role: for much of history Jews were barred from the political stage, as Curiel was in Egypt, and so what influence they had was 'hidden from view and ... behind the scenes'.[34] (This fact has, of course, encouraged endless conspiracy theories about secret cabals of Jews running the world.)

Blake and Curiel seem to have found clandestinity thrilling and glamorous. Curiel incarnated the image of 'a professional revolutionary', recalled one of his admiring underground colleagues.[35] A more sceptical militant once scolded him for his 'man-of-the-shadows cinema'.[36] The South African writer, fantasist and anti-apartheid activist Breyten Breytenbach, who got help from Solidarité, described how at their final meeting in France, Curiel 'dramatically decided to tell me his real name. Like removing the last barrier between us. In one of those faceless apartments where we used to rendezvous, he wrote his name on a slip of paper, showed to me, and then destroyed it. (He did not swallow it!).'[37]

Like Blake, Curiel took it for granted that the struggle for the cause required violence. Radicals of their generation saw themselves as the spiritual descendants of the violent wartime resistance to the Nazis, Curiel's son Gresh told me.[38] But Curiel, like Blake, had no personal taste for violence. He always kept himself at a remove from it. Most of the groups that Solidarité helped did their killings in faraway Third World countries. Curiel lamented Palestinian hijackings, and considered Europe's 1970s' terrorist movements odious and idiotic.[39] Perrault says 'he never in his life carried a firearm'.[40]

Nonetheless, on 21 June 1976 the conservative French newsweekly Le Point devoted a cover story to Curiel headlined 'The Boss of the Networks of Aid to Terrorists'.[41] The piece cited about twenty supposed terrorist organisations he was helping and added, 'Curiel is in constant liaison with the KGB.'[42] The article was riddled with factual errors. Even so, Le Point's claims – made mid-Cold War, while terrorists were killing people all over western Europe – had the effect of demonising Curiel.

Le Point followed up in 1977 with a long (and equally inaccurate) article about Blake. The magazine claimed that after 'months of research' it had made 'the stupefying, sensational discovery: in almost all intelligence services, the files of Blake and Curiel are now placed side by side'.

Le Point breathlessly revealed their family relationship (already revealed in Britain some years previously). The magazine claimed that Curiel had recruited his adolescent cousin into the local Communist scene in 1930s Cairo. Blake, explained Le Point, dreamed of emulating Curiel, of 'acting in the shadow, becoming the invisible hero, the deus ex machina and the martyr of history'.[43] The article implied that Curiel's relationship with Blake lent force to the magazine's earlier accusation that Curiel was a KGB agent.

Blake in Moscow read both the *Point* pieces – 'especially', he once recalled with a chuckle, 'the article that said it was him who recruited me'. He added, 'As for the rest, I didn't know anything about it, but I didn't think he was an agent of the KGB.' In Moscow, he often thought of his cousin in Paris: 'I thought it would please him that my life had taken this turn. But I didn't know. Obviously I couldn't put myself in touch with him. It probably wouldn't have been difficult, but I thought that in my position, it wouldn't be prudent.'[44] Curiel never seems to have tried to contact Blake in Moscow either.

In October 1977, after the German magazine *Der Spiegel* had repeated *Le Point*'s accusations, two policemen called at Curiel's flat on rue Rollin on Paris's Left Bank with an order to expel the stateless man to the French countryside.[45] In January 1978 he was allowed to return to Paris. On 4 May 1978, Curiel lunched on a ham sandwich and cup of coffee with his wife, Rosette. At 2 p.m. he got into the lift of his apartment building to go out to a yoga lesson. When he reached the ground floor, he was gunned down inside the lift by two unknown men. He was sixty-three years old.

Stambouli, who jumped into his car and sped to Curiel's flat on hearing the news, remembered his friend once predicting he would die violently. 'That's how I would like to finish', Curiel had added. 'It's the most beautiful death: that of a soldier.'[46] Like Blake, he seems to have seen his life's work as a war on an invisible front.

An hour after the assassination, an anonymous phone call to the Agence France-Presse agency dictated the following message: 'The KGB agent Henri Curiel, militant of the Arab cause, traitor to the France that adopted him, has definitively ceased his activities.' It was signed 'Delta'.[47] The phrase 'KGB agent' confirmed the suspicions of many of his friends that *Le Point*'s allegations had effectively condemned him to death.[48]

In a Cape Town jail Breytenbach claims that a senior police officer told him, 'We got Curiel, you're the next.' Breytenbach writes, 'I remembered then, and still do now, their all-obliterating fascination with, and the hatred they had for Curiel. As if by eliminating one man they could destroy what they considered to be a menacing network of conspiracy against them.'[49] The stateless Egyptian Jew made a perfect hate figure for the global political right.

Twenty-six days after his 'extermination', *Der Spiegel* published an apology 'for having made accusations against Henri Curiel that were later revealed to be without foundation'.[50] A French government commission investigated Curiel's alleged support for terrorism, and found that 'these particularly serious accusations were not accompanied by any proof, nor even the beginning of proof'.[51] At the urging of Curiel's son Gresh, Blake asked the KGB whether it had employed Curiel. The KGB told Blake it had not.[52] But then it would say that, wouldn't it? The CIA in a 'top secret' report on 'Soviet Support for International Terrorism and Revolutionary Violence' in 1981 expressed uncertainty as to whether the 'Curiel Apparat' had had Soviet links. Its best evidence seems to have been 'a source with contacts to the Apparat' who in 1964 'had been told by an Apparat member that the organization received extensive funding from Moscow'.[53]

Nobody has ever been convicted for Curiel's murder. However, in 2015 *Le roman vrai d'un fasciste français* (*The True Novel of a French Fascist*) was published. Its author, René Resciniti de Says had died three years earlier. In the book he recounts having been part of the commando team that killed Curiel. He says they acted on orders from Pierre Debizet, leader of the Service d'Action Civique, a far-right terrorist squad of the 1970s. The book claims that the killers obtained the murder weapons from the Parisian prefecture of police and returned them there afterwards. Even the phone call to the press agency was made from the prefecture, writes Resciniti de Says.

Gresh suspects the South African regime was also involved.[54] After Resciniti de Say's book appeared, Curiel's family called for the murder case to be reopened. But nobody was put on trial.

Cynicism and Christmas Pudding

In Wormwood Scrubs and then in Moscow, Blake went about twenty years without seeing his three sons. When he was jailed in 1961, Anthony and James were small boys and Patrick still in the womb. As Blake told me the story, Gillian and the boys soon rebounded from the trauma of his arrest. She married the man for whom she had divorced Blake, 'and that was a very happy marriage. Her husband was a very, very nice man who was a very good father for my children ... That man had cancer and he died a couple of years ago, but that family is very close.'[1]

But Blake's separation from his sons anguished him. Only in their teens were they told that Blake was their biological father.[2] Then, some time in the early 1980s, the middle son, James, who was then twenty-four-years-old, decided he wanted to meet him.[3] Blake recalled:

> James had served in the English army, he was a trooper in the Life Guards. By then he was already demobilised and he was the first of my sons who came with my mother to

[East] Germany. I met him there for the first time, and we talked and became very good friends. So that was quite an event.[4]

James said of that first visit: 'I went there determined that he would not be my father but I came away sure he was and liking him. After talking to him I understood where he was coming from.'[5] Later, at James's urging, Anthony and Patrick came to see their dad in Moscow.[6] Blake and his Russian son Misha collected the two young Englishmen at Belorusskaya train station. Blake told Olink:

Then they sat here all evening and they – *[Blake stops, and by the sound of it is weeping. He drinks something, then continues talking].* We sat here till deep in the night *[coughing]* and they, I told them everything, explained everything *[he is audibly sobbing].*

But they understand everything well, and although they didn't agree with me, we built up a very good understanding, and the sign of that is that they *[speaking loudly and firmly, apparently in order to stifle his sobs]* want to come here every year and see me.[7]

Blake would always be grateful to Gillian for 'never saying a bad word about me to our children'.[8]

One thing he and his sons had in common was Christianity.[9] It scarcely mattered that his had lapsed somewhat and theirs had not. His youngest English son, Revd Patrick Butler (the surname comes from his stepfather), had even fulfilled Blake's early vocation by becoming a church minister in Hampshire.[10] It is noteworthy that two of Blake's sons had taken on the most traditional possible British establishment roles, as if to make up for their father's treachery. Blake appears to have been proud of their choices: he kept a picture of James in army uniform on his desk.[11]

Blake marvelled to me: 'And now they come here regularly! I have nine grandchildren, and apart from one who lives here, they all live in England. ... It's such a wonder, you must agree ... that things have ended up so well with my sons in England.'[12] Misha and his son had even attended James's wedding in Limerick,[13] Sean Bourke's home town, where they met Gillian. In Blake's words: 'I have been granted the good fortune to have a new family while not losing the old family.'[14]

On the other hand, he did not see his mother in her final years. By her nineties she was no longer strong enough to visit him in Moscow. The KGB offered to make him a false western passport so that he could visit her in her Rotterdam care home, but he didn't dare take the risk.[15] His fellow Dutch Muscovite Derk Sauer tried to pull strings with former Dutch prime minister Ruud Lubbers, but was told that if the UK found out that Blake was in the Netherlands, the Dutch would have no choice but to hand him over.[16] Ida, who did visit the Netherlands in the dying days of the USSR, reported back to her husband that Dutch pensioners lived better than Russian government ministers.[17]

For the ageing Blake, family had come to matter more than ideology. His political ideals had petered out during his years in Moscow. The man of conviction had become a sceptic, even a cynic. He stopped striving for paradise, and learned to enjoy the simple things: loving relationships, and the privileges of the Soviet *nomenklatura*. This didn't mean luxury – in Soviet times the Blakes still queued for basics such as meat and went short of sugar – but the odd KGB food parcel was welcome.[18] Kalugin recalled: 'The Englishman was friendly and grateful

21. Blake at home in Moscow (c. 1997). Note
the Christian icon on the wall.

for the extra money and perks we gave him.'[19] After Communism fell, Blake also received dollars from relatives in the West.[20]

He drank English tea with milk in the morning while listening to the BBC.[21] Every year he made British Christmas pudding from a recipe in *The Times*, although he missed English whipped cream.[22] Sauer's family brought him Dutch syrup waffles and got him a satellite dish so that he could watch Dutch TV. Practically the first programme the old royalist got to see was Princess Juliana's funeral in 2004.[23] He wasn't even averse to the British royal family: a journalist visiting his Moscow flat in 1991 spotted a plate commemorating Charles and Diana's wedding.[24]

Another pleasure of his old age was reading. He couldn't afford subscriptions to the British press,[25] but he loved history and fiction, especially Chekhov and Gogol. We chatted about le Carré (also a favourite of Philby and Maclean), whose early novels are set in almost exactly the milieu and era that Blake had inhabited in his SIS days. The hero of *The Spy Who Came In from the* Cold (1963) – a novel set in the Berlin that Blake had then recently vacated – is actually a British suspected double agent who grew up in the Netherlands. After the novel appeared, Graham Greene wrote to le Carré's publisher, Victor Gollancz: 'I suppose it's asking too much of you to tell me even in confidence what [the author's] real name is? My only possible guess is that Blake has taken to writing novels during his first year [of his] sentence!'[26]

Blake told me, 'Well I think le Carré's books are very good, very good!'

Me: Did you know him?

Blake: No, never. I don't know if he wrote to me once, I can't remember.

Me: Does he describe the milieu as it is?

Blake: Yes, I think so.

Me: Aren't you a character in one of his books?

Blake: No I don't think he wrote about me, not as far as I know.

Me: *Tinker, Tailor, Soldier, Spy* has just been made into a big movie.

Blake: Very good book!

Me: It was already a TV series with Alec Guinness.

Blake: Alec Guinness played –

Me: Played Smiley.

Blake: Played Smiley. Yes, yes, yes. He was a very good actor. In England they had, and have, lots of good actors.[27]

Moscow, for all its shortcomings, became something of a long rest cure for Blake. His life from 1936 to 1966 had been turbulent and scary. Being a double agent was stressful. But by the time he got to Moscow he no longer had to worry about being exposed, because it had already happened.

In 1990 he wrote, 'The twenty-four years I have lived in this country have been the most stable and happy period in my life.'[28] That year Randle and Pottle came to see him in Moscow, for the first time since they had helped him escape. It was the celebration Blake had wished for that night in 1966 when he said goodbye to the Randle family in their camper van on the Berlin highway. Now the old friends reminisced over champagne in Blake's flat.[29] Pottle passed on a friendly message from Blake's long-ago prison visitor in the Scrubs, Roger Falk, and Blake wrote Falk a polite letter in neat round script from Moscow:

> I remember with pleasure our many talks and your sympathetic attitude and kindness to me and my wife in the difficult days of our divorce. I hope that my escape did not lead to any difficulties for you. There was no reason why it should have, but one never knows in cases like this.[30]

In fact, a week or two after Blake's escape, Falk had taken the precaution of tearing the page recording his visits out of the Scrubs' visitors' book.[31]

Pottle later reported back from Moscow:

22. Michael Randle and Pat Pottle in 1991 after being
acquitted of helping Blake escape from jail, even though
they had admitted in court that they had done it.

I don't care what anyone says. George Blake had carved
out some sort of normal life with a second wife. I refuse
to believe he would be better off rotting in some English
jail. Having seen him and his family, I believe what we did
was completely justified.[32]

Randle and Pottle, who had been identified by Bourke's
book in 1970, were finally tried for their role in the escape
in 1991. Blake testified for them by videotape from Moscow.
Pottle, who was representing himself, told the Old Bailey
courtroom:

What did George do that sets him apart from other spies
uncovered at that time? He was not really British, was
he? Not of the old school, not one of us. Deep down, he

was a foreigner, and half-Jewish to boot. He was never part of that privileged undergraduate set at Cambridge in the 1930s. Not like dear old Kim ... or dear old Anthony [Blunt].[33]

The jury acquitted Pottle and Randle, against the judge's instructions.[34] The *Sun* commented, in an editorial headlined 'Stinkers of the Bailey': 'The 1,000-year old jury system, one of the glories of our legal system, is marred by the disgraceful acquittal of ... this odious pair.'[35]

After Pottle died in 2000, Blake's son James came to the memorial service. 'Somebody recognised him,' Randle said later, 'so we invited him to say a few words.'[36] James passed on condolences and best wishes from his 'deeply grateful' father, and added his own tribute: 'For myself it is much more pleasant to visit my father in Moscow than to visit him in Wormwood Scrubs. Thank you.'[37]

Back in Moscow, Blake had spent the final years of the USSR trying to salvage some remnants of his Communist dreams. He concluded that human beings were not good enough for Communism, and that the USSR had to adopt 'values based on capitalist principles'.[38] Yet he hoped it would be possible to reconcile bits of the two systems. Derk Sauer recalls a dinner party with the Blakes and Kalugins at Blake's flat on Moscow's Prospect Mira in about 1991: 'Kalugin was a fervent supporter of Gorbachev and Yeltsin – just like Blake, incidentally. How optimistic we were that evening!'[39] Blake once travelled from his dacha to Moscow to vote for Yeltsin, telling Ida, 'I didn't imagine I'd ever leave the dacha to vote.'

Meanwhile he also stayed close to his old employers. In the summer of 1991, as the USSR was collapsing, he praised the KGB as 'one of the few Soviet institutions which was not corrupt. The KGB was to the Communist Party what the Jesuit order was to the Catholic Church.'[40] Yet the attempted KGB coup of August 1991 appalled him. On the morning of the coup, he told a friend: 'If they keep power, the Soviet Union won't even be a third-world but a fourth-world country. A backward country with a dangerous bomb.' He had always disdained the hardliners of the KGB's domestic security service. He considered his own section, the foreign intelligence service, far more 'progressive' and unfairly tarnished by the crimes of the domestic KGB, just as he thought MI6 in Britain had a 'much more cosmopolitan view of life' than the internal security service MI5.[41]

His life became more turbulent again after the collapse of the Soviet Union – which he likened to the end of the British empire.[42] Wolf, the East German spy chief, remarked: 'The peculiar sadness of Blake's fate is that he lost his homeland not just once, when he fled England, but twice, when the Soviet Union collapsed.'[43] In fact, he lost it three times, starting with his flight from the Netherlands in 1942.

The new post-Soviet political climate did allow him to publish his autobiography, No Other Choice (1990), a work long in the making before glasnost finally made its publication possible. Some early versions had been edited by a skilled Anglophone journalist, Kim Philby. Rufina Philby recalls him working on it on a typewriter in the Blakes' dacha in 1970.[44]

The first version was to be called No Abiding City, a reference to Blake's cosmopolitanism. Robin Denniston, a British publisher who read it in a Moscow office under the supervision of Soviet officials in 1970, had found it tedious and 'hardly publishable'.[45] He thought the author 'a bit of a prig'.[46]

The book idea was revived in the late 1980s after the British literary agent Andrew Nurnberg, on a plane to Moscow, happened to read a newspaper article about an interview Blake had given to Soviet television.[47] Nurnberg recalled:

> I thought, 'Bloody hell! George Blake! How amazing that a man like this is alive and I might be able to meet him.' I knew who he was, that he was this huge traitor. Nobody had ever heard of him since he'd been there [in Moscow].

Nurnberg, who spoke Russian, had recently begun selling western books to the Soviet copyright agency VAAP. He asked VAAP for an introduction to Blake. Within thirty-six hours Blake showed up at the VAAP offices. 'Will you write a book?' asked Nurnberg, and Blake replied, 'Oh yes, I think it could be possible.' Nurnberg doesn't recall him mentioning that he had already written it. The publisher Anthony Cheetham of Random Century signed Blake up for a hefty advance of £33,650, plus another £55,000 to be paid on publication.[48]

The literary agent and the double agent met several more times, and talked about faith and Communism. 'He was a very genial fellow, a highly intelligent man,' Nurnberg told me. 'He did his damnedest to persuade me that Communism would prevail. The only reason it hadn't yet, he'd say, was that it's come too early.'

No Other Choice is an elegantly written book (which may be Philby's legacy). It focuses on Blake's own motivations but reveals little detail either about the KGB or, more surprisingly, about SIS. Nurnberg said: 'He had of course signed the Official Secrets Act. As far as I remember [in the book] he didn't break the Official Secrets Act.' Blake later explained that in the book, he had tried to show his former British colleagues respect: 'I did not want to rubbish them, the way Philby did.

All espionage is difficult. Only those who do it can appreciate how difficult it is.'

The academic Philip Davies calls No Other Choice 'a far more understated and far less self-serving account than Philby's memoir'.[49] The Russian edition became a best-seller, although that didn't make Blake any money, given the collapse of the Soviet economy.[50] But the book's reception in Britain was 'a little muted', said Nurnberg, 'probably because of this reaction to arguably the biggest traitor to this country writing a book. There was very understandable resentment.' Denniston noted: 'A hostile reception and poor sales were coupled with a libel action threatened by Anthony Cheetham's father-in-law, Kenneth de Courcy [Blake's old upper-class prison chum], which left the publishers with a deficit.'[51]

And there was another problem. As Nurnberg recalled it, a certain British journalist, who had long hoped to interview Blake, was angry to see that the publishers had granted the interview to Phillip Knightley instead. The slighted journalist complained to his MP, who raised the issue in the Commons of whether Blake should be allowed to make money out of his treachery. The government then began a long-running attempt to block the book's British royalties. The House of Lords finally ruled in 2000 that he shouldn't receive payment for the book. However, in 2006 the European Court of Human Rights in Strasbourg judged that the British government owed him £3,500 in damages because the long proceedings had violated his human rights. (The ruling did not please British tabloids.[52]) Still, the vast bulk of his royalties was denied to him.

The immediate post-Soviet era was hard on Blake. Moscow's sudden capitalist frenzy appalled him.[53] He also had a scare when Britain requested his extradition from the new Russian state. His neighbours at the dacha offered to hide

23. In the 1970s and 80s, Blake was a frequent guest of the East German Stasi, to which he had betrayed so many British agents. The Stasi was always proud to welcome a visiting celebrity, especially one who spoke fluent German.

him.[54] There were rumours that he was planning to flee to his old stamping ground North Korea, but Blake said, 'I would rather go back to Wormwood Scrubs.'[55] The state newspaper *Rossiyskaya Gazeta* would recall later that 'hotheads' in the early 1990s' Russian government considered expelling Blake, and that 'he lived through several unpleasant months'.[56] The Russians asked Britain to release twenty former Soviet agents in return for Blake, but nothing came of it.[57] He himself claimed to have been sure all along that his hosts wouldn't hand him over.

Even after the USSR disappeared, he always kept on the right side of the KGB and its main successor, the FSB. He occasionally gave lectures to Russian spies (or 'scouts', in Russian security parlance). He also continued to help other Anglophone traitors cope with life in Moscow. Edward Lee Howard, the only CIA agent to defect to the USSR, said in 1998:

> The KGB encourages us to meet other defectors ... George Blake is one of my closest friends and I regret never meeting Kim Philby before he died. George really saved me. He came to my dacha in 1989. I was going through a very bad patch. He sat down in his little English bow tie and told me to pull myself together. That my family could manage very well without me, and the most important thing was to find some useful employment.[58]

In 2000 the head of Russia's foreign intelligence service, Sergey Lebedev, said the seventy-eight-year-old Blake was 'still working actively for the good of Russian intelligence'.[59]

When I asked Blake whether in Moscow he had continued working for the KGB, he replied, 'Huh?'

Me: You worked for the KGB here, didn't you?

Blake: No, well, not directly anyway. Yes I have, eh – no, I have – of course I have good relations and so on, very good relations. They look after me very well.

Me: They arranged this house for you.

Blake: This house and my flat in Moscow, they arranged all that. Yes, yes, that's why I say they look after me very well, and they also looked after Donald very well, and Guy Burgess; he died, but they looked after him very well too. In that regard they are very grateful and they feel obliged to look after us well.[60]

He had told the Stasi that, when he had first arrived in Moscow, he expected the KGB to look after him for 'a few weeks, a few months', but he thought that he would then have to fend for himself. After all, he and the other British defectors to Moscow had 'no more direct use today', he acknowledged in 1977.[61]

However, he said, the KGB had never stopped caring. 'That is, I think, something quite new in the history of – let's use that word – espionage. I know it's not a nice word, but I don't know another word for it.'[62] The KGB's 'remarkable' lifelong generosity to its former double agents was very unlike the usual relationship between secret service and former agent, he told the Stasi:

> You might have personal empathy for him, you might value his work, but when it comes to it, in the best case he gets a sum of money and the case is closed. Auf Wiedersehen, and he can live as he wants ... I have had many experiences in my life, but for me this [treatment by the KGB] has been the greatest experience.[63]

Still, he didn't like Putinist government by former KGB goons. His old friend Kalugin had fled to the US to escape Putin, and had been sentenced in absentia to fifteen years for treason.[64] All that Blake would say to me about Putin was that when he turned eighty he had been to see the president: 'Yes, yes, yes! He invited me. Gave me a decoration.'[65] The day we spoke in 2012, Blake saw no political salvation anywhere in Putin's authoritarian Russia: 'The Communist Party is the only real party here at the moment. The other parties are really fake parties. But the Communists cling to that old image, let's say, of Stalinism, and there's not much future in that either.'[66]

'Tragic I Am Not'

Six months after my interview with Blake, in November 2012, the state celebrated his ninetieth birthday. The Zvezda TV channel broadcast a documentary that opens with the question, 'Who is he really, a *mister* [i.e., an Englishman] or a comrade?' In it Blake says modestly, 'I feel I am neither hero nor traitor' and also: 'I'm a cosmopolitan. Maybe I mostly feel Dutch.' However, the film concludes triumphantly: 'Even in England he was a foreigner. But here he is ours.'[1]

By that time, writes Sauer, he had acquired an 'almost iconic status' in Russia.[2] Putin sent the birthday boy a telegram saying that he had a place in the 'constellation of strong and courageous men'. In the president's words, 'You and your colleagues made an enormous contribution to the preservation of peace, to security, and to strategic parity. This is not visible to the eyes of outsiders.'[3] Blake was almost certainly more moved by the visit of his ex-wife Gillian, with their British sons, nearly fifty years after she had last seen him in Wormwood Scrubs. The two old people made peace with each other.[4]

On Blake's ninety-fifth birthday, in November 2017,

24. Poster from the 2018 production of *Cell Mates*. Simon Gray's 1995 play returned to the stage in Hampstead, a short walk from Pat Pottle's flat in which Bourke and Blake had hidden after their escape. Gray suggests a suppressed homoerotic love between the two fugitives.

Russia's foreign intelligence service, the SVR, issued a statement in his name. He was quoted as saying that the SVR must 'save the world in a situation when the danger of nuclear war and the resulting self-destruction of humankind again have been put on the agenda by irresponsible politicians'.[5] (He was presumably referring to the faceoff between Donald Trump and the North Korean dictator Kim Jong-un.) The SVR's chief Sergei Naryshkin praised Blake as 'a reliable comrade, a man of great wisdom ... and a skilful teacher.'

In an interview on Russian state TV, the ninety-five-year-old said he still believed in socialism: 'If I didn't believe in it I'd be dead already.' His age, he continued, was 'a lot for a person and yet very little for the history of humanity.' He said he had not regretted his life 'for a moment', and looked to the future 'with optimism'.[6]

I suspect that neither his own words nor the eulogies meant much to Blake anymore.

In old age he had acquired something he had lacked in youth: the ability to find happiness in the here and now, beyond either power or ideas. In a Russian TV interview in 2011 he had sounded more negative than in his official statements, describing the present as a cynical era in which beliefs scarcely mattered any more: 'Young agents have it tougher than we did. In my time, many worked for the idea … Today no one believes in such ideas, you can only attract people using spite, black-mail and money.'[7]

By the time I met Blake, he had spent more than half his life doing not very much in Moscow. He had become an anachro-nism, a historical curiosity.

'Didn't you miss adventure?' I asked. 'You'd been a man of the world, you went everywhere, and now –'

'No, I didn't miss it,' Blake interrupted. 'I think I'd had enough of adventure. And life here was an adventure in itself.'

Didn't he miss the Netherlands, or Britain? Wouldn't he like to go for a stroll in Rotterdam?

'Yes. Or in England, in London. Of course I'd like that, but I know it's not possible so I don't think about it. As I said, I have always been able to resign myself to fate.'[8]

Anyway, even if he could somehow have got to London, he had gone too blind to see it. After losing his eyesight, Blake relied on Ida to read to him, invariably in Russian. He also listened to classical music and the BBC World Service, and he enjoyed neighbourhood life. He pointed me to a little house just across from his garden. He said he and Ida had given it to a poor family from central Asia. The house had been run down, so the Blakes had helped the family pay for renova-tions, and had given them a car, and lent them money for a second car. Blake said, 'We are very happy that they are here, it's always good to have someone here, and at night and so on. And [*laughs*] they are happy with us.'[9]

I had read that most of the nearby houses belonged to officials in the Russian intelligence services, but he denied it.

This is a very international community here, there are many people from – what's it called? – Turkestan and so on, Tajikistan. And I have very good relations with neighbours, because I walk every day here, twice a day, mornings and evenings, on this road. Back and forth. Ida thinks, and she's right, that I must keep moving, not sit for too long. Whether it's good weather or bad, we pay no attention to that. And doggie comes with us – also an important member of the family.[10]

I asked what the dog was called. Blake chuckled uncomfortably, then said, 'Wait a moment – I'll tell you later.'[11] Clearly I couldn't keep him much longer. We had been talking for a couple of hours. His voice was starting to fade. I asked if I could take some photographs of him in the garden.

Blake: Fine, certainly, certainly. Well, what's your judgement now? [*Laughs*] Are you astonished by everything I have told you, or eh, did you know it all beforehand, or –

Me: I had –

Blake: Well, at least –

Me: I had expected a more tragic figure.

Blake: Ahhhh! Yes. Hahahaha. Tragic I am not.

Me: No, you're affable.

Blake: Hahaha! Tragic I am not, but had you expected that?

Me: Yes. You have lived through a lot.

Blake: Yes.

Me: You took very difficult decisions.

Blake: Yes.

Me: You lived in a time of life and death, in Berlin, in Korea.

Blake: Yes, that is true. But that is the way it went.[12]

I said I was impressed by how he had managed to adapt and to find happiness. It must have been difficult, I remarked.

Blake: Difficult but possible.

Me: Apparently so, yes.

Blake [*laughs*]: Why do you think it would be difficult? That depends entirely on the person. The one finds it difficult, and the other doesn't ... I think many people will think that, eh – that the life that I have led, that I didn't deserve that life, but that is the way it went.[13]

His appeals to determinism seemed to have become instinctive.

I would like to say that I recorded the older Blake's fullest and deepest assessment of his life, but in fact the Dutch journalist Hans Olink did. In 1999, at the end of his four-part radio series, he had asked Blake the great question: 'Was it all worthwhile?' Blake had replied:

Yes, I believe it was worthwhile, for me, for two reasons. Firstly because I thought – and still think – that the communist experiment (and it always was an experiment) was worth trying. It was a very noble experiment. And had it succeeded, it would of course have been a great step forward for humanity ...

And I have no regrets at all at having dedicated my life, or a large part of my life, to that. I also don't regret that that has made my life – I have to say – an interesting life. I'm grateful for that. And [I am grateful] for having been able to meet and get to know well many very interesting and exceptional people. Those people were Maclean, Philby, they were the people who aided my escape, they were many other people whom I got to know here, and even people in jail. People to whom I think back fondly, and many situations that were really quite exceptional.

But of course I also have a feeling of guilt. Guilt in the first place towards my family, my wife, my children – although they have forgiven me; towards my mother and sisters who faced a great many difficulties because of eh my actions. And of course also, to some degree, regret and guilt towards those – my colleagues in the English service, and others who trusted me, and whose trust I disappointed. So I cannot get away from that feeling of regret. But on the other hand, as I say, I think I did it for something that maybe was worthwhile in the history of humanity, and that – although it has caused lots and lots of suffering – maybe was also something from which humanity learned a lot, and that maybe in future centuries might turn out to have been useful.[14]

Neither in the interview with Olink nor in any other context did he once express any regret about the agents he betrayed, at least not explicitly. Sauer believes that after Blake was disillusioned first by Communism and later by Putinism, he 'became ever more remorseful about his role as a spy, but distancing himself from it was a bridge too far.'[15]

I had asked all my questions. The half-blind little geriatric took his cane, raised himself from the sofa and went out into the sunlit garden, where I took some very bad photographs of him and of Ida and the dog (who turned out to be called Lyusha). As Blake sat posing happily, he began to reminisce, speaking English for Ida's benefit.

> Blake: My son [Misha] was two years old when we came here. We started off in the summer and then gradually we started coming here in the winters as well because we like skiing in the woods and, eh – eventually, we moved in here altogether and my son lives in our flat in Moscow. That's how it happened, gradually. Everything in life happens gradually.
>
> Me: You speak English with a Dutch accent.
>
> Blake: Yes, that is true. [*Laughs*] I cannot deny it, and I don't want to.[16]

One day his ashes would be strewn in the woods around the dacha. Blake said:

> I will explain it to you very simply – I hope. I don't believe in life after death. When we die, it's the end of everything, and therefore there is no hell and there is no heaven and there is no reward and no punishment, there is nothing. We aren't there any more. Just like the grass and the leaves of trees that fall off and rot and aren't there any more ... That is my true belief.[17]

But surely, I asked, he would have a sort of afterlife as a historical figure? Blake replied: 'I don't think about that. Because nobody knows how history will continue and what will come of that. No, I don't have such thoughts. That is of no importance to me.'[18]

We were done. In just a few minutes in the garden the mosquitoes had bitten me to shreds. Some summer days, said Blake, it was so bad you had to wrap yourself up as if it were winter. But today he had been OK, he said. 'Maybe they don't like the taste of my blood.'[19]

That weekend there were anti-Putin protests all over Moscow, and without mentioning the president's name, Blake warned me that this might delay my drive to the airport.

I asked if there was anything Dutch I could send him from the West. He chuckled: 'How would you want to send it? That's quite a complicated affair.'[20] But if it were possible, he added politely, he would appreciate some Dutch herring or cheese. I said I'd look into sending it, and at that moment I fully intended to.

Blake, Ida and Lyusha came out into the lane behind the house to wave me off. Blake pointed to a yellow villa opposite: 'People from Turkestan, from Bukhara, live there.'

The exotic name made me think of Blake's childhood neighbourhood in Rotterdam. 'You've come a long way from Spangen,' I said.

He gripped my arm and said in Russian, '*Dasveedanya*', 'Goodbye'.

'*Tot ziens*', 'Till later', I said in Dutch.

Afterwards, Blake phoned Sauer to say that we had had a very enjoyable conversation.[21]

I must admit that the feeling was mutual. Colonel Blake had charmed me. I flew home to Paris and told my wife about this gentle, fascinating, cerebral, cosmopolitan and baffling old man. She pointed out that he seemed to have killed forty people. It sounded, she said, as if he had managed to con me too. I thought about it, and in the end I didn't send him the herring.

Afterword

Blake spent much of his final year sheltering inside his dacha in a woolly hat and mittens. The coronavirus was cutting through Russia, slaying many of the last survivors of the country's Great Patriotic War against Nazi Germany, though Russian deaths from the disease were grossly underreported. Blake and Ida – herself ailing by then – lived in isolation, watched over by the SVR foreign intelligence agency, their son Misha, and a Tajik guard-cum-handyman.

Despite the circumstances, Blake was enjoying the old age that he had denied to dozens of his victims. He appears to have remained cheery and alert to the end. 'I feel strong,' he told his friend Sauer in December 2019. 'With a bit of luck I'll get to a hundred.' He didn't see himself as a hero (though the Russian state did), but he was a contented man.[1]

His death, at the age of ninety-eight, was reported on Boxing Day 2020. No details of the cause were given. The Rotterdammer was buried in the Troyekurovskoye cemetery's Alley of Heroes in western Moscow, under his Russian name Gyorgi Bekhter, to the strains of the Russian national anthem and gun salutes from a military guard of honour, which wore masks against the virus. 'Colonel Blake was a brilliant professional of a special kind and courage,' eulogised Vladimir Putin.[2] The SVR said Blake 'sincerely loved our country and admired our people's achievements during World War Two'.[3] The UK's Foreign, Commonwealth and Development Office refused to comment on his death.[4]

Acknowledgements

I will for ever be grateful to Derk Sauer in Moscow for putting me in touch with George Blake. Many thanks also to Jana Bakunina, Carl Bromley, Gareth Brown, Claire Browne, George Carey, Teresa Cherfas, Emma Crates, Penny Daniel, Christian Dellit, Jack Farchy, Quentin Falk, Marc Favreau, Andrew Franklin, Bonnie Green, Alain Gresh, Shirley Haasnoot, Pauline Harris, Adam Kuper, Leila Kuper, Richard Kuper, Ana Lankes, Simon Lister, Ton van Luin, Henri Mamarbachi, Nathaniel McKenzie, Andrew Nurnberg, Philippe Sands, Tom Sauer, Marijke Schussler-Sol, Adam Shatz, Jan Maarten Slagter, David Stafford, Matthew Taylor, Henk ter Borg, Ellen Verbeek, Gordon Wise, Valentina Zanca and, above all and always, Pamela Druckerman.

Notes

When a note cites a book but not a specific page number, it is because I found the reference through Google Books and no page number was provided. Notes marked 'GB' denote the Dutch transcript of my interview with Blake in May 2012, which can be found online at www. TheHappyTraitor.com/blake-interview. The reference 'GB49', for example, denotes page 49 of the transcript.

Chapter 1: Finding Blake

1. Nigel West, *At Her Majesty's Secret Service: The Chiefs of Britain's Intelligence Agency, MI6* (Frontline Books, Barnsley, 2016).
2. Account of the break-out in Roger Hermiston, *The Greatest Traitor: The Secret Lives of Agent George Blake* (Aurum Press, London, 2013), pp. 286–7; and in George Blake, *No Other Choice* (Simon & Schuster, New York, 1990), pp. 230–33.
3. Kevin O'Connor, *Blake, Bourke & The End of Empires* (Prendeville, London, 2003), pp. 187–8.
4. Louis Mountbatten, 'Report of the Inquiry into Prison Escapes and Security'.
5. Giles Playfair, 'Wormwood', *Spectator*, 30 January 1969.
6. Michael Randle and Pat Pottle, *The Blake Escape: How We Freed George Blake – And Why* (Harrap, London, 1989), pp. 112–13.

7. Peter Deeley, 'Blake the Spy Escapes from Scrubs Cell', *Observer,* 23 October 1966.

8. George Blake, *No Other Choice*, pp. 18–19.

9. Ellen Verbeek, 'Spion voor een verloren zaak', *HP/De Tijd*, 13 September, 1991.

10. Robert Mendick and Tom Parfitt, 'My Father the Russian Spy, by Anglican Curate from Guildford', *Sunday Telegraph*, 11 November 2012.

11. GB49 [GB denotes the Dutch transcript of the interview].

12. GB41.

13. GB56–7.

14. Robert Cecil, *A Divided Life: A Biography of Donald Maclean* (William Morrow, New York, 1989), p. 156.

15. Roland Philipps, *A Spy Named Orphan* (Bodley Head, London, 2018), p. 375.

16. Ian Buruma, 'The Weird Success of Guy Burgess', *New York Review of Books,* 22 December 2016.

17. Stasi archive, MfS Sekr. Neiber 81, 'Eine grossartige Begegnung'.

18. Stasi archive, MfS Arbeitsbereich NEIBER, 'Vortrag für die Auswertung des Besuches von George Blake', 1977.

19. Blake, speech to Stasi, probably 1980, Stasi online archive, Bundesbeauftragte für die Unterlagen des Staatssicherheitsdienstes der ehemaligen Deutschen Demokratischen Republiks, MfS HV A/ Vi/15.

Chapter 2: An Ordinary Dutch Boy

1. GB2.

2. Hermiston, *The Greatest Traitor,* p. 3.

3. Blake, *No Other Choice,* pp. 28, 32.

4. Hermiston, *The Greatest Traitor,* p. 3.

5. Sean Bourke, *The Springing of George Blake* (Viking Press, New York, 1970), p. 210.

6. Blake, *No Other Choice*, pp. 27–30.

7. Hans Olink, *Meesterspion George Blake*, OVT radio programme, part 1.

8. Blake, *No Other Choice*, p. 30, and Hermiston, *The Greatest Traitor*, p. 3.

9. Hermiston, *The Greatest Traitor*, pp. 315–16.

10. E. H. Cookridge, 'George was schuchter in gezelschap van vrouwen', *De Telegraaf*, 19 January 1967.

11. Wim A. Van Geffen, 'We noemden hem Poek', *De Telegraaf*, 30 December 1961.

12. Cookridge, 'George wilde later theologie studeren', *De Telegraaf*, 20 January 1967.

13. Blake, speech to Stasi, 1981, Bundesbeauftragte für die Unterlagen des Staatssicherheitsdienstes der ehemaligen Deutschen Demokratischen Republiks, MfS HV A/Vi/80–81.

14. Blake, speech to Stasi, probably 1980.

15. Blake, *No Other Choice*, p. 34.

16. GB20.

17. Blake, *No Other Choice*, p. 107.

18. Ibid., pp. 54–5, 35.

19. GB54.

20. Olink, *Meesterspion George Blake*, part 2.

21. Blake, *No Other Choice*, p. 109.

22. Randle and Pottle, *The Blake Escape*, p. 43.

23. GB29–30.

24. Blake, *No Other Choice*, pp. 36–7.

25. Ibid., p. 4.

26. Olink, *Meesterspion George Blake*, part 1.

27. Hermiston, *The Greatest Traitor*, p. 8.

Chapter 3: A Jewish Mansion in an Arab City

1. Gilles Perrault, *Un homme à part* (Bernard Barrault, Paris, 1984), p. 48.

2. Ibid., p. 60.

3. Hermiston, *The Greatest Traitor*, pp. 9–11.

4. Perrault, *Un homme à part*, pp. 48–9.

5. Ibid., p. 50.

6. Gilles Perrault, 'Henri Curiel, citoyen du tiers-monde', *Le Monde Diplomatique*, April 1998.

7. Perrault, *Un homme à part,* p. 59.

8. Ibid., pp. 52–3.

9. Gillian Blake, 'Portret van een spion', *De Telegraaf,* 23 December 1961.

10. Blake, *No Other Choice,* p. 44.

11. Ibid., p. 39.

12. Perrault, *Un homme à part*, p. 55.

13. Perrault, 'Henri Curiel, citoyen du tiers-monde'.

14. Perrault, *Un homme à part*, p. 72–3.

15. Mehdi Lallaoui, *Henri Curiel: Itinéraire d'un combattant de la paix et de la liberté*, Mémoires Vives productions, Paris, 2001.

16. Perrault, *Un homme à part*, p. 60.

17. Blake, *No Other Choice,* pp. 44–5, and Eiji Nagasawa, 'Henri Curiel: A Jewish Egyptian Dedicated to Peace and Socialism', *Mediterranean Review*, vol. 9, no. 1 (June 2016), p. 83.

18. Perrault, *Un homme à part,* p. 73.

19. Blake, *No Other Choice,* p. 45.

20. Perrault, 'Henri Curiel, citoyen du tiers-monde'.

21. Perrault, *Un homme à part*, p. 74.

22. James C. Riley, 'Bibliography of Works Providing Estimates of Life Expectancy at Birth and Estimates of the Beginning Period of Health Transitions in Countries with a Population in 2000 of at Least 400,000' at http://www.lifetable.de/data/rileybib.pdf.

23. Perrault, *Un homme à part*, p. 75.

24. Perrault, 'Henri Curiel, citoyen du tiers-monde'.

25. Piotr Cherkasov, 'Vtoraya Zhizn Gomera', *Izvestia*, 21 May 2003.

26. Nagasawa, 'Henri Curiel', pp. 83–4.

27. Blake, *No Other Choice*, p. 45.

28. See, for instance, Christopher Andrew, *The Defence of the Realm: The Authorized History of MI5* (Penguin, London, 2010), p. 488.

29. Perrault, *Un homme à part*, p. 85.

30. Joel Beinin, *The Dispersion of Egyptian Jewry: Culture, Politics, and the Formation of a Modern Diaspora* (American University in Cairo Press, Cairo, 2005), p. 143.

31. Ibid.

32. Adam Shatz, unpublished essay on Henri Curiel, undated.

33. Perrault, *Un homme à part*, p. 108.
34. Nagasawa, 'Henri Curiel', p. 86.
35. Olivier Roy, 'International Terrorism', BKA autumn conference, 18–19 November 2015.
36. Olink, *Meesterspion George Blake*, part 1.
37. Blake, *No Other Choice*, p. 45.
38. Ibid.

Chapter 4: Deception Becomes Daily Habit

1. Perrault, *Un homme à part*, p. 569.
2. This paragraph is based on Blake, *No Other Choice*, pp. 49–51.
3. Blake, speech to Stasi, probably 1980.
4. Blake, *No Other Choice*, p. 55.
5. GB16.
6. Olink, *Meesterspion George Blake*, part 1.
7. Blake, *No Other Choice*, p. 146.
8. Blake, speech to Stasi, probably 1980.
9. Hermiston, p. 25.
10. Ibid., p. 58.
11. N. M. Westerbeek van Eerten-Faure, *En de 'Rücksack' stond altijd klaar... dagboek van een doktersvrouw in oorlogstijd* (Doetinchem, Mr. H. J. Steenbergen-Stichting, 2015), pp. 148–9.
12. Olink, *Meesterspion George Blake*, part 1.
13. GB17.
14. GB17 and GB19.
15. Unsigned, 'Operation "Gold" und andere ...', *Neues Deutschland*, 18 February 1970 (translation in the East German party newspaper of Blake's coming-out interview in the Soviet newspaper *Izvestia*).
16. Blake, *No Other Choice*, pp. 60–62.
17. Hermiston, *The Greatest Traitor*, p. 30.
18. Westerbeek van Eerten-Faure, 'En de "Rücksack" stond altijd klaar...', p. 161.
19. Ibid., p. 178.
20. Hermiston, *The Greatest Traitor*, pp. 41–2.
21. Olink, *Meesterspion George Blake*, part 1.

22. Marijke Huisman, *Mata Hari (1876–1917): de levende legende* (Verloren Verleden, Hilversum, 1998), pp. 9–17.

23. Perrault, *Un homme à part*, p. 62.

Chapter 5: A Legendary Centre of Hidden Power

1. Blake, *No Other Choice,* p. 82.

2. Blake, speeches to Stasi, 1980 and 1981.

3. Blake, *No Other Choice,* pp. 83–5.

4. Tom Bower, *The Perfect English Spy* (St Martin's Press, New York, 1995), p. 260.

5. Blake, *No Other Choice,* pp. 84–6.

6. Olink, *Meesterspion George Blake*, part 1.

7. Blake, speech to Stasi, 1981.

8. GB17.

9. Olink, *Meesterspion George Blake*, part 1.

10. Blake, *No Other Choice,* pp. 91–2.

11. Blake, speech to Stasi, 1981.

12. O'Connor, *Blake, Bourke & The End of Empires,* p. 44.

13. Blake, speech to Stasi, probably 1980.

14. Ibid.

15. Blake, speech to Stasi, 1981.

16. Olink, *Meesterspion George Blake*, part 1.

17. George Carey, *George Blake: Masterspy of Moscow*, BBC TV documentary, screened on BBC4, 22 March 2015.

18. Blake, *No Other Choice*, p. 99.

19. Hermiston, *The Greatest Traitor,* p. 67.

20. E. H. Cookridge, *George Blake: Double Agent* (Ballantine Books, New York, 1982), p. 50.

21. Blake, speeches to Stasi, 1980 and 1981.

22. Blake, speech to Stasi, 1981.

23. Unsigned, 'Operation 'Gold' und andere …', *Neues Deutschland*.

24. Blake, *No Other Choice*, p. 102.

25. Blake, speech to Stasi, probably 1980.

26. Cookridge, *George Blake,* p. 50 and p. 54–5.

27. Rebecca West, *The New Meaning of Treason* (Viking Press, New York, 1964), p. 303.

28. Blake, *No Other Choice,* p. 99.

29. Hermiston, *The Greatest Traitor,* p. 70.

30. Ben Macintyre, *A Spy among Friends: Kim Philby and the Great Betrayal* (Crown Publishers, New York, 2014), p. 234.

31. Cookridge, *George Blake,* pp. 70–71.

32. Carey, *George Blake: Masterspy of Moscow.*

33. GB20.

34. Stasi archive, MfS Sekr. Neiber/Tb/1, Blake, speech to Stasi, 1976.

35. Eleanor Wachtel interview, *John le Carré on War, Terror and His New Biography,* CBC Radio (Canada), 29 November 2015.

36. Guido Knopp, *Top-Spione: Verräter im Geheimen Krieg* (Goldmann, Munich, 1997), p. 132.

37. Simon Gray, *Plays Five* (Faber and Faber, London, 2010), p. 34.

38. Ibid., p. 133.

39. Blake, speech to Stasi, probably 1980.

40. GB24–5.

41. Information on Hill from A. D. P. Briggs, 'Obituary: Dame Elizabeth Hill', *The Independent,* 6, January 1997; Anthony Cross, 'Hill, Dame Elizabeth Mary', *Oxford Dictionary of National Biography*: http://www.oxforddnb.com/view/article/64000; R. Auty, L. R. Lewitter and A. P. Vlasto (eds), *Gorski Vijenac: A Garland of Essays Offered to Professor Elizabeth Mary Hill* (Modern Humanities Research Association, Cambridge, 1970); and D. M. Thomas, 'A War of Soft Words', *Guardian,* 16 November 2002.

42. Blake, *No Other Choice,* p. 105.

43. Jonathan Haslam, *Near and Distant Neighbours: A New History of Soviet Intelligence* (Oxford University Press, Oxford, 2015), p. 187.

44. Blake, speech to Stasi, 1981.

Chapter 6: The Prisoner Converts

1. Blake, *No Other Choice,* pp. 109–11.

2. Blake, speech to Stasi, probably 1980.

3. Blake, speech to Stasi, 1976.

4. Hermiston, *The Greatest Traitor*, pp. 85–6; Randle and Pottle, *The Blake Escape,* p. 248; and Carey, *George Blake: Masterspy of Moscow.*

5. Blake, speech to Stasi, probably 1980.

6. Perrault, *Un homme à part,* pp. 571–2.

7. Blake, *No Other Choice,* p. 111.

8. Ibid.

9. Blake, speech to Stasi, probably 1980.

10. Blake, *No Other Choice,* p. 118.

11. Blake, speeches to Stasi, 1980 and 1981.

12. Carey, *George Blake: Masterspy of Moscow.*

13. Blake, *No Other Choice,* pp. 115–16.

14. Blake, speech to Stasi, probably 1980.

15. Ibid.

16. Blake, *No Other Choice,* p. 126.

17. http://hansard.millbanksystems.com/written_answers/1961/may/10/foreign-service-security#S5CV0640P0_19610510_CWA_28.

18. Blake, speech to Stasi, Erfurt, 1977; and Blake, *No Other Choice,* pp. 132–4

19. Cookridge, *George Blake,* p. 91.

20. H. Montgomery Hyde, *George Blake Superspy: The Truth behind Blake's Sensational Escape to Moscow* (Futura, London, 1988), p. 38.

21. Cookridge, *George Blake,* p. 93.

22. Blake, *No Other Choice,* pp. 134–5.

23. Blake, speech to Stasi, 1981.

24. Hermiston, *The Greatest Traitor,* pp. 100, 105.

25. Steve Vogel, *Betrayal in Berlin: The True Story of the Cold War's Most Audacious Espionage Operation* (Custom House, New York, 2019), p. 7.

26. Richard Norton-Taylor, 'George Blake Now Prepared to Talk after Decades of Silence', *Guardian,* 19 September 1990.

27. Evan Osnos, 'The Risk of Nuclear War with North Korea', *New Yorker,* 18 September, 2017.

28. Blake, speech to Stasi, 1976.

29. Ibid.

30. Blake, *No Other Choice,* pp. 135–6.

31. Blake, speech to Stasi, probably 1980.

32. T. Rees Shapiro, 'George Blake, notorious Cold War double agent who helped Soviets, dies at 98', *Washington Post,* 26 December 2020.

33. Cookridge, *George Blake*, p. 99.

34. Blake, speech to Stasi, probably 1980.

35. Blake, *No Other* Choice, p. 137.

36. GB22–3.

37. Blake, speech to Stasi, 1981.

38. Blake, speech to Stasi, 1976.

39. Blake, speech to Stasi, 1977.

40. Knopp, *Top-Spione*, p. 134.

41. Blake, speech to Stasi, probably 1980.

42. Cookridge, *George Blake,* pp. 94–104.

43. Blake, speech to Stasi, probably 1980.

44. GB24.

45. Blake, speech to Stasi, 1976.

46. Blake, speech to Stasi, 1981.

47. Blake, speech to Stasi, probably 1980.

48. Hermiston, *The Greatest Traitor,* pp. 131–3.

49. Helen Womack, 'British Traitor George Blake "Hooked by KGB Sweets"', *Independent,* 18 April 1992.

50. Unsigned, 'Food Won Spy, ex-KGB Man Says', Reuters, 19, April 1992.

51. Vogel, *Betrayal in Berlin*, p. 47.

52. Blake, *No Other Choice*, p. 110.

53. Olink, *Meesterspion George Blake*, part 2.

54. Thomas Grant, *Jeremy Hutchinson's Case Histories* (John Murray, London, 2016), p. 60.

55. Joanne Levine, 'Former Double Agent Left Out in the Cold', *St Petersburg Times,* 14 July 1992.

56. GB21.

57. Ibid., p. 126.

58. Simon Kuper, 'From Cambridge Spies to Isis Jihadis', *Financial Times,* 1 April 2016.

59. Piotr Cherkasov, *IMEMO: Portret na fone epokhi* (Ves' mir, Moscow, 2004). All translations from Russian texts are by Jana Bakunina.

60. Bower, *The Perfect English Spy*, p. 272.

61. Ibid., p. 261.

62. Bourke, *The Springing of George Blake*, p. 278.

63. Angelo Codevilla, 'KGB: The Inside Story, by Christopher Andrew and Oleg Gordievsky', *Commentary*, 1 February 1991.

64. Blake, *No Other Choice*, pp. 129–31.

65. Carey, *George Blake: Masterspy of Moscow*.

66. Elliott Shiff and David Stein, 'George Blake, Master of Deception', Episode 7 of *Betrayal!*, Associated Producers, 2004.

Chapter 7: Lunchtime Spy

1. Hermiston, *The Greatest Traitor*, pp. 136–8.

2. Vogel, *Betrayal in Berlin*, p. 79.

3. Blake, *No Other Choice*, p. 152.

4. Knopp, *Top-Spione*, p. 133.

5. Carey, *George Blake: Masterspy of Moscow*.

6. Vogel, *Betrayal in Berlin*, p. 84.

7. Hermiston, *The Greatest Traitor*, p. 150.

8. Cookridge, *George Blake: Double Agent*.

9. John le Carré, 'Fifty Years Later', *The Spy Who Came In from the Cold* (Penguin, London, 2014), p. 280.

10. John le Carré, *The Pigeon Tunnel: Stories from My Life* (Penguin, London, 2016).

11. John le Carré, *Tinker, Tailor, Soldier, Spy* (Penguin, London, 2011), Introduction.

12. Randle and Pottle, *The Blake Escape*, p. 156.

13. Tennent H. Bagley, *Spymaster: Startling Cold War Revelations of a Soviet KGB Chief* (Skyhorse Publishing, New York, 2015).

14. David Stafford, *Spies beneath Berlin* (John Murray, London, 2003), p. 76.

15. Ibid.

16. Chapman Pincher, *Too Secret, Too Long* (St Martin's Press, New York, 1984), p. 371.

17. Unsigned, 'Operation "Gold" und andere ...', *Neues Deutschland*.

18. Blake, *No Other Choice*, pp. 17–18.

19. Blake, speech to Stasi, probably 1980.

20. Mark Franchetti, 'Revealed – Blake's Bus Ride of Betrayal', *Sunday Times*, 14 November 1999.

21. Bagley, *Spymaster*.

22. Blake, speech to Stasi, 1976.

23. Ibid.

24. Unsigned, 'Operation "Gold" und andere ...', *Neues Deutschland*.

25. Bagley, *Spymaster*.

26. Stafford, *Spies beneath Berlin*, p. 78.

27. Knopp, *Top-Spione*, p. 159.

28. Blake, speech to Stasi, 1976.

29. Austin B. Matschulat, 'Coordination and Cooperation in Counterintelligence', CIA Historical Review Program, 2 July 1996: https://www.cia.gov/library/center-for-the-study-of-intelligence/kent-csi/vol13no2/html/v13i2a05p_0001.htm.

30. Michael Evans, 'Macmillan Struck Secret Deal to Jail Blake for 42 Years', *The Times,* 9 March 1995.

31. Fritz Wirth, 'Noch immer keine Spur von George Blake ...', *Welt am Sonntag,* 20 August 1967.

32. Stephen Dorril, 'George Blake exemplified the desolation, waste and treachery of the Cold War', *Guardian*, 27 December 2020.

33. Carey, *George Blake: Masterspy of Moscow*.

34. Bower, *The Perfect English Spy*, p. 262.

35. Shiff and Stein, 'George Blake, Master of Deception'.

36. Hermiston, *The Greatest Traitor*, pp. 150–55.

37. Blake, *No Other Choice*, p. 164.

38. GB6.

39. Cookridge, *George Blake*, p. 120.

40. Ibid., p. 121.

41. Blake, *No Other Choice*, pp. 164–5.

42. Cookridge, pp. 121–2.

43. Carey, *George Blake: Masterspy of Moscow*.

44. GB31–2.

45. Knopp, *Top-Spione*, p. 178.

46. Blake, speech to Stasi, 1981.

Chapter 8: A Mole in Berlin

1. Paul Maddrell, *Spying on Science: Western Intelligence in Divided Germany 1945–1961* (Oxford University Press, Oxford, 2006), pp. 144–5.

2. David Milner Woodford, 'Oral History', Imperial War Museums, produced 18 November 1999, at http://www.iwm.org.uk/collections/item/object/80018317.

3. Patrick Major, *Behind the Berlin Wall: East Germany and the Frontiers of Power* (Oxford University Press, Oxford, 2010), p. 31.

4. Stafford, *Spies beneath Berlin*, p. 95.

5. Vogel, *Betrayal in Berlin*, p. 18.

6. Bundesbeauftragte für die Unterlagen des Staatssicherheitsdienstes: 'Audiobeitrag: Vortrag von George Blake' http://www.bstu.bund.de/DE/BundesbeauftragterUndBehoerde/Aktuelles/spionagetunnel_altglienicke.html.

7. Vogel, *Betrayal in Berlin*, p. 16.

8. Ibid., pp. 110–11 and p. 122.

9. Ibid., p. 79.

10. GB13.

11. Stafford, *Spies beneath Berlin,* p. 45.

12. Hermiston, *The Greatest Traitor,* p. 176.

13. Blake interview by Sylvie Braibant, TV5Monde.com, released online on 8 August 2011.

14. Cookridge, *George Blake*, p. 124.

15. Vogel, *Betrayal in Berlin*, p. 66.

16. Stasi archive, 'Vortrag für die Auswertung des Besuches von George Blake', 1977.

17. Maddrell, *Spying on Science,* p. 130.

18. Ibid., p. 267.

19. Blake, speech to Stasi, probably 1980.

20. Blake, speech to the Stasi, 1976.

21. Vogel, *Betrayal in Berlin*, p. 76.

22. Knopp, *Top-Spione*, p. 140.

23. Bundesbeauftragte für die Unterlagen des Staatssicherheitsdienstes der ehemaligen Deutschen Demokratischen Republiks: 'Podiumsveranstaltung in der Schule der Hauptverwaltung Aufklärung des MfS in Belzig mit George Blake. Ausschnitt aus einer Videoaufzeichnung von 1980'. http://www.bstu.bund.de/DE/BundesbeauftragterUndBehoerde/Aktuelles/spionagetunnel_altglienicke.html.

24. Vogel, *Betrayal in Berlin*, p. 112.

25. Knopp, *Top-Spione,* p. 164.

26. Stafford, *Spies beneath Berlin*, p. 99.

27. Vogel, *Betrayal in Berlin*, p. 176.

28. Stafford, *Spies beneath Berlin*, pp. 185–7.

29. Unsigned, 'The Berlin Tunnel', CIA, November 21, 2012: https://www.cia.gov/about-cia/cia-museum/experience-the-collection/text-version/stories/the-berlin-tunnel.html.

30. GB13.

31. Oleg Gordievsky, 'No Laughing Boy', *Times Literary Supplement,* 14 November 1997.

32. Markus Wolf and Anne McElvoy, *Man without a Face* (PublicAffairs, New York, 1997), p. 99.

33. Knopp, *Top-Spione*, p. 150.

34. CIA, 'Clandestine Services History: The Berlin Tunnel Operation 1952–1956', 24 June 1968 at https://www.cia.gov/library/readingroom/docs/CIA-RDP07X00001R000100010001–9.pdf.

35. Bagley, *Spymaster.*

36. Stafford, *Spies beneath Berlin,* p. 187.

37. Bagley, *Spymaster.*

38. Bundesbeauftragte für die Unterlagen des Staatssicherheitsdienstes: 'Audiobeitrag', http://www.bstu.bund.de/DE/BundesbeauftragterUndBehoerde/Aktuelles/spionagetunnel_altglienicke.html.

39. Sergei Nilau, *Dve zizni Georgi Bleika*, Zvezda television, 2012.

40. Haslam, *Near and Distant Neighbours.*

41. Stafford, *Spies beneath Berlin*, p. 150.

42. Gordievsky, 'No Laughing Boy'.

43. Knopp, *Top-Spione,* pp. 146–7.

44. Ibid., p. 188.

45. Christopher Andrew and Vasili Mitrokhin, *The Sword and the Shield: The Mitrokhin Archive and the Secret History of the KGB* (Basic Books, New York, 2000), p. 400.

46. Chapman Pincher, *Treachery: Betrayals, Blunders and Cover-Ups: Six Decades of Espionage* (Mainstream Publishing, Edinburgh, 2011), p. 64.

47. Vogel, *Betrayal in Berlin*, p. 252.

48. Richard J. Aldrich, *GCHQ: The Uncensored Story of Britain's Most Secret Intelligence Agency* (HarperPress, London, 2010), p. 175.

49. Sam Benstead and Jonathan Hacker, *Spies beneath Berlin*, National Geographic/Arte TV documentary, 2011.

50. Knopp, *Top-Spione*, pp. 147–8.

51. Ibid., p. 150.

52. Stasi archive, East German newspaper, probably based in Frankfurt an der Oder, 27 April 1956.

53. Stasi archive, ADN news agency, East Berlin, 25 April 1956.

54. Vogel, *Betrayal in Berlin*, p. 310.

55. CIA, 'A Look Back … The Berlin Tunnel: Exposed', 26 June 2009: https://www.cia.gov/news-information/featured-story-archive/the-berlin-tunnel-exposed.html .

56. Blake, speech to Stasi, probably 1980.

57. Stafford, *Spies beneath Berlin*, pp. 184–9.

58. Carey, *George Blake: Masterspy of Moscow*.

59. Stafford, *Spies beneath Berlin*, p. 132.

60. Vogel, *Betrayal in Berlin*, p. 201 and p. 206.

61. Unsigned, 'V: The Berlin Tunnel', CIA, 4 February 2014: https://www.cia.gov/library/center-for-the-study-of-intelligence/csi-publications/books-and-monographs/on-the-front-lines-of-the-cold-war-documents-on-the-intelligence-war-in-berlin-1946-to-1961/art-7.html.

62. Unsigned, 'The Berlin Tunnel', CIA.

63. Stafford, *Spies beneath Berlin*, p. 141.

64. Vogel, *Betrayal in Berlin*, pp. 220–22.

65. Ibid., p. 214 and p. 467.

66. Stafford, *Spies beneath Berlin*, p. 193.

67. Adam Hochschild, 'The Golden Years of United Fruit', *Times Literary Supplement*, 17 September 1999.

68. GB13.

69. Stafford, *Spies beneath Berlin*, p. 195.

Chapter 9: The Game is Up

1. E. H. Cookridge, 'Geständnis in Beirut', *Der Spiegel*, issue 5, 1968, p. 121.

2. Hermiston, *The Greatest Traitor,* p. 218.

3. Blake, speech to Stasi, probably 1980.

4. Hermiston, *The Greatest Traitor,* p. 201.

5. Grant, *Jeremy Hutchinson's Case Histories,* p. 61.

6. Juliette Desplat, 'A British "Spy School" in the Middle East?', National Archives, 3 March 2017, at http://blog.nationalarchives.gov.uk/blog/british-spy-school-middle-east-centre-arab-studies/ .

7. David Gladstone, 'Recollections of David Gladstone CMG' (2015), at https://www.chu.cam.ac.uk/media/uploads/files/Gladstone.pdf.

8. Desplat, 'A British "Spy School" in the Middle East?'

9. Ibid.

10. Ibid.

11. Montgomery Hyde, *George Blake Superspy,* p. 51.

12. O'Connor, *Blake, Bourke & The End of Empires,* p. 141.

13. Hugh Thomas, 'Shamrock and Sickle', *Washington Post,* 11 October 1970.

14. Edward Jay Epstein, [untitled], *The New York Times,* 28 September 1980.

15. Bagley, *Spymaster.*

16. Hermiston, *The Greatest Traitor,* p. 211.

17. Bower, *The Perfect English Spy,* p. 259.

18. Vogel, *Betrayal in Berlin,* pp. 349–50.

19. Pincher, *Too Secret, Too Long,* pp. 251–2.

20. Stafford, *Spies beneath Berlin,* p. 181.

21. Matschulat, 'Coordination and Cooperation in Counterintelligence'.

22. Bower, *The Perfect English Spy,* p. 259.

23. Hermiston, *The Greatest Traitor,* pp. 221–2.

24. Knopp, *Top-Spione,* p. 161.

25. GB32.

26. Knopp, *Top-Spione,* p. 162.

27. Blake, speech to Stasi, probably 1980.

28. Ibid.

29. GB33.

30. Blake, speech to Stasi, probably 1980.

31. Blake, *No Other Choice,* p. 198.

32. Blake, speech to Stasi, 1977.

33. Blake, *No Other Choice*, pp. 194–5.
34. Blake, speech to Stasi, probably 1980.
35. Ibid.
36. Blake, *No Other Choice*, p. 197.
37. Blake, speech to Stasi, 1977.
38. Knopp, *Top-Spione*, p. 159.
39. Bagley, *Spymaster*.
40. Gordon Corera, 'Kim Philby, British Double Agent, Reveals All in Secret Video', *BBC News*, 4 April 2016.
41. Bower, *The Perfect English Spy*, p. 265.
42. Carey, *George Blake: Masterspy of Moscow*.
43. Montgomery Hyde, *George Blake Superspy*, pp. 54–5.
44. Pincher, *Too Secret, Too Long*, p. 254.
45. Gordon Corera, *The Art of Betrayal: Life and Death in the British Secret Service* (Hachette UK, London, 2011).
46. Grant, *Jeremy Hutchinson's Case Studies*, p. 49.
47. Blake, *No Other Choice*, p. 198.
48. Blake, speech to Stasi, probably 1980.
49. Olink, *Meesterspion George Blake*, part 3.
50. Hermiston, *The Greatest Traitor*, p. xvii.
51. Andrew, *The Defence of the Realm*, p. 489.
52. Corera, *The Art of Betrayal*.
53. Randle and Pottle, *The Blake Escape*, p. 25.
54. Bower, *The Perfect English Spy*, pp. 265–6.
55. Hermiston, *The Greatest Traitor*, p. 229.
56. Bower, *The Perfect English Spy*, p. 266.
57. Blake, *No Other Choice*, p. 199.
58. Ibid., pp. 199–200.
59. Randle and Pottle, *The Blake Escape*, p. 250.
60. Ibid., p. 267.
61. Le Carré, *The Pigeon Tunnel*.
62. Adam Sisman, *John le Carré: The Biography* (Bloomsbury, London, 2015), p. 216.
63. Private email from John de St Jorre, 14 February 2017.
64. Le Carré, *The Pigeon Tunnel*.
65. Corera, *The Art of Betrayal*.

66. Cookridge, *George Blake*, p. 23.

67. Richard Donkin, 'Full-Time Aspirations', *Financial Times*, 24 July 1996.

68. Le Carré, *Tinker, Tailor, Soldier, Spy*, Introduction.

69. BBC Radio 4, *Best of Today, John Le Carre: The return of master spy George Smiley*, 7 September 2017.

70. Philip Marchand, 'The Last Cold War Novel', *Toronto Star*, 17 November 1990.

71. West, *The New Meaning of Treason*, p. 295.

72. Hermiston, *The Greatest Traitor*, p. 127.

73. Carey, *George Blake: Masterspy of Moscow*.

74. Hermiston, *The Greatest Traitor*, p. 172.

75. Paul Geoffrey Methven, 'Why Was the Profumo Affair So Damaging to the Government?', MA dissertation, University of Exeter, 2006. p. 18.

76. Matthew Denning, *Cover Stories: Narrative and Ideology in the British Spy Thriller* (Routledge, London, 2014), pp. 91–2.

77. https://www.mi6-hq.com/sections/movies/dn_production.php3.

78. Haslam, *Near and Distant Neighbours*.

79. Ibid.

80. Grant, *Jeremy Hutchinson's Case Histories*, pp. 42–3. Klaus Fuchs, a German-born atomic scientist who had fled to Britain, was convicted in 1950 of passing atomic secrets to the USSR. The Italian nuclear physicist Bruno Pontecorvo had been working on the British nuclear energy project at Harwell, doing secret work on reactors, when he fled with his family to the Soviet Union in 1950.

81. Bower, *The Perfect English Spy*, p. 269.

82. Andrew, *The Defence of the Realm*, p. 489.

83. Aldrich, *GCHQ*, p. 176.

84. Ibid., p. 238.

85. Stewart Alsop, 'CIA: The Battle for Secret Power', *Saturday Evening Post*, 13 July 1963.

86. Knopp, *Top-Spione*, p. 128.

87. Corera, *The Art of Betrayal*.

88. Bower, *The Perfect English Spy*, p. 267.

89. http://hansard.millbanksystems.com/commons/1961/may/04/ security-procedures-case-of-george-blake.

90. Andrew, *The Defence of the Realm*, p. 493.

91. Bower, *The Perfect English Spy*, p. 305.

92. Stafford, *Spies beneath Berlin*, p. 92.

93. Pincher, *Too Secret, Too Long*, pp. 254–5.

94. Bower, *The Perfect English Spy*, p. 262.

95. Ibid., p. 50.

96. Blake, speech to Stasi, probably 1980.

97. Cookridge, *George Blake*, p. 183.

98. Wirth, 'Noch immer keine Spur von George Blake …'.

99. West, *The New Meaning of Treason*, p. 295.

100. Randle and Pottle, *The Blake Escape*, p. 251.

101. Corera, *The Art of Betrayal*.

102. Geoffrey Robertson, 'Lord Hutchinson of Lullington obituary', *Guardian*, 13 November, 2017.

103. Pincher, *Treachery*, p. 62.

104. Randle and Pottle, *The Blake Escape*, p. 273.

105. Blake, speech to Stasi, probably 1980.

106. Ibid.

107. Hermiston, *The Greatest Traitor*, p. 250.

108. Blake, speech to Stasi, probably 1980.

109. Ibid.

110. Randle and Pottle, *The Blake Escape*, p. 24.

111. Grant, *Jeremy Hutchinson's Case Histories*, pp. 63–4.

112. Hansard, House of Lords, 9 May 1996, column 205.

113. Cookridge, *George Blake*, p. 135.

114. Andrew, *The Defence of The Realm*, p. 491.

115. Knopp, *Top-Spione*, p. 169.

116. Cabinet, 'Conclusions of a Meeting of the Cabinet held at Admiralty House, S.W.1, on Thursday, 4th May, 1961, at 11 a.m.', at http://discovery.nationalarchives.gov.uk/details/r/ D7664102#imageViewerLink.

117. Dominic Kennedy, 'The Spy Who Came In for Rough Justice', *The Times*, 1 February 2016.

118. Grant, *Jeremy Hutchinson's Case Histories*, p. 68.

119. Jack Profumo, the secretary of state for war, resigned in 1963 after accusations that he had shared a mistress (Christine Keeler) with the naval attaché at the Soviet embassy.

120. Grant, *Jeremy Hutchinson's Case Histories,* pp. 43–4.

121. GB14–15.

Chapter 10: The Human Cost

1. Andrew, *The Defence of the Realm*, p. 633.

2. Hermiston, *The Greatest Traitor*, p. 252.

3. Chapman Pincher, 'Leakers I Have Known', *Spectator,* 12 September 1998.

4. Montgomery Hyde, *George Blake Superspy*, p. 19, and Randle and Pottle, *The Blake Escape*, p. 253.

5. Randle and Pottle, *The Blake Escape*, p. 255.

6. Bower, *The Perfect English Spy*, pp. 268–9.

7. Randle and Pottle, *The Blake Escape,* p. 253.

8. Carey, *George Blake: Masterspy of Moscow.*

9. Le Carré, *Tinker, Tailor, Soldier, Spy*, Introduction.

10. Shiff and Stein, 'George Blake, Master of Deception'.

11. Norton-Taylor, 'George Blake Admits Doing Great Damage to British Intelligence', *Guardian*, 19 September 1990.

12. Camilla Redmond, 'This Week's Archive Hour', *Guardian*, 4 August 2009.

13. Vogel, *Betrayal in Berlin*, p. 373.

14. Le Carré, *The Pigeon Tunnel.*

15. Kathy Lally, 'Former Spy Blake Says World Not Mature Enough for Communism', *Baltimore Sun,* 16 January 1992.

16. Stephen Handelman, 'Communism Failed, Spy Admits', *Toronto Star,* 16 January 1992.

17. Blake, *No Other Choice*, p. 174.

18. Knopp, *Top-Spione*, p. 177. My translation from the German.

19. Ibid.

20. Montgomery Hyde, *George Blake Superspy*, p. 180.

21. Carey, *George Blake: Masterspy of Moscow.*

22. Alan Judd, 'Why Did He Do It?', *Spectator,* 20 April 2013.

23. Norton-Taylor, 'George Blake Admits Doing Great Damage to British Intelligence'.

24. Grant, *Jeremy Hutchinson's Case Histories*, pp. 73–4.

25. Knopp, *Top-Spione*, p. 178.

26. West, *The New Meaning of Treason*, p. 311.

27. Knopp, *Top-Spione*, p. 178.

28. Kalugin, *Spymaster*, pp. 204–7.

29. *Cold War*, Turner Broadcasting System, and *Spies*, BBC, episode 21.

30. Hermiston, *The Greatest Traitor*, p. 241.

31. Matschulat, 'Coordination and Cooperation in Counterintelligence'.

32. Ibid.

33. Klaus Taubert, 'Stasi-Entführung: Stiller Tod im "Gelben Elend"', *Der Spiegel*, 25 June 2010.

34. Matschulat, 'Coordination and Cooperation in Counterintelligence'.

35. Blake, *No Other Choice*, p. 209.

36. Matschulat, 'Coordination and Cooperation in Counterintelligence'.

37. Dorril, 'George Blake exemplified the desolation, waste and treachery of the Cold War', *Guardian*.

38. Randle and Pottle, *The Blake Escape*, p. 263.

39. Unsigned, 'A Look Back ... CIA Asset Pyotr Popov Arrested,' CIA historical document, 20 June 2013 at https://www.cia.gov/news-information/featured-story-archive/2011-featured-story-archive/pyotr-popov.html.

40. Ibid.

41. Unsigned, 'The Capture and Execution of Colonel Penkovsky, 1963', CIA, 30 April 2013: https://www.cia.gov/news-information/featured-story-archive/2010-featured-story-archive/colonel-penkovsky.html.

42. Blake, speech to Stasi, probably 1980.

43. Phillip Knightley, 'Janet Chisholm: Fighting the Cold War in Moscow', *Guardian*, 12 August 2004.

44. Nigel West, *Cold War Counterfeit Spies: Tales of Intelligence – Genuine or Bogus?* (Frontline Books, Barnsley, 2016), p. 113.

45. Bagley, *Spymaster*.

46. Carey, *George Blake: Masterspy of Moscow*.

47. Ibid., and email from Carey, 16 February 2016.

48. Unsigned, 'Keine Nachsicht für Feinde unserer Ordnung,' *Der Spiegel*, 26 July 1976.

49. Jan-Philipp Wölbern, *Der Häftlingsfreikauf aus der DDR 1962/63– 1989: Zwischen Menschenhandel und humanitären Aktionen* (Vandenhoeck & Ruprecht, Göttingen, 2014).

50. Hermiston, *The Greatest Traitor*, pp. 181–2.

51. GB5.

52. Stasi archive, 'Notiz über das Abschlussgespräch zwischen dem Genossen Minister und dem Stellvertreter des Vorsitzenden des KfS und Leiter der Verwaltung Kader des KfS der UdSSR, Gen. G.J. Ageew', Berlin, 19 November 1985.

53. GB12.

54. GB54–5.

55. Randle and Pottle, *The Blake Escape*, p. 50.

Chapter 11: Espionage, Balls and Rackets

1. Geoff Andrews, *Agent Molière: The Life of John Cairncross, the Fifth Man of the Cambridge Spy Circle* (I. B. Taurus, London, 2020), pp. 133–4.

2. Philipps, *A Spy Named Orphan*, pp. 2, 146, 150, 155–7, 191, 201–2.

3. Andrew Lownie, author of *Stalin's Englishman: The Lives of Guy Burgess,* speaking at the American Library, Paris, 16 March 2016.

4. Philipps, *A Spy Named Orphan*, pp. 70–71.

5. Ibid., pp. 83–4, 125–6.

6. Vogel, *Betrayal in Berlin*, p. 141.

7. Andrew, *The Defence of the Realm,* pp. 846–7.

8. Olink, *Meesterspion George Blake*, part 4.

9. Ibid.

10. Vogel, *Betrayal in Berlin*, pp. 129–31.

11. David E. Murphy, *What Stalin Knew: The Enigma of Barbarossa* (Yale University Press, New Haven, 2006), p. 87.

12. Vogel, *Betrayal in Berlin*, p. 132.

13. Robert Cottrell, 'Russia, NATO, Trump: The Shadow World', *New York Review of Books,* 22 December 2016.

14. Ibid.

15. Andrew, *The Defence of the Realm,* p. 851.

16. Richard Dearlove podcast, 'Talking Politics', 30 March 2017, at https://www.acast.com/talkingpolitics/richarddearlove
17. Neal Ascherson, 'Which le Carré Do You Want?', *New York Review of Books,* 13–26 October 2016.
18. Paul Foot, 'So What If He Was?', *London Review of Books*, 25 October 1990.
19. Unsigned, 'George Blake, notorious British double-agent for the Soviets, dies at 98'. CBC Radio, 29 December 2020.
20. Geoffrey Wheatcroft, 'Spies Who Watched Spies Who Watched Spies', *Sunday Times,* 5 October 1997.
21. Bourke, *The Springing of George Blake*, p. 281.
22. Grant, *Jeremy Hutchinson's Case Histories,* p. 61.
23. Richard M. Bennett and Katie Bennett – AFI Research, 'UK Intelligence and Security Report August 2003', retrieved from Wikileaks, Cryptome Documents, on 7 March 2017.
24. Andrew, *The Defence of the Realm*, pp. 641–3.
25. Ibid., pp. 538–40.

Chapter 12: Foreign Traitor

1. Vogel, *Betrayal in Berlin*, p. 45.
2. George Steiner, 'The Cleric of Treason', *New Yorker,* 8 December 1980.
3. Richard Davenport-Hines, *An English Affair: Sex, Class and Power in the Age of Profumo* (William Collins, London, 2013), pp. 218–22.
4. Ibid., pp. 228–34.
5. Carey, *George Blake: Masterspy of Moscow*.
6. Blake, *No Other Choice*, p. 187.
7. Ibid., p. 139.
8. Macintyre, *A Spy among Friends*, pp. 234–5.
9. Ibid., p. 62.
10. Montgomery Hyde, *George Blake Superspy*, p. 31.
11. Macintyre, *A Spy among Friends,* p. 248.
12. Ibid.
13. Pincher, *Too Secret, Too Long*, p. 281.
14. 'Obituaries: John Cairncross', *Independent*, 9 October 1995.
15. Blake, *No Other Choice,* p. 211.

16. Carey, *George Blake: Masterspy of Moscow.*
17. Macintyre, *A Spy Among Friends,* pp. 263–4.
18. Pincher, *Too Secret, Too Long,* p. 254.
19. Hermiston, *The Greatest Traitor,* p. 42.
20. Grant, *Jeremy Hutchinson's Case Histories,* p. 59
21. Vogel, *Betrayal in Berlin,* p. 356.
22. GB27.
23. GB29.
24. GB39–40.
25. GB43–44.
26. Christian Caryl, 'Back from the Cold,' *New York Review of Books,* 23 November 2017, p. 29.
27. Unsigned, 'Obituary: Double agent George Blake dies in Moscow, aged 98', *The Times,* 26 December 2020.
28. Philip Davies, *MI6 and the Machinery of Spying: Structure and Process in Britain's Secret Intelligence* (Routledge, London, 2004).
29. Roger Berthoud, 'Unsere Spione sind die besten', *Die Zeit,* 4 March 1988.

Chapter 13: Headstands in Jail

1. Randle and Pottle, *The Blake Escape,* p. 212.
2. Blake, *No Other Choice,* pp. 201–2.
3. Blake, speech to Stasi, probably 1980.
4. Andrew, *The Defence of the Realm,* pp. 485–6.
5. Ibid., p. 486.
6. Ibid.
7. Blake, *No Other Choice,* pp. 213–14.
8. Hermiston, *The Greatest Traitor,* p. 264.
9. Andy Roberts, *Albion Dreaming: A Popular History of LSD in Britain* (Marshall Cavendish, London, 2008), p. 120.
10. Michael Hollingshead, *The Man Who Turned on the World* (Blond & Briggs, London, 1973).
11. Andy Roberts, *Divine Rascal: On the Trail of LSD's Cosmic Courier, Michael Hollinghead* (Strange Attractor Press, London, 2019), pp. 140–42.

12. Roy Walmsley, *Special Security Units,* Home Office Research Study no. 109, at http://library.college.police.uk/docs/hors/hors109.pdf, p. 7.
13. Nigel West, *At Her Majesty's Secret Service: The Chiefs of Britain's Intelligence Agency, MI6* (Casemate Publishers, Oxford, 2016).
14. Hermiston, *The Greatest Traitor,* p. 262.
15. Cookridge, *George Blake*, p. 102.
16. Randle and Pottle, *The Blake Escape*, p. 175.
17. Pat Pottle, 'Gray's Betrayal of the Truth about Blake the Spy', *Guardian,* 17, February 1995.
18. Randle and Pottle, *The Blake Escape*, p. 23.
19. Deeley, 'Blake the Spy Escapes from Scrubs Cell'.
20. Unsigned, 'Obituary of Alan Maclean', *Daily Telegraph,* 2 October 2006.
21. Quoted in Randle and Pottle, *The Blake Escape*, p. 47.
22. Ibid., p. 49.
23. Richard Tomlinson, 'The Big Breach', manuscript, retrieved from Wikileaks, Cryptome Documents, on 7 March 2017.
24. Randle and Pottle, *The Blake Escape,* pp. 8–10, 24, 26.
25. Ibid., p. 275.
26. BBC World Service, 'Witness: George Blake Escapes', 24 October 2011.
27. Randle and Pottle, *The Blake Escape*, p. 22.
28. Ibid., pp. 45–6.
29. Ibid., p. 285.
30. Shiff and Stein, 'George Blake, Master of Deception'.
31. Randle and Pottle, *The Blake Escape*, p. 26.
32. Hermiston, *The Greatest Traitor,* pp. 261–2.
33. Unsigned, 'Operation "Gold" und andere …', *Neues Deutschland.*
34. Blake, speech to Stasi, 1976.
35. Knopp, *Top-Spione*, p. 170.
36. Blake, speech to Stasi, 1976.
37. Robert Verkaik, 'The Blake Escape', *Independent,* 23 August 2008.
38. Hermiston, *The Greatest Traitor*, pp. 266–7, and Mountbatten, 'Report of the Inquiry into Prison Escapes and Security'.
39. Roger Falk, 'Chocs and chats with Blake', *Hampstead and Highgate Express,* 9 June 1989.

40. Mountbatten, 'Report of the Inquiry into Prison Escapes and Security'.

41. Nigel West, *The Circus: MI5 Operations 1945–1972* (Stein and Day, New York, 1983), p. 259.

42. Mountbatten, 'Report of the Inquiry into Prison Escapes and Security'.

43. Randle and Pottle, *The Blake Escape,* p. 131.

44. Ibid., pp. 28–9.

45. Ibid., p. 136.

46. Mountbatten, 'Report of the Inquiry into Prison Escapes and Security'.

47. GB7.

48. O'Connor, *Blake, Bourke & The End of Empires*, p. 214.

Chapter 14: Straight out of Hitchcock

1. Victor Cherkashin and Gregory Feifer, *Spy Handler: Memoir of a KGB Officer* (Basic Books, New York, 2014), pp. 68–70.

2. Blake, speech to Stasi, 1976.

3. Kieran Fagan, 'Escape of the Century – or Farce?', *Irish Times*, 10 May 2013.

4. Ben Macintyre, 'Spies on stage: the story behind Simon Gray's "Cell Mates"', *The Times*, 27 November 2017.

5. Fagan, op cit.

6. Blake, *No Other Choice,* pp. 224–5.

7. Blake, speech to Stasi, 1976.

8. Randle and Pottle, *The Blake Escape,* p. 42.

9. Bourke, *The Springing of George Blake*, p. 11.

10. Vogel, *Betrayal in Berlin*, p. 416.

11. Montgomery Hyde, *George Blake Superspy*, p. 75.

12. Bourke, *The Springing of George Blake,* pp. 31–43.

13. Knopp, *Top-Spione*, pp. 171–2.

14. Nilau, 'Dve zizni Georgi Bleika'.

15. Bourke, *The Springing of George Blake,* p. 86; and Randle and Pottle, *The Blake Escape*, p. 66.

16. Hermiston, *The Greatest Traitor,* p. 281.

17. Blake, speech to Stasi, 1976.

18. Blake, speech to Stasi, 1977.

19. Blake, speech to Stasi, 1976.

20. Randle and Pottle, *The Blake Escape*, pp. 105–6.

21. Blake, *No Other Choice,* p. 231.

22. Account of the break-out in Hermiston, *The Greatest Traitor,* pp. 286–9.

23. Mountbatten, 'Report of the Inquiry into Prison Escapes and Security'.

24. Giles Playfair, 'Wormwood', *Spectator*, 30 January 1969.

25. Randle and Pottle, *The Blake Escape*, p. 123.

26. Ibid., pp. 112–13.

27. Bourke, *The Springing of George Blake,* p. 178.

28. Vogel, *Betrayal in Berlin*, p. 428.

29. Alan Watkins, 'An Influx of One-Legged Romanian Roofers and Plumbers? Someone Had to Pay', *Independent on Sunday,* 14 January 2007.

30. Mountbatten, 'Report of the Inquiry into Prison Escapes and Security'.

31. Gill Bennett, 'What's the Context? 22 October 1966: Spy George Blake Escapes from Wormwood Scrubs', Blog: History of Government, 21 October 2016, at https://history.blog.gov.uk/2016/10/21/whats-the-context-22-october-1966-spy-george-blake-escapes-from-wormwood-scrubs/.

32. Mollie Panter-Downes, 'Letter from London', *New Yorker*, 14 January 1967.

33. Unsigned, 'Der Fall Blake vor dem Unterhaus', *Frankfurter Allgemeine Zeitung*, 2 November 1966.

34. John Campbell, *Roy Jenkins: A Well-Rounded Life* (Random House, London, 2014).

35. Unsigned, 'Der Fall Blake vor dem Unterhaus'.

36. Mountbatten, 'Report of the Inquiry into Prison Escapes and Security'.

37. Peter Jenkins, 'Prisoners Likely to be Losers after Breakout of IRA Terrorists', *Independent*, 9 July 1991.

38. Kennedy Fraser, 'Walled City', *New Yorker*, 5 April 1969.

39. Blake, *No Other Choice,* p. 220.

40. Alfred Hitchcock, *Hitchcock on Hitchcock,* vol. 1: *Selected Writings and Interviews* (University of California Press, Oakland, 2014), p. 61.

41. David Freeman, *The Last Days of Alfred Hitchcock* (Pavilion, London, 1985), p. 8.

42. François Truffaut, *Hitchcock* (Simon & Schuster, New York, 1985), p. 343.

43. Mystery Man, 'Script Review – "Hitch's Short Night"', http://mysterymanonfilm.blogspot.fr/2009/01/script-review-hitchs-short-night.html.

44. Freeman, *The Last Days of Alfred Hitchcock*, pp. 15–16.

45. Ibid., p. 44.

46. Ibid., p. 66.

47. Ibid., p. 68.

48. Truffaut, *Hitchcock*, p. 344.

49. Freeman, *The Last Days of Alfred Hitchcock,* p. 246.

50. Ibid., p. 226.

51. Blake, speech to Stasi, 1976.

52. Knopp, *Top-Spione,* pp. 171–2.

53. Randle and Pottle, *The Blake Escape*, p. 85.

54. Ibid., pp. 140–41.

55. O'Connor, *Blake, Bourke & The End of Empires*, p. 198.

56. Pincher, *Too Secret, Too Long,* p. 255.

57. 'George Blake Escape from Wormwood Scrubs', *Reporting 67,* ITN News, 1 January 1967, clip 7; www.itnsource.com/shotlist/BHC_ITN/1967/01/01/X01016704/

58. Barrie Penrose, 'Author Knew of Spy Escape Plot', *Sunday Times,* 29 January 1989.

59. Barrie Penrose, 'Blake Escape – Questions for Redgrave', *Sunday Times,* 15 November 1987.

60. Nick Cohen, 'Cleared Blake Escape Pair Win Hearts of the Jury', *Independent,* 27 June 1991.

61. Randle and Pottle, *The Blake Escape,* p. 127.

62. Barrie Penrose and Jonathan Leake, 'The Shoplifters' Vicar Hid Fugitive Spy Blake', *Sunday Times,* 16 March 1997.

63. Randle and Pottle, *The Blake Escape,* p. 129.

64. Michael Beloff, 'Sprinters', *Times Literary Supplement,* 27 April 2012.

65. Randle and Pottle, *The Blake Escape,* pp. 160–61.
66. Andrew, *Defence of the Realm,* p. 538.
67. Randle and Pottle, *The Blake Escape,* p. 109.
68. Ibid., pp. 151–2.
69. Ibid., pp. 137, 146.
70. Pottle, 'Gray's Betrayal of the Truth about Blake the Spy'.
71. Randle and Pottle, *The Blake Escape,* pp. 215, 223.
72. O'Connor, *Blake, Bourke & The End of Empires,* p. 209.
73. Ibid., p. 144.
74. Knopp, *Top-Spione,* p. 174; and Randle and Pottle, *The Blake Escape,* pp. 144–5.
75. Pottle, 'Gray's Betrayal of the Truth about Blake the Spy'.
76. Randle and Pottle, *The Blake Escape,* p. 162.
77. Ibid., p. 75.
78. Ibid., p. 164.
79. Ibid., pp. 155, 167.
80. Ibid., p. 175.
81. Nilau, 'Dve zizni Georgi Bleika'; and Randle and Pottle, *The Blake Escape,* p. 177.
82. Randle and Pottle, *The Blake Escape,* p. 177.
83. Ibid., pp. 180–81.
84. Ibid., pp. 178–83.
85. Knopp, *Top-Spione,* p. 175.
86. Blake, speech to Stasi, 1976.
87. Bagley, *Spymaster.*
88. Ibid.
89. 'George Blake Escape from Wormwood Scrubs', *Reporting 67,* clip 7.
90. Verkaik, 'The Blake Escape'.

Chapter 15: Someone Who Adjusts Easily

1. Unsigned, 'Spion Blake achter het Ijzeren Gordijn?', *Leidsch Dagblad,* 7 April 1967.
2. Ibid.
3. Verkaik, 'The Blake Escape'.
4. Shiff and Stein, 'George Blake, Master of Deception' .

5. Andrew Lownie, *Stalin's Englishman: Guy Burgess, the Cold War and the Cambridge Spy Ring* (St Martin's Press, New York, 2016), p. 282.

6. Bower, *The Perfect English Spy*, p. 384.

7. Blake, *No Other Choice*, p. 249.

8. Derk Sauer, Foreword to planned Dutch translation of *The Happy Traitor*, October 2017.

9. Olink, *Meesterspion George Blake*, part 4.

10. O'Connor, *Blake, Bourke & The End of Empires*, p. 253.

11. Barry, 'Double Agent, Turning 90, Says, 'I Am a Happy Person''.

12. Mark Trevelyan, 'British Defector Clings to Beliefs', Reuters, 8 September 1991.

13. Ibid.

14. Olink, *Meesterspion George Blake*, part 4.

15. Clem Cecil, 'How I Became a Lunchtime Spy for Moscow', *The Times,* 14 May 2003.

16. West, *At Her Majesty's Secret Service.*

17. Bourke, *The Springing of George Blake,* p. 282.

18. Blake, speech to Stasi, 1981.

19. GB38.

20. GB10–11.

21. O'Connor, *Blake, Bourke & The End of Empires*, p. 214.

22. Ibid., p. 254.

23. Ibid., p. 255.

24. GB8.

25. Hermiston, *The Greatest Traitor,* p. 325.

26. Richard Boudreaux, 'Putin Sings with Deported Agents', *Wall Street Journal,* 26 July 2010.

27. Blake, *No Other Choice,* p. 30.

28. Randle and Pottle, *The Blake Escape,* pp. 165, 188–9.

29. Blake, *No Other Choice,* p. 246.

30. O'Connor, *Blake, Bourke & the End of Empires*, p. 212.

31. Ibid., p. 217.

32. Bourke, *The Springing of George Blake,* p. 256.

33. Ibid., p. 257.

34. Ibid., p. 260.

35. Ibid., p. 289.

36. O'Connor, *Blake, Bourke & The End of Empires*, p. 213.

37. Bourke, *The Springing of George Blake*, p. 360.

38. Gray, *Five Plays*, p. 80.

39. DPA, 'Befreier des Spions Blake aus Moskau heimgekehrt', *Süddeutsche Zeitung*, 26 October 1968.

40. AP/UPI, 'Fluchthelfer des britischen Spions Blake verhaftet', *Berliner Tagesspiegel*, 1 November 1968.

41. O'Connor, *Blake, Bourke & The End of Empires*, p. 243.

42. Randle and Pottle, *The Blake Escape*, p. 209.

43. Bourke, *The Springing of George Blake*, p. viii.

44. O'Connor, *Blake, Bourke & The End of Empires*, p. 239.

45. Randle and Pottle, *The Blake Escape*, p. 214.

46. Unsigned, 'Obituaries: Patrick Pottle', *Daily Telegraph*, 4 October 2000.

47. Randle and Pottle, *The Blake Escape*, pp. 163–4.

48. Hermiston, *The Greatest Traitor*, p. 335.

49. Kevin O'Connor, 'A Death in January', Documentary on One, RTE Radio, 1983.

50. Randle and Pottle, *The Blake Escape*, p. 221.

51. Ibid., p. 236.

52. Ed Moloney and Bob Mitchell, 'The George Blake Escape: An Interesting If Troubling Postscript', Thebrokenelbow.com, 6 July 2013.

53. Kalugin, *Spymaster*, p. 159.

54. O'Connor, *Blake, Bourke & The End of Empires*, p. 276.

55. Unsigned, 'Sean Bourke Helped Blake Flee, Wrote Book on Spy', Associated Press, 28 January 1982.

56. O'Connor, 'A Death in January'.

57. O'Connor, *Blake, Bourke & The End of Empires*, p. 328.

58. Unsigned, 'Moeder van spion Blake bij familie in Haarlem', *Het Vrije Volk*, 25 November 1967.

59. Olink, *Meesterspion George Blake*, part 4.

60. O'Connor, *Blake, Bourke & The End of Empires*, p. 254.

61. Cecil, 'How I Became a Lunchtime Spy for Moscow'.

62. Ibid.

63. Montgomery Hyde, *George Blake Superspy*, p. 177.

64. Blake, *No Other Choice*, pp. 214, 262–3.

65. Hermiston, *The Greatest Traitor,* p. 324.

66. Rufina Philby, *The Private Life of Kim Philby: The Moscow Years* (Fromm International, New York, 2000), p. 24.

67. GB27.

68. Norton-Taylor, 'George Blake Now Prepared to Talk After Decades of Silence'.

69. O'Connor, *Blake, Bourke & The End of Empires*, p. 326.

70. Kalugin, *Spymaster*, p. 159.

71. Ibid., pp. 159–60.

72. Macintyre, *A Spy among Friends,* p. 270.

73. Unsigned, 'Soviet Introduces its Spy in *Izvestia*', *New York Times*, 15 February 1970.

74. Unsigned, 'Operation 'Gold' und andere…', *Neues Deutschland*.

75. CIA, 'The President's Daily Brief', 25 February 1970, at https://www. cia.gov/library/readingroom/docs/DOC_0005977317.pdf.

76. Tim Milne, *Kim Philby: A Story of Friendship and Betrayal* (Biteback Publishing, London, 2014).

77. O'Connor, *Blake, Bourke & The End of Empires*, p. 257.

78. Grant, *Jeremy Hutchinson's Case Histories*, p. 71.

79. Shaun Walker, 'The Spy Who Stayed Out in the Cold: George Blake at 90', *Independent*, 6 November 2012.

80. Andrew and Mitrokhin, *The Sword and the Shield*, p. 411.

81. Christopher Marcisz, 'The Spies Who Loved', *Russian Life,* 1 July 2006.

82. PBS interview with George Blake, 1999, at http://www.pbs.org/ redfiles/kgb/deep/interv/k_int_george_blake.htm.

83. Philby, *The Private Life of Kim Philby,* pp. 59, 314.

84. GB8.

85. Macintyre, *A Spy among Friends*, p. 238.

86. Hermiston, *The Greatest Traitor,* pp. 326–7.

87. Philby, *The Private Life of Kim Philby*, p. 25.

88. Ibid., p. 30.

89. Ibid., pp. 26–7.

90. Ibid., pp. 49–50.

91. Cecil, 'How I Became a Lunchtime Spy for Moscow'.

92. Philby, *The Private Life of Kim Philby*, p. 56.

93. Blake, *No Other Choice,* Introduction, p. vi.

94. Barry, 'Double Agent, Turning 90, Says, "I Am a Happy Person"'.

95. Philby, *The Private Life of Kim Philby,* p. 56.

96. GB33–4. Philby's father was Hillary St John Bridger Philby, a famous Arabist whose second wife was a slave girl presented him by the king of Saudi Arabia.

97. Tom Parfitt, 'Moscow Diner Spies a Chance to Serve Up Dish of Soviet Nostalgia', *The Times,* 28 May 2016.

98. Bower, *The Perfect English Spy,* p. 384.

99. Stasi archive, MfS Arbeitsbereich NEIBER, 'George BLAKE', 1976.

100. Phillip Knightley, 'A Spymaster Recalls the Twists of the Game', *Independent on Sunday,* 27 July 1997.

101. Philby, *The Private Life of Kim Philby,* p. 56.

102. O'Connor, *Blake, Bourke & The End of Empires,* p. 269.

103. John F. Burns, 'Donald Maclean of Spy Fame Dies', *New York Times,* 12 March 1983.

104. Cecil, *A Divided Life,* p. 165

105. O'Connor, *Blake, Bourke & The End of Empires,* p. 256.

106. Cecil, *A Divided Life,* p. 177.

107. Kalugin, *Spymaster,* p. 160.

108. Ibid., p. 162.

109. O'Connor, *Blake, Bourke & The End of Empires,* p. 271.

110. Blake, *No Other Choice,* p. 266.

111. Philipps, *A Spy Named Orphan,* p. 161.

112. Vogel, *Betrayal in Berlin,* pp. 44–5.

113. Ibid., p. 42.

114. Ibid., p. 161.

115. Cecil, 'How I Became a Lunchtime Spy for Moscow'.

116. GB8.

117. Philipps, *A Spy Named Orphan,* p. 185.

118. Verbeek, 'Spion voor een verloren zaak'.

119. Blake, *No Other Choice,* pp. 265, 271–2.

120. Blake, speech to Stasi, 1981.

121. Nilau, 'Dve zizni Georgi Bleika'.

122. GB26.

123. Olink, *Meesterspion George Blake*, part 4

124. Mike Gruntman, *Enemy among Trojans: A Soviet Spy at USC* (self-published, 2010).

125. Cherkasov, *IMEMO: Portret na fone epokhi*.

126. Olink, *Meesterspion George Blake*, part 4.

127. Cherkasov, *IMEMO: Portret na fone epokhi*, pp. 348 ff.

128. GB9.

129. Ibid.

130. Again, Blake got the facts about his friend wrong. Maclean died on 6 March. Philipps, *A Spy Named Orphan*, p. 378.

131. Cherkasov, 'Vtoraya Zhizn Gomera'.

132. Blake, *No Other Choice*, p. 148.

133. Ibid., p. 270.

Chapter 16: Henri Curiel, A Parallel Life

1. Perrault, *Un homme à part*, pp. 120–21.

2. Ibid., p. 314.

3. Ibid., pp. 125–6.

4. Ibid., p. 199.

5. Shatz, unpublished essay.

6. Perrault, *Un homme à part*, p. 220.

7. Nagasawa, 'Henri Curiel', p. 88.

8. Shatz, unpublished essay.

9. Perrault, *Un homme à part*, p. 90

10. Nagasawa, 'Henri Curiel', p. 89.

11. Ibid., p. 88.

12. Perrault, *Un homme à part*, p. 331.

13. Lallaoui, *Henri Curiel*.

14. Perrault, *Un homme à part*, pp. 440–41.

15. Ibid., p. 332.

16. Ibid., p. 207.

17. Ibid., p. 333.

18. Ibid., p. 454.

19. Ibid., p. 496.

20. Ibid., p. 402.

21. Ibid., p. 301.

22. Ibid., p. 419.

23. Ibid., p. 472.

24. Ibid., p. 476.

25. Ibid., p. 436.

26. Ibid., p. 434.

27. Ibid., p. 437.

28. Ibid., p. 112.

29. Ibid., p. 529.

30. Ibid., pp. 541–2.

31. Cherkasov, *IMEMO: Portret na fone epokhi*.

32. Nagasawa, 'Henri Curiel', pp. 91–2.

33. Beinin, *The Dispersion of Egyptian Jewry*, p. 163.

34. Hannah Arendt, *The Origins of Totalitarianism* (Houghton Mifflin Harcourt, Orlando, 1973), p. 108.

35. Perrault, *Un homme à part*, p. 306.

36. Ibid., p. 419.

37. Breyten Breytenbach, *The True Confessions of an Albino Terrorist* (McGraw-Hill, New York, 1986), p. 111.

38. Interview with Alain Gresh, Paris, 10 May 2017.

39. Perrault, *Un homme à part*, p. 560–61.

40. Ibid., p. 16.

41. Ibid., pp. 545–6.

42. Ibid., p. 557.

43. Ibid., pp. 570–71.

44. Lallaoui, *Henri Curiel*.

45. Perrault, *Un homme à part*, p. 574.

46. Ibid., p. 25.

47. Ibid., pp. 17–24.

48. Ibid., p. 16.

49. Breytenbach, *The True Confessions of an Albino Terrorist*, pp. 54–5.

50. Perrault, *Un homme à part*, p. 575.

51. Ibid., p. 579.

52. Lallaoui, *Henri Curiel*.

53. CIA, 'Soviet Support for International Terrorism and Revolutionary Violence', 27 May 1981, at https://www.cia.gov/library/readingroom/docs/CIA-RDP90T00155R000200010009-2.pdf.

54. Interview with Gresh.

Chapter 17: Cynicism and Christmas Pudding

1. GB7.
2. Unsigned, 'Obituary: Double agent George Blake dies in Moscow, aged 98', *The Times*, 26 December 2020.
3. Blake, *No Other Choice*, p. 278.
4. GB5.
5. Unsigned, 'Obituary: Double agent George Blake dies in Moscow, aged 98', *The Times*.
6. Hermiston, *The Greatest Traitor*, p. 330.
7. Olink, *Meesterspion George Blake*, part 4.
8. Verbeek, 'Spion voor een verloren zaak'.
9. Blake, *No Other Choice*, pp. 278–9.
10. http://www.churchontheheath.org.uk/whos-who/.
11. David Loyn, 'A Traitor's Apologia', *Spectator*, 5 July 1991.
12. GB6; GB30.
13. O'Connor, *Blake, Bourke & The End of Empires*, p. 334.
14. Olink, *Meesterspion George Blake*, part 4.
15. Dido Michielsen, *Moscow Times: het Russische avontuur van Derk Sauer en Ellen Verbeek* (Nieuw Amsterdam, Amsterdam, 2013).
16. Sauer, Foreword to planned Dutch translation of The *Happy Traitor*.
17. Verbeek, 'Spion voor een verloren zaak'.
18. Norton-Taylor, 'George Blake Now Prepared to Talk after Decades of Silence'.
19. Kalugin, *Spymaster*, p. 159.
20. Verbeek, 'Spion voor een verloren zaak'.
21. Loyn, 'A Traitor's Apologia' and Ellen Verbeek, 'Spion voor een verloren zaak'.
22. Clem Cecil, 'George Blake Dreams of Cream for his Christmas Pud', *The Times*, 14 May 2003.
23. Michielsen, *Moscow Times: het Russische avontuur*.
24. Loyn, 'A Traitor's Apologia'.
25. Cecil, 'How I Became a Lunchtime Spy for Moscow'.
26. Sisman, *John le Carré*, p. 253.
27. GB41–3.

28. Blake, *No Other Choice*, p. 253.

29. Stewart Payne and Adrian Shaw, 'Champagne Traitor Blake Tells His Story', *Evening Standard*, 25 June 1991.

30. Blake letter to Roger Falk, 15 February 1990.

31. Roger Falk, 'Chocs and chats with Blake', *Hampstead and Highgate Express*, 9 June 1989.

32. Cohen, 'Soviet Spy George Blake Will Appear on Video at Old Bailey Trial'.

33. O'Connor, *Blake, Bourke & The End of Empires*, p. 319.

34. Cohen, 'Cleared Blake Escape Pair Win Hearts of the Jury'.

35. Auberon Waugh, 'Another Voice', *Spectator*, 5 July 1991.

36. Mendick and Parfitt, 'My Father the Russian Spy, by Anglican Curate from Guildford'.

37. O'Connor, *Blake, Bourke & The End of Empires*, p. 340.

38. Verbeek, 'Spion voor een verloren zaak'.

39. Sauer, Foreword to planned Dutch translation of *The Happy Traitor*.

40. Trevelyan, 'British Defector Clings to Beliefs'.

41. Verbeek, 'Spion voor een verloren zaak'.

42. Ibid., p. 327.

43. Wolf and McElvoy, *Man Without a Face*, p. 102.

44. Philby, *The Private Life of Kim Philby*, p. 27.

45. Robin Denniston, 'Three Kinds of Hero: Publishing the Memoirs of Secret Intelligence People', in *Intelligence and National Security*, vol. 7, 1992, p. 113.

46. Montgomery Hyde, *George Blake Superspy*, pp. 178–9.

47. Quotations from Andrew Nurnberg are from an interview in London, 28 February 2017.

48. European Court of Human Rights, 'Case of Blake v. the United Kingdom', Strasbourg, 26 September 2006 at hudoc.echr.coe.int/app/conversion/pdf/?library=ECHR&id=001-76995...

49. Davies, *MI6 and the Machinery of Spying*.

50. O'Connor, *Blake, Bourke & The End of Empires*, p. 335.

51. Denniston, 'Three Kinds of Hero', p. 124.

52. Geneviève Roberts, 'Ministers Told to Pay £3,500 Damages to George Blake, *Independent*, 27 September 2006.

53. Olink, *Meesterspion George Blake*, part 4.

54. Verbeek, 'Spion voor een verloren zaak'.

55. Ian Glover-James, 'Blake Vows to Stay in Moscow', *Sunday Times,* 5 January 1992.

56. Vladimir Isachenko, 'Russia Honors Soviet Spies', *Associated Press,* 13 November 2007.

57. Interview with Sylvie Braibant, TV5Monde.com, released online on 8 August 2011.

58. Georgina Wroe, 'Blake's Heaven on Golden Pond', *Scotland on Sunday*, 8 March 1998.

59. Unsigned, 'British Spy Blake "Still Working for Moscow"', BBC Monitoring Newsfile, 19 December 2000.

60. GB35.

61. Blake, speech to Stasi, 1977.

62. Blake, speech to Stasi, 1976.

63. Blake, speech to Stasi, 1981.

64. Sauer, Foreword to planned Dutch translation of *The Happy Traitor.*

65. Ibid.

66. GB10.

Chapter 18: 'Tragic I Am Not'

1. Nilau, 'Dve Zizni Georgi Bleika'.

2. Sauer, Foreword to planned Dutch translation of *The Happy Traitor*

3. Alec Luhn, 'Ex-British double agent says Russian spies must save world', *Daily Telegraph*, 10 November, 2017.

4. Robert D. McFadden, 'George Blake, British Spy Who Betrayed the West, Dies at 98', *The New York Times*, 26 December 2020.

5. AFP, 'British double agent who spied for USSR says he's still a socialist', i24news.tv, 10 November, 2017.

6. Barry, 'Double Agent, Turning 90, Says, "I Am a Happy Person"'.

7. Ilona Egiazarova, 'Znakomtes: George Bleik', Vokrug TV, 11 April 2011.

8. GB27.

9. GB50.

10. GB36.

11. Ibid.

12. GB44–5.

13. GB37–8.
14. Olink, *Meesterspion George Blake*, part 4.
15. Sauer, Foreword to *De vrolijke verrader*, Dutch translation of *The Happy Traitor*.
16. GB45–6.
17. GB25–6.
18. GB54.
19. GB55.
20. GB51.
21. Sauer, foreword to planned Dutch translation of *The Happy Traitor*.

Afterword

1. Derk Sauer, 'De oude dubbelspion George Blake is niet kapot te krijgen', *Het Parool*, 8 December 2019.
2. Robert D. McFadden, 'George Blake, British Spy Who Betrayed the West, Dies at 98', *The New York Times*, 26 December 2020.
3. Unsigned, 'British Cold War Double Agent George Blake Dies in Moscow', *Agence France-Presse*, 26 December 2020.
4. Vladimir Isachenkov, 'British double agent George Blake dies in Russia at 98', *Associated Press*, 26 December 2020.

Select Bibliography

There is much that we still do not know about Blake. MI6 has not opened its file on him. Early writings on him – notably E. H. Cookridge's books and the section about him in Rebecca West's extremely readable *The New Meaning of Treason* (1964) – are full of errors.

Blake, Bourke & The End of Empires (2003), a rich but curiously overlooked book by the Irish journalist Kevin O'Connor, contains material from several interviews with Blake. O'Connor, a Limerick man himself, also deepens our knowledge of Sean Bourke. In German, Guido Knopp's *Top-Spione* (1997), based on a well-funded TV series for the ZDF channel, draws on interviews with Blake and other KGB officials in Moscow in the 1990s – exactly the time when these people were freest to talk. The long interview or series of interviews that Blake gave to the Dutch radio journalist Hans Olink in 1999 – hitherto unknown to non-Dutch-speakers – was also very useful.

All translations from Dutch, German and French sources are mine. In addition, I have used passages from Russian texts, courtesy of Jana Bakunina's translations.

Since 2013 our knowledge of Blake has greatly increased thanks to Roger Hermiston's biography, George Carey's BBC documentary, Steve Vogel's deeply researched account of the Berlin tunnel, *Betrayal in Berlin*, and the old CIA man Tennent Bagley's posthumous book *Spymaster* (based largely on conversations with Blake's late KGB handler, Sergei Kondrashev).

The most reliable guides to British intelligence that I have found are Christopher Andrew and Tom Bower.

Books and Articles

Books

Christopher Andrew, *The Defence of the Realm: The Authorized History of MI5* (Penguin, London, 2010)

Christopher Andrew and Vasili Mitrokhin, *The Sword and the Shield: The Mitrokhin Archive and the Secret History of the KGB* (Basic Books, New York, 2000)

Tennent H. Bagley, *Spymaster: Startling Cold War Revelations of a Soviet KGB Chief* (Skyhorse Publishing, New York, 2015)

George Blake, *No Other Choice* (Simon & Schuster, New York, 1990)

Sean Bourke, *The Springing of George Blake* (Viking Press, New York, 1970)

Tom Bower, *The Perfect English Spy* (St Martin's Press, New York, 1995)

Victor Cherkashin and Gregory Feifer, *Spy Handler: Memoir of a KGB Officer* (Basic Books, New York, 2014)

Piotr Cherkasov, *IMEMO: Portret na fone epokhi* (Ves' mir, Moscow, 2004)

E. H. Cookridge, *George Blake: Double Agent* (Ballantine Books, New York, 1982)

Gordon Corera, *The Art of Betrayal: Life and Death in the British Secret Service* (Hachette UK, London, 2011)

David Freeman, *The Last Days of Alfred Hitchcock* (Pavilion, London, 1985)

Thomas Grant, *Jeremy Hutchinson's Case Histories* (John Murray, London, 2016)

Simon Gray, *Plays Five* (Faber and Faber, London, 2010)

N. M. Westerbeek van Eerten-Faure, *En de "Rücksack" stond altijd klaar... dagboek van een doktersvrouw in oorlogstijd* (Doetinchem, Mr. H. J. Steenbergen-Stichting, 2015)

Jonathan Haslam, *Near and Distant Neighbours: A New History of Soviet Intelligence* (Oxford University Press, Oxford, 2015)

Roger Hermiston, *The Greatest Traitor: The Secret Lives of Agent George Blake* (Aurum Press, London, 2013)

Alfred Hitchcock, *Hitchcock on Hitchcock,* vol. 1: *Selected Writings and Interviews* (University of California Press, Oakland, 2014)

Marijke Huisman, *Mata Hari (1876–1917): de levende legende* (Verloren Verleden, Hilversum, 1998)

Oleg Kalugin, *Spymaster: My Thirty-Two Years in Intelligence and Espionage against the West* (Basic Books, New York, 2009)

Guido Knopp, *Top-Spione: Verräter im Geheimen Krieg* (Goldmann, Munich, 1997)

Ben Macintyre, *A Spy among Friends: Kim Philby and the Great Betrayal* (Crown Publishers, New York, 2014)

H. Montgomery Hyde, *George Blake Superspy: The Truth behind Blake's Sensational Escape to Moscow* (Futura, London, 1988)

Louis Mountbatten, 'Report of the Inquiry into Prison Escapes and Security', in *Reports Commissioners: Prisons to Science Research,* session 18 April 1966–27 October 1967, Volume XLVII, London

David E. Murphy, *What Stalin Knew: The Enigma of Barbarossa* (Yale University Press, New Haven, 2006)

Kevin O'Connor, *Blake, Bourke & The End of Empires* (Prendeville, London, 2003)

Gilles Perrault, *Un homme à part* (Bernard Barrault, Paris, 1984)

Rufina Philby, *The Private Life of Kim Philby: The Moscow Years* (Fromm International, New York, 2000)

Roland Philipps, *A Spy Named Orphan: The Enigma of Donald Maclean* (The Bodley Head, London, 2018)

Chapman Pincher, *Too Secret, Too Long* (St Martin's Press, New York, 1984)

Chapman Pincher, *Treachery: Betrayals, Blunders and Cover-Ups: Six Decades of Espionage* (Mainstream Publishing, Edinburgh, 2011)

Michael Randle and Pat Pottle, *The Blake Escape: How We Freed George Blake – And Why* (Harrap, London, 1989)

Adam Sisman, *John le Carré: The Biography* (Bloomsbury, London, 2015)

David Stafford, *Spies beneath Berlin* (John Murray, London, 2003)

Steve Vogel, *Betrayal in Berlin: The True Story of the Cold War's Most Audacious Espionage Operation* (Custom House, New York, 2019)

Markus Wolf and Anne McElvoy, *Man without a Face* (PublicAffairs, New York, 1997)

Articles

Ellen Barry, 'Double Agent, Turning 90, Says, "I Am a Happy Person"', *New York Times*, 12 November 2012

Gillian Blake, 'Portret van een spion', *De Telegraaf,* 23 December 1961

Tom Bower, 'Obituaries: John Cairncross', *Independent,* 9 October 1995

Clem Cecil, 'How I Became a Lunchtime Spy for Moscow', *The Times,* 14 May 2003

E. H. Cookridge, 'George was schuchter in gezelschap van vrouwen', *De Telegraaf,* 19 January 1967

E. H. Cookridge, 'George wilde later theologie studeren', *De Telegraaf,* 20 January 1967

Edward Jay Epstein, [untitled], *The New York Times,* 28 September 1980

Wim A. Van Geffen, 'We noemden hem Poek', *De Telegraaf,* 30 December 1961

Dominic Kennedy, 'The Spy Who Came In for Rough Justice', *The Times*, 1 February 2016

Aly Knol, 'George Blake, "de beste man van de KGB"', *Het Vrije Volk,* 30 April 1988

Simon Kuper, 'From Cambridge Spies to Isis Jihadis', *Financial Times,* 1 April 2016

Austin B. Matschulat, 'Coordination and Cooperation in
    Counterintelligence', CIA Historical Review Program, 2 July 1996:
    https://www.cia.gov/library/center-for-the-study-of-intelligence/
    kent-csi/vo113no2/html/v13i2a05p_0001.htm

Robert Mendick and Tom Parfitt, 'My Father the Russian Spy, by
    Anglican Curate from Guildford', *Sunday Telegraph*, 11 November
    2012

Paul Geoffrey Methven, 'Why Was the Profumo Affair So Damaging
    to the Government?', unpublished MA dissertation, University of
    Exeter, 2006

Ed Moloney and Bob Mitchell, 'The George Blake Escape: An
    Interesting If Troubling Postscript', Thebrokenelbow.com, 6 July
    2013

Richard Norton-Taylor, 'George Blake Now Prepared To Talk after
    Decades of Silence', *Guardian*, 19 September 1990

Richard Norton-Taylor, 'George Blake Admits Doing Great Damage to
    British Intelligence', *Guardian*, 19 September 1990

Hans Olink, 'George Blake, Meesterspion'. *VPRO Gids*, Netherlands,
    3 July 1999

Gilles Perrault, 'Henri Curiel, citoyen du tiers-monde', *Le Monde
    Diplomatique*, April 1998

Pat Pottle, 'Gray's Betrayal of the Truth about Blake the Spy',
    Guardian, 17 February 1995

Olivier Roy, 'International Terrorism: How Can Prevention and
    Repression Keep Pace?', BKA autumn conference, 18–19
    November, 2015

George Steiner, 'The Cleric of Treason', *New Yorker*, 8 December 1980

Ellen Verbeek, 'Spion voor een verloren zaak', *HP/De Tijd*, 13
    September 1991.

Robert Verkaik, 'The Blake Escape', *Independent*, 23 August 2008

Audio and visual material and other speeches

BBC World Service, 'Witness: George Blake Escapes', 24 October 2011

George Blake speech to Stasi, Bundesbeauftragte für die Unterlagen
    des Staatssicherheitsdienstes der ehemaligen Deutschen
    Demokratischen Republiks, MfS Sekr. Neiber/Tb/1, 1976

George Blake speech to Stasi, Bundesbeauftragte für die Unterlagen
des Staatssicherheitsdienstes der ehemaligen Deutschen
Demokratischen Republiks, MfS HV A/Vi/15, probably 1980
George Blake speech to Stasi, Bundesbeauftragte für die Unterlagen
des Staatssicherheitsdienstes der ehemaligen Deutschen
Demokratischen Republiks, MfS HV A/Vi/80–81, probably 1981
Sylvie Braibant interview with Blake, TV5Monde.com, released online
on 8 August 2011
George Carey, *George Blake: Masterspy of Moscow*, BBC TV
documentary, screened on BBC 4, 22 March 2015
Mehdi Lallaoui, *Henri Curiel: Itinéraire d'un combattant de la paix et
de la liberté*, Mémoires Vives productions, Paris, 2001
Hans Olink, 'Meesterspion George Blake,' OVT radio programme
in four parts, broadcast July 1999. http://www.npogeschiedenis.
nl/ovt/afleveringen/1999/Ovt-04-07–1999/Meesterspion-George-
Blake-deel-1.html
Elliott Shiff and David Stein, 'George Blake, Master of Deception',
Episode 7 of *Betrayal!*, Associated Producers, 2004
Turner Broadcasting System and BBC, 'Spies', Episode 21 of BBC TV
series *Cold War*, 1998
Eleanor Wachtel interview, 'John le Carré on war, terror and his new
biography (encore episode)', Canadian Broadcasting Company, 29
November 2015

List of Illustrations

While every effort has been made to contact copyright-holders of illustrations, the author and publishers would be grateful for information about any illustrations where they have been unable to trace them, and would be glad to make amendments in further editions.

Index